Winds of Change

Winds of Change

Geopolitics and the World Order

Azam Gill

Writers Club Press
San Jose New York Lincoln Shanghai

Winds of Change
Geopolitics and the World Order

Writers Club Press
an imprint of iUniverse.com, Inc.

For information address:
iUniverse.com, Inc.
5220 S 16th, Ste. 200
Lincoln, NE 68512
www.iuniverse.com

ISBN: 0-595-20016-8

Printed in the United States of America

DEDICATION

Dedicated to *La Belle France*, my land of adoption, for succor and the *de jeure* and *de facto* liberty of expression: where most things wonderful in my life happened, and to whom I owe more than I can express or ever repay.

EPIGRAPH

For what is a man advantaged, if he gain the whole world, and lose himself, or be cast away? Be not conformed to this world, but be ye transformed by the renewing of your mind—be in the world, not of the world, and render therefore unto Caesar the things which are Caesar's; and unto God the things that are God's. He that is without sin among you, let him first cast a stone...

Luke 9:25, Romans 12:2, Matthew 22:21, John 8:7

CONTENTS

The section heading indicates the subject heading of the articles. Within this heading, the title of each article is followed by its date of publication.

ACKNOWLEDGEMENTS

First and foremost, the successive editors-in-chief of *The National Educator*, Jim Townsend and Muazzam Gill, whose help, guidance, and cogent remarks were indispensable. My only sister, Shaista-Apa, for her emotional and material generosity. My late parents, to whom I owe my education and more than I can mention.

My friend Jean-Christophe Leveque, for liberal access to his meticulous research files, sharp analytical mind, formidable memory for world events and generosity in picking up the tab in restaurants.

Friends in the *Amicale des Anciens de la Legion Etrangere* in Grenoble, for their sharp-witted comments and analyses, and help with translations.

My wife, Miranda and the children, Nathanael, Fiona and Matthieu for letting me get on with it, and listening to me.

The faculty and students of the GEA Department, Grenoble University, for the memorable atmosphere I worked in, which allowed me to synthesize my writing interests and teaching. Mr Benoit, Mr and Mrs Spalanzani, Mr. Palumbo, Mrs. Robbez Masson, Mr. Michel and Mr. Patoglia, and the secretaries—Françoise, Christine, Valerie and Pascale—deserve a special mention.

Aunty Ellen, Isabel Courant and Jean-Louis Ricciardelli for their stimulating discussions, gastronomical hospitality and constant help and encouragement.

And could I ever forget to mention Certified Public Accountant Pierre Ahidzi and his pointed remarks on world affairs?

The Agus and the Mumfords, for their hospitality and intelligent table conversations

I owe the following Grenoble Libraries a special debt of thanks: The GEA Department, Lycée Champollion, Municipal Library, The Institute of Political Science, The Inter-University Library of Grenoble.

In Paris, the British Council Library and the American Library.

On the French Riviera, the Documentation Center of the *Centre d'Instruction Naval*, St Mandrier, and the University of Var Library. For their invaluable assistance, a debt of thanks is also owed to friend and brother-in-arms, Warrant Officer Eric Demdjian, former commando in the Franch navy special forces, Mssrs Christophe Gire, Olivier Rollé, Matthieu Dufoulon and Pierre Cato of the *Centre d'Instruction Naval* and Rifka Kielson of iuniverse.

INTRODUCTION

It was no Fool's Day prank. An American spy plane had been forced to land at a Chinese airfield, and the crew and aircraft had been detained. The shock of the resulting U.S.-China row over the spy plane in spring 2001 brought the new U.S. administration into sharp focus, generating fears of a new cold war. Washington's unabashed recognition of India as a principal instrument of policy in Asia and South Asia had U.S. analysts busy, while its firm line over the Middle East raised further anxiety.

All these issues did not suddenly parachute into the Oval Office overnight. They are leftovers from previous U.S. administrations, both Republican and Democrat, but in recent history, corresponding to the period of my columns, the American people had entrusted the Democrats with their overseas national interest. The Democratic team was composed of very intelligent appointees of high academic repute, hampered by the constraints of youthful ideology they were unwilling to abandon in the face of a changed world, the public opinion of which, however, they managed to turn to their advantage.

The rough seas encountered by the Clinton administration's foreign policy towards the European Union and its member countries and Asia, especially China, India and Pakistan—its floundering on the issue of East Asian neo-Confucianism, and its confusion over the application of human rights. Its "special relationship" with Britain, French unilateral decisions, the rise of German influence, and the Indo-Russian-Chinese tripartite, as well as the looming issue of terrorism and what to do about it formed the ethos of my columns written for *The National Educator* between 1993 and 2000, which constitute the pages of this book. George Bush had announced a New World Order after the Gulf War, and the American people had chosen Mr. Clinton to manage it.

In 1991, conservative leadership enabled the American people to recover in the sands of the Middle East what they had lost in the jungles of Vietnam. In the Presidential election of 1992, they expressed their gratitude by choosing a Vietnam-era refusenik Commander-in-Chief over former fighter pilot and CIA Director George Bush. From 1993 to 2000, neither the United States' Commander-in-Chief, nor its Defence or Foreign Secretaries had a military background. Twelve years of conservative leadership were replaced by eight years of left-wing values deemed "progressive" by the politically correct. Progress towards the ideal welfare state is not at the centre of the dispute between conservative and progressive. How to achieve it and at what expense delineates the difference. For the progressives, it is redistribution of wealth by legislation: for the conservatives, it is the natural outcome of enforcing values of character, responsibility and competitiveness. Liberal and Keynesian policies find themselves being kicked around on the same pitch, with conservatives and progressives fighting to claim credit for serving up the tastiest morsels.

Both sides have been helped by the explosion of Information Technology, and they master it equally well to excercise influence and disseminate propaganda. Neither side would have been capable of reining in the anguish of laid-off employees resulting directly from the turf wars and mega-mergers of the IT industry. Its revolutionary consequences reach as far as India and China.

Relations with France were marked by the latter's dogged pursuit of a foreign policy firmly entrenched within the Western Alliance, yet refusing to abandon its doctrine of *la difference française, its sole protection against being taken for granted. The rest of the European Union was not far behind in its criticism of the United States' pursuit of a clumsy policy against rogue nations*: it is not the policy itself that the EU countries question, but the pursuit of double standards to wrest trade benefits for the United States. In France itself, the National Front made astounding news: from 0.74 percent of the national vote in 1974, it went up to 15 percent in 1995! The alarm in Europe maintained the National Front at the centre of concern for political analysts, and occupied a prominent place in the columns of *The National Educator*, including an exclusive interview of Monsieur Jean Marie Le Pen.

In February 1998, Operation Desert Thunder was launched to bomb Iraq. However noble and clear-headed the intentions of the U.S. administration, the act failed to convince the world of the absence of a link between economic sanctions, punitive air strikes, and Mr. Clinton's woes brought on by his excess of libido.

Led by the United States, policies of nuclear deterrence successively evolved into those of arms limitation, nuclear non-proliferation and nuclear counter-proliferation. They were unsuccessful in their implementation, from the resumption of nuclear tests by France to the emergence of two new nuclear powers in South Asia.

With the rest of Asia, America had to ride a seesaw with Taiwan and the People's Republic of China at the other end. In 1996, the Chinese dropped the Boeing deal in the American lap, while gaining points with the European Union. Although the Chinese were unable to barge their way into the World trade Organization (WTO) at the 1997 summit of the Asia Pacific Economic Cooperation (APEC), the U.S. Administration failed to convince Asian countries to open up their Information Technology markets in infrastructure.

By about 1998, it was becoming apparent that poor and backward countries could bypass a renaissance or industrial revolution by clever handling of Information Technology and disinformation through the western media for their own ends, the Gulf War being a clear example, followed by the periodic surges in optimism concerning Iran's imminent return to the western fold.

During the same period, the U.S. announced its "strategic partnership" with China, although ideologically, institutionally, socially and politically they have nothing in common, except perhaps a balance of trade heavily in China's favor. Consequently, a grateful China moved closer to Russia, allowing the former to benefit from the transfer of military technology.

The NATO Alliance has seen significant changes over the past eight years. Its eastward expansion under the aegis of Partnership for Peace had a rocky start in 1994, and has not seen smooth sailing since. Partly, this is due to a two-speed alliance of Warren Christopher's "meritocracy", with poor relatives casting furtive glances from the end of the table. The Europeans have their Western European Union, as much a competitor as a partner of NATO, and with plans for the European Defense Force, the current U.S. administration will have ample opportunity to earn its spurs.

Neither the European Union nor the United States can, however, count coup over their handling of the Balkans, partially because it is hard to determine who is wittingly or unwittingly supporting Muslims, the Orthodox Church, or the Roman Catholic Church. One of the consequences has been the rise of Bosnia and Albania as drug-running nerve centers, while providing battle experience to Islamic mercenaries of every hue. The outcome of the Balkan mess has been a diaspora of refugees directed at western European countries, putting to test the very fabric of their moral order. Perhaps this confusion was maintained by the left-ward swing of Europe during the past eight years—inspiration from across the Atlantic? In 1998, thirteen of the EU's fifteen Member states were led by left-wing governments or coalitions. Whatever the case, left-wing ideology finds it difficult to accommodate factors of religion in its analyses—unless it is as a destructive, superstitious force retarding progress. The Marxist-inspired dialectic of the mainstream left-wing only admits economic conditions and the social environment as the causes of human misery. The functioning of such analyses requires different levels of a problem to be reduced to the victim-perpetrator relationship, which has obscured the treatment of other, highly relevant factors affecting the Balkan mix.

The single European currency has now become the Euro, but is still at the centre of fierce debate. Indeed, the General election of 2001 in the United Kingdom refocused on the controversy. The EU has not yet emerged from a classic wait-and-see situation. This, of course, has not stopped it from exercising foreign policy from China to Latin America. Its Achilles heel will always be its composition of sovereign states, that, in their national interests, will unhesitatingly take unilateral decisions to forge bilateral ties.

These past few years, that has been the case with the American Middle East peace initiative, born in confused presumption of received, untested ideas of non-consensual ideology, and muddling along because of the U.S.' inability to include competent allies. Although it is now upto the Republicans to pull the fat from the fire, can they deliver? And if so, will the delivery be premature or miscarried?

While Germany, the self-proclaimed "tutor" of the old members of the Habsburg Empire, warmly regards the possibility of a renascent MittelEuropa hidden within the EU, Russia under Putin needs to be taken very seriously. Unfettered by a morally exigent public, its Chechnya quagmire has as yet neither threatened its social fabric nor posed a challenge to its political stability. That allows Russian nationalism to prosper and seek alliances with forces fearful of American hegemony.

The syntheses of the past eight years lack of success are most visible by taking into account a singular, indisputable fact—the terrorists retain the initiative, and we are only on the defensive.

It was the unfolding of these events, and their interaction with U.S. foreign policy at the centrepiece that define a single theme uniting the various topics my columns were devoted to.

The articles are grouped by subject, which constitute the section headings on **The United States, Nato, The European Union, France, Germany, The United Kingdom, Russia, Asia** and **Terrorism**. The chronological order of each article is indicated by the date of publication. An exhaustive General Index and a Bibliography of documents read and consulted are provided. Since press sources tend to be confidential, there are no end-notes, but if bona fide researchers write to the author, care of the publishers, they should get a response.

SECTION ONE—THE UNITED STATES

As The Clinton-Gore Welfare State Grows, Destruction Nears—November 1993.

The modern welfare state is less than fifty years old. From the renaissance until Britain's Insurance Act of 1911, the application of reason was enough to define enlightenment. Although such enlightenment was elitist and concern for the have-nots figured prominently on its agenda, redistribution of wealth did not. Empathy for the poor was based on an interest in character, responsibility and competitiveness. Poor honest folk, by dint of character and competence, upheld the validity of social mobility. The remnants were taken care of by charitable Christians. While Darwin and Spencer revealed the scientific theories of natural selection, Charles Dickens' and Jack London's moral clout kept them within bounds.

The internal dynamism of an industrial revolution fuelled external influence—the feedback from colonial markets revealed it. The cyclic process spawned Great Powers, Karl Marx and corpses rotting in the trenches of the Great War.

The prevailing ethics within European industrial powers espoused competition with the ethos on responsibility. They also allowed Marxist ideas to acquire an audience and gain a following. The failure of the Soviet experiment showed up K. Marx in only seven decades: a spiteful philosopher. Over 150 million Soviet subjects were required to realize his posthumous revenge on a handful of capitalists.

Britain, the great colonial empire, started using up its collateral on the eve of World War I. By the end of World War II, there was even less to go around. The labour Party chose this moment to further decrease the national collateral by divesting Britain of its colonies when they were perhaps most needed. This lofty idealism rising from empty coffers went on to edify the welfare state. The benefits of this state were to be lifelong, and its umbrella benevolently sheltered the very immigrants whose lives are now threatened by echoes from hollow coffers.

Western European welfare states are thus hastily trying to reorder the dimensions of this concept in an effort to rescue it from extinction. They have done their history homework, and are ready to bite the bullet.

The huge, expensive welfare program of the United States reflects the situation the Europeans were in at the end of WW-II. Today, the end of the Cold War has left the U.S. staring at its budget deficit. Decision makers have deemed this moment appropriate to increase the privileges of their constituents. If the American decision continues on the European path, later U.S. governments will have to face up to the consequences. Granting privileges results in a happy populace. Reducing privileges leads to a disgruntled electorate. The Democrats have put into motion a series of events similar to those started by Britain's labour government after WW-II.

This decision is not statesmanlike but political. If the democrats had the wisdom and foresight to postpone their welfare program to better times, they might not be in power. The republicans would steal a march on them, and that would never do.

The collapse of the USSR has turned the world's moral spotlight on the U.S., which should not blink under the glare, but maintain resolute leadership. America is in a unique position of being able to mutate outdated expectations to the demands of today's moral order. By reacting to anticipated criticism, the U.S. is losing the opportunity of replacing the old moral order with a new one.

The welfare state launched by Britain's 1911 Insurance Act is no longer pertinent or workable. People's welfare, and the long-term economic well being of a people and a way of life are still valid. Courageous leadership and sagacious advice should recognize this fact, reorder priorities, and resist the lure of the European economic trap.

Don't Be Dazzled By The Hype—August 1994.

Interactive and multimedia are the latest terms being tossed around with conviction to remind stock market investors that information technology has not yet reached its watershed. TCI and Bell Atlantic's expected merger at the beginning of the year caused speculators to salivate. When the merger fell through, it was a reminder of information science's vulnerability to press hype. The estimated financial size of the interactive, multimedia and telecom market is around 300 billion dollars. Louis-Jacques Campanyo, ALCATEL (Europe's biggest telecom company)'s director for international affairs, warns: "Until the year 2001…more lines (phone, cable, fiber-optic) will be installed in Asia and Latin America than in the industrialized nations."

The temptation to reach out to new markets is understandable. Historian Paul Kennedy in *Rise and Fall of the Great Powers, points out the emerging importance of the Pacific Rim, but without advocating disinvestments in the EU*, as the Clinton Administration's seesaw policy sees fit. Following suit, western companies are blindly investing in Communist China with a total disregard of guarantees. The surfeit of enthusiasm discounts the continuity of the anticommunist struggle, which is fancifully thought to be over. Upheavals in China are only to be expected.

That allows U.S. to take a closer look at the U.S.-EU market possibilities. The interactive, multimedia telecom market hyped up with the U.S. fiber-optic highway endorsed by Al Gore, has also distorted perspectives in the EU. EC business leaders and governments are scrambling to lay their own infrastructure of fiber-optic cables.

These U.S.-EC decisions are based on the assumption that the infrastructure itself determines its optimisation. It is a false premise as software companies led by Bill Gates' Microsoft have proved: updated software on existing hardware eliminates the need to replace the infrastructure. Similarly, state of the art software and integrated circuits should, at the least, question the value of laying new cables. Somewhere along the line, chip manufacturers have failed to convince financiers of the superfluity of new lines faced with more powerful chips. Radio and television will, in the future, be transmitted by wire. Phone calls will be beamed. When the load of phone calls using existing cables is subtracted, it approximately doubles their capacity. This cable capacity further increases in proportion to the power of the chips used to transmit information.

However, the convergent policies of government and business leaders from Singapore to the United States focus only on the laying of fiber-optic lines. The shift of phone networks to satellite and the advent of super chips seem to have escaped the attention of government and big business. The market is already splitting up along lines of multinational interest. In Europe, Deutsche Bunderpost Telekom and France Telecom have formed Eunetcom to provide services. Britain, as usual, is straining its eyes across the Atlantic horizon: British Telecom have teamed up with EDS.

Confusion of information has led to limited understanding and application. The idea is not to lay more lines, but to send more information along existing lines.

Technological change in laboratories is a spawn of massive investment, not forthcoming for chips. As such, in the field of integrated circuits, no dramatic thunderclap has been heard, and governments are unable to appreciate the consequences of a super chip. U.S. Vice President Al Gore, reputedly information science literate, claims that the "Data Super Highway (is the) most important marketplace of the 21st century."

Nuclear Tests Show Chinks In Clinton Policy—
August 1995.

France has announced a resumption of nuclear tests. If the Pentagon is inclined to resume testing, the French decision opens a tidy little loophole allowing the U.S. to test new warheads from the "moral high ground" Margaret Thatcher is said to have suggested to Ronald as the basis for his confrontations with the "evil empire". If the Pentagon has no plans to test a nuclear warhead, then the French decision only draws attention to the chinks in Bill Clinton's European policy.

Charles de Gaulle withdrew France from joint NATO command in 1960 and instituted an independent nuclear deterrent. Last year, more than three decades later, Francois Mitterand, France's socialist president, suspended nuclear tests in order not to "offend the world". A year after this announcement, Gaullists ousted the socialists by a clear majority. Within a month of his presidency, Jacques Chirac, the new president, brushed aside Clinton's overtures to membership of a high technology, mythical post-nuclear club by announcing tests lasting until 1996.

China apart, the declared nuclear powers had agreed to the three-year moratorium on nuclear testing masterminded by the Bush administration. Resumption of nuclear testing by France aligns it with China. Reaction from different quarters of the world has been mixed. Germany's chancellor Helmut Kohl "respects" the decision, whereas China silently applauds it. French nuclear tests are conducted in the Pacific, and accordingly, Australia, New Zealand and the South Pacific Forum which groups the independent island states of the Pacific are raising Cain over the issue. On June 17th, the French consulate in Perth, Australia was destroyed by explosion and fire. Responsibility was claimed by an "obscure" group called the Pacific Popular Front. Mediagenic acts of anti-French spite in bad taste quickly followed.

They were gleefully reported by the German and British press. The Germans are exercising discretion over the French decision, especially since Jacques Chirac called the Franco-German partnership "necessary, but not sufficient... no Europe without Britain". Jacques Chirac's remarks coupled with Mrs. Thatcher's recent approbation on French TV of Mr. Chirac as a fellow-conservative are not enough to decrease Britain's gall at the American snub. At the beginning of the year, the White House's announcement that Germany was the most important country in Europe was aimed at Britain and not France. Followed by Gerry Adams' visit to the White House, it was a clear indication that the United States felt it no longer needed Britain's navigational skills to steer across the diplomatic seas. Squirming under the snub, the British press have released their pent-up frustration on the French decision. Their past status is based on a myth of empire perpetuated by themselves. According to Paul Kennedy's authoritative *The Rise and Fall of Empires, the British empire* lasted only sixty-odd years (from 1856 to 1914), and before that, France was the richest country in the world. It is worth remembering this conflict between illusion and reality when studying Franco-British relations.

With Germany, the consequences of the French decision to continue nuclear tests is less complex. Germany has avoided criticizing the French decision, tacitly defining France's future role in a common European defense based on the Western European Union and NATO. According to Jean-Christophe Leveque, recently elected deputy mayor of Pommiers la Plaçette, the French decision to resume nuclear testing "marks, on the European landscape, a shift of the military and strategic balance Germany towards France". The European Union of the future would thus bestow economic power on Germany, and executive power on France with Britain as back up.

Domestically, the decision has not really hurt the Gaullists. With the anti-Chirac ultra-nationalist National Front winning a record 15 percent of the national vote in the first round of the presidential elections, and 30 percent of the vote in 14 towns of more than 30,000 inhabitants in the first round of the municipal elections, the Gaullists cannot afford to be seen as Washington's wimps. By declaring a suspension of nuclear testing on moral grounds, Mr. Mitterand, known among intimate political circles as "the Florentine", laid a classic trap for his successor on the lines of Kautilya's *Arthashastra (Indian work on statecraft, and reportedly one of the preoccupations of Dr Henry Kissinger's* doctoral dissertation). The laying of the trap suggests that Mitterand knew the socialists would not win the next election, and confirms that he underestimated Gaullist mettle and overestimated Clinton's diplomatic prowess.

In *Leaders* Richard Nixon observes "De Gaulle's greatest fear was that France would suffer the fate of nations that once made history and now only observe it". France has survived post-empire traumatic stress with remarkable aplomb, retaining a prominent place among the Group of 7. Britain, its neighboring rival, is successfully sliding towards observer status with the end of the cold war. After the Gulf War, Bush managed to draw France closer to Washington, and a moratorium on nuclear testing was one of the concessions to American diplomacy coaxed by a conservative President from a socialist counterpart. The tidy little applecart left over by the Republicans has been upset by the haywire diplomacy of the current administration. BBC TV World Service ran a series in April unequivocally suggesting that the United States' interest in the moratorium was neither moral nor strategic, but financial. It seeks to sell post-nuclear military technology, including battlefield robots, in order to recover massive investment made in this field. This explains why CIA director John Deustch's credibility as a salesman of state of the art non-nuclear military technology has been undermined to the point of ridicule. After the Gulf war, Bush managed to draw France closer to Washington, and a moratorium on nuclear testing was one of the concessions to American diplomacy coaxed by a conservative. That has not been the effect of Washington's diplomatic bungling on the Franco-German relationship, which just might have been helped into entering the preliminary stages of a Sumo wrestling match, with each opponent making ritual gestures of intimidation. While Helmut Kohl is often compared with a sumo wrestler, and Jacques Chirac himself is a keen fan of the sport, Bill Clinton has no pretensions to even assistant-referee status.

Trade War Ahead For U.S.-China?—June 1996.

If China's MFN status with the U.S. is not renewed on June 4, it will not be in reaction to China's choice of Airbus over Boeing. The $2 billion deal was announced five years ago when Helmut Kohl, the German Chancellor, visited Beijing to smoothen Chinese feathers ruffled by the French decision to sell Mirage fighters to Taiwan. France and Germany are majority shareholders in Airbus at 37.5percent each. Announcing the decision to buy Airbus to Helmut Kohl strengthened China's relations with the European Union, ensured EU support for membership of the World Trade Organization and left intact their rhetoric on the sale of French Mirage fighters to Taiwan. Since an announcement is not binding, the Chinese led Boeing to believe that they might actually win the plum contract. By dropping Boeing, the Chinese have gained face with the EU and slapped America on the wrist for granting the Taiwanese Premier a visa and sending warships to the China Sea during the recent Chinese live-fire exercises off Taiwan.

Following the Euro-Asian Trade Summit in Bangkok on February 28 (April issue of *The National Educator*) the Chinese Prime Minister, Li Peng, visited France on April 10 to conclude the Airbus contract and other deals. China will buy thirty A320 Airbuses and three A340 transport air-craft from Airbus for $2 billion. France will also export cereals to China over the next two years, and has granted the People's Republic $200 million worth of credit to quadruple the production capacity of the Franco-Chinese Citroen car-manufacturing plant in China.

France, Germany and Japan are among the biggest financial sponsors of China, offering loans practically written-off after a time lapse. Under a system of franchising, a public works project is financed by the company awarded the contract. The company may earn a profit on the project with-in an agreed time limit, after which ownership automatically reverts to the Chinese. China's controlled liberalization has not changed the fundamentals of Mao Zedong's policy, urging autonomy in the means of production.

Since China opened up some of its regions to foreign investment, the United States has been its biggest trading partner, prompting grumbles from the British and concern within the EU leading to a flurry of visits to Beijing by Sir Leon Brittan, the EU's British Trade Commissioner. The Chinese like the rest of East Asia would like to decouple human rights from trade. By being granted Most Favored Nation status, China has accomplished just that with the United States. At the Euro-Asian Summit, the leaders of the EU accepted the de facto separation of human rights and trade. After signing the trade agreements on April 10 in Paris, Li Peng was due for a state banquet hosted by the French Premier, Alain Juppé. Li Peng kept Alain Juppé waiting from (reportedly) one to two hours until reassured that the French Premier would not evoke human rights.

Lately, it has been observed that foreign investment in China has fallen. The carpetbaggers who rode the first euphoria have come up against the Mao Zedong principle of autonomy of production: China will not be a big market for western consumer goods. China only welcomes foreign investment when it allows it to—eventually—own the means of production. While buying Airbuses the Chinese are also eager to purchase the German-owned Dutch aircraft company Fokker, which went bankrupt shortly before the Paris signatures. Chinese acquisition of Fokker would provide them with access to western technology and a base of operations in the EU. German shares in Airbus are held by DASA, (actually Mercedes), which owns now-bankrupt Fokker: transfer into Chinese hands would allow the Germans to get rid of excess financial baggage in exchange for giving the Chinese a foothold in Europe, much like Britain offered the Japanese.

China is looking at far horizons, but might want to pay more attention at home. The selective opening up of thirty provinces, regions and self-administered cities has caused economic disparity, increased disunity and led to clashing import-export policies. There is a five-year plan to fix internal boundaries, the absence of which is causing friction between provinces over the ownership of natural resources. The power of certain regions to decide their own taxation is leading to provincial monopolies encouraged by bribes in high places. And the large Muslim population of China, mainly concentrated in Xinjiang province (which holds a large number of nuclear sites) bordering Pakistan, Afghanistan and Central Asia, strains its eyes across the Celestial Mountains in search of its Islamic soul. Historically, warring provinces struggling against economic disparity have fuelled Chinese disunity, and not Yugoslavia-type religious and ethnic strife.

"Will China disintegrate?" is the question asked by the British weekly *The Economist* on the cover of its April 26 issue. *The Economist* refers to a study undertaken by the Pentagon last year, which concluded that there was a 50 percent chance of China seeing a Soviet-style break-up. Perhaps that is why the Indian government has optimistically maintained a 20,000 force of Tibetan commandos at its expense for the past 35 years (*National Educator*, February 1994).

China's Most Favored Nation status with the U.S. comes up for renewal on June 4, the World Trade Summit in Singapore is due in December, and China is aware of the U.S. presidential election on the same horizon. If China's MFN status is renewed, the Chinese will offer a lucrative deal to the U.S. This would then strengthen China's position with the EU and the U.S. with a view to gaining support for membership of the WTO.

U.S. Administration Bows To China's Power — January 1997.

This year's APEC Summit of 18 Pacific countries took place in Manila from 22 to 25 November, attended by a U.S. President unfettered by re-election worries. Bill Clinton had hoped to achieve his niche in history by convincing the Asian countries to open up the Information Technology markets in infrastructure and reduce the fundamental tensions gripping U.S.-China relations. China had hoped to bargain its way into the World Trade Organization (*National Educator* April, May and June 1996). Despite the optimism of American and Chinese spokesmen, neither government was successful. Warren Christopher, the out-going Secretary of State, reassured the Chinese that "no single issue would dominate the agenda of future U.S.-China talks". Accordingly, a Chinese spokesman congratulated Bill Clinton for choosing "dialogue" over "confrontation". Although Mike McCurry, the White House spokesman, understandably referred to the exchange of U.S. and Chinese Heads of State in 1997 and 1998 as "one step ahead in strategic relations", Winston Lord, often considered the U.S. State Department's foremost authority on China, was cautious. He warned of "serious difficulties" with China over Human Rights, Non-proliferation, Piracy of intellectual property and Commerce. Lisa Ranso, *BBC World Service* correspondent covering the Manila Summit, reported only "qualified support" for Bill Clinton's demand to open up Asia's information technology market, and China's prospects of sliding into the World Trade Organization, as "bleak".

The U.S. administration has over-rated the dimensions of the Asian Pacific market, and retains hazy notions about the Middle East, Africa and the Latin American Mercosur, while ignoring the European Union.

In *The Times* August 20, 1996 issue, Anatole Kaletsky, in his article "Tiger, Tiger, are you burning out?" concluded that the Asian Pacific rim was approaching its economic watershed in relation to the EU and the U.S.A. Paul Krugman, the MIT economist, titled his now celebrated article in *Foreign Affairs* "The Myth of Asia's Miracle", and has always considered the Tigers' economic miracle a mirage. Adi Ignatius, writing in *The Far Eastern Economic Review,* believes that double-digit growth in Asia is over. The British weekly *The Economist* reported on November 9, 1996 that the Asian economy had entered a period of decline. In the first half of this year, export growth in Asia decreased to 7 percent compared with 28 percent in the corresponding period in 1995. According to the Asian Development Bank, Japan's weaker yen has made it more competitive against the Tigers, whilst China and Indonesia seek to "cool" their economies by containing economic expansion. The Tigers' erstwhile low-wage edge is now a disadvantage: "wages account for less than 5 percent of the cost…Far more value may be added by nimble staff who can quickly redesign a product".

The future of the Middle East's oil-producing economies will be determined by the car industry. Undersea oil and low emission engines will limit the Middle East's importance to that of a politically turbulent region.

Africa's future as a plump trading partner remains blurred as the continent reels under successive political shocks to its psyche. East Europe is said to be a bustling market, but closer scrutiny reveals a mixture of individual entrepreneurs, organized crime and corrupt officials. It is still in the process of evolving into a stable, long-term partner offering wide-ranging mutual benefits. Latin American Mercosur is developing within its own confines. Communication within and with outside trading partners needs to be streamlined before economic coherence can focus on trade relations with mature trading zones.

The European Union, with its cultural history of trade, links with the United States, economic maturity and sophisticated trade practices, offers unparalleled possibilities of equal opportunity. Volker Ruhe, the German defense minister, declared in November "Americans want to be relieved of their job in Europe and Europeans want a stronger identity". In this perspective the French President's diplomatically premature remark about "co-sponsorship" with the United States assumes relevance (*National Educator*, November '96). Decreased American defense involvement in Europe should be complemented by economic involvement—a natural extension of historical and cultural roots. Max Weber's Protestant work ethic retains its integrity on either side of the Atlantic, the decision-making process remains identical, and the concept of liberty is a common denominator. G.M. Tamas, the Hungarian political philosopher, writing from Budapest in *Magyar Narancs*, affirms that the French ideal of republican liberty by revolution is the prevailing logic of the continent, a perfect parallel to the American idea of liberty. Cultural profiles determine conflict or cooperation.

Samuel Huntington, writing in *Foreign Affairs* in 1993, observed that "... the greatest divisions among humankind and the dominating source of conflict will be cultural". In his *The Closing of the American Mind* Harold Bloom, nearly a decade ago, reminded Americans of the imperative of retaining their European cultural perspectives. Although cultural heterogeneity is an elegant argument, it may lead to political chaos. In *The Social Virtues and the Creation of Prosperity*, Francis Fukuyama defines "high-trust" and "low-trust" societies, by which definition the U.S. and the European Union are, natural "high-trust" allies as opposed to the neo-Confucian "low-trust" model.

The New York Times rates China as President Clinton's "greatest challenge". Jacques Attali, the left-wing ex-President of the European Bank for Research and Development, was interviewed in the December issue of *Paris Match*, about his latest book *Paths of Wisdom* and Henry Kissinger's book *Diplomacy. He assessed China as the U.S.'s "principal villain in the next fifteen years". By over-emphasizing Asia's importance and appeasing Chinese ambitions, Mr. Clinton seeks to deny his successors their niche in history, perhaps in pursuit of youthful vows tak*en in an era of Anti-

Americanism. Directing political, economic and diplomatic energy towards the European Union would be statesmanship beyond the call of duty to party politics.

Incoherence Of U.S. Foreign Policy Disturbs Allies—January 1998.

The western alliance has regularly found itself at odds with France. Along with Germany, one of the European Union's two key countries, France conducts a foreign policy, which does not always suit the United States. Since the implosion of the Soviet Union, the western alliance recognized the emerging threat from rogue nations. Led by France, EU countries shared this prognostic. However, since the EU is not a sovereign entity, each member country feels free to pursue its bilateral interests, which might include a rogue nation now and then, to Washington's occasional ire. This can lead to mutual hostility when the U.S. itself decides to nurture its economic interests with a rogue nation. Cross-Atlantic flare-ups over Cuban and Iranian embargoes are a case in point.

Peer competitors like China and Russia rather than rogue nations now figure at the top of the Pentagon's catalogue of future threats. While this definition is waiting to be translated into foreign policy, it leaves U.S. allies free to pursue their bilateral interests. Allies cannot be expected to lend support to a void. When a foreign policy does emerge (possibly after the next election, despite the probability of Mr. Clinton's premature departure) it will need to be sold to the allies: they will have to be wooed and not whistled into a last-minute parade. Washington's onus of responsibility is thus humbling.

By-passing the time-honored ritual of courting evokes vague suspicions of the dreaded medieval *droit de seigneur*, distressing Europeans' peace of mind. Since 1992, U.S. foreign policy has been on a downslide. Its vision cannot be shared because there isn't enough of it to go around. The awe-some military and economic power of the U.S. has been clumsily, and even—whether by accident or intent—flauntingly mishandled.

EU intellectual circles are not pro-Iraqi, but the effect of the Iraqi embargo on Iraq's citizenry leads them to focus on what they perceive as American hegemony, and ignore whatever lofty benignness it might hide. It is widely felt that the smooth running of a nation's bilateral relations should not be held hostage to an ally's indecision and myopia.

Feeling threatened by one force, France has historically maneuvered a second one into the problem to dissipate pressure. Thus, in the 16th century, François I of France cultivated an alliance with Turkey to keep the Germans at bay: a useful partnership renewed on and off since then. When Napoleon Bonaparte invaded Egypt, Turkey formed an alliance with Russia to check Napoleon, but when Napoleon invaded Russia, Turkey withdrew its opposition! Even today, the Franco-Turkish alliance works well for both countries: while France pursues its interests in Central Asia, Turkey has an alternative to U.S. support in the western alliance. At the close of the 19th century, France even overcame its historical distaste for all creatures Anglo and Saxon, offering Britain the Entente Cordial designed to rein in the Kaiser.

The French pursuit of independence in bilateral relations with China and Russia does not seek new alliances to replace existing relations, but wishes to deter the U.S. from taking a position that opens it to charges of hegemony. This is, of course, in the U.S.' own interests. In Africa, French interests have felt the hot breath of American business. The U.S. call for a pan-African peacekeeping force, Mobutu's ouster, and his successor Kabila's subsequent grant of mineral exploration rights to an Arkansas company are interpreted as a desire to make an occupied seat vacant. Truman followed the same policy after World War II, but the cold war took the focus off his strategy. Madeline Albright's weeklong African tour in December further confirms apprehensions in Europe. The American Secretary of State's spokesman, James Healy, clearly described the purpose of the tour to include promotion of "American business".

Last year, Boeing's deal with China left Europe's Airbus in the lurch, and investor countries grinding their teeth. American-led mergers in telecommunications and the defense industry threaten domestic telecommunications operators and the defense industry of the European Union. While the EU's advanced tactical fighter aircraft is in the works, the Americans look like being able to dominate the coming two decades with their Joint Strike Fighter, Osprey tilt-rotor aircraft and Comanche stealth helicopters. So, there is also that pie of which everybody wants a share to eat and keep.

France has a historical responsibility towards its people to ensure a cockerel in the Sunday dinner-pot of every French home. Unlike Britain's delusion of "imperial responsibility", France applies De Gaulle's definition of his beloved country as a middle-rate power refusing to accept spectator status in the global theatre. The 7th Francophone Conference was held in Hanoi from November 14-16th 1997, and Boutros Boutros Ghali, former United Nations secretary general, appointed its General Secretary. Both are deliberate choices. If the United States occupies space left vacant by the French, then it had better watch its back! French speakers will weave multi-lateral relations from Vietnam to the Middle East, and hope to proceed towards mutual economic benefit. The derisive invective dribbled by sectors of the British press about *La Francophonie* only sought to divert attention from the subdued flop of the Commonwealth.

France seeks to realize its own-self-image rather than confront the United States with an alliance of countries with which it has little natural affinity. On the eve of the Gulf War, lady Thatcher reportedly soothed a worried George Bush about France's perceived vacillations. France, she is reported to have said, "will hum and haw, but when the ship sails, she will be on it".

"Clinton Loser" Says Euro Press—February 1998.

European newspapers, riveted by the sex scandal surrounding President Clinton, widely predict that he will be fatally wounded, even if he manages to cling to power.

Clinton's presidency has been plunged into its deepest crisis by allegations that he had an affair with trainee Monica Lewinsky, and then urged her to lie about it to investigators. Some papers fear that the U.S. leader, who denies wrongdoing, is more likely to turn his military might against Iraq's Saddam Hussein to divert attention from the scandal.

The French liberal daily, *Liberation*, portrays Clinton howling with pain after his wife placed a mousetrap on his penis. Everything indicates that the President has handed himself to his enemies on a platter, the newspaper said.

"Clinton might manage to save his job. Politically, however, his is finished already," said Germany's daily *Frankfurter Raund Schau*. "He can forget his ambitious domestic projects. Plans are already being made in the corridors of power for the time after Clinton. As a weak president at home, he will also lose influence abroad."

In another cartoon, Spain's *El Mundo* showed Hillary Clinton brandishing a pair of scissors and saying to her husband ..."We're going to have to take drastic measures to insure you finish your term without further hiccups."

Il Foglio, a new center-right newspaper in Italy, said the uncertainty was weakening U.S. markets and the dollar.

In a front-page headline, unusual in its crudity even in Italy, *Il Foglio* wrote: "A mere blow job can make Wall Street collapse."

Turin's *La Stampa* newspaper, in an editorial headlined "If the Emperor Becomes Lame," said Clinton must think carefully before ordering the use of force to punish Iraq for obstructing U.N. arms inspectors.

"If the president, even without the U.N.'s consent, decides that the moment has come to use force against Iraq, would it be seen as trying to divert attention from his domestic scandal?" the editorial said.

Spain's *El Pais* said the worst possible consequence of the crisis would be "the search for an international crisis to enable (Clinton) to retake the reins."

British media were divided over whether Clinton's credibility was irreparably damaged, or whether the frenzy over his alleged sexual adventures was a sign of political correctness gone mad.

The Guardian, saying these are "desperate times calling for desperate measures" urged Hillary Clinton to "break with her instincts and tell the truth."

But the paper said Clinton should not be forced out of office. "She (Hillary) should take the high-risk gamble of admitting her husband's weakness—a fact universally accepted long ago—but asking the American people whether they believe that trait should trigger the second presidential disgrace in a generation."

The mass-circulation *Sun* said Clinton's credibility "has dropped faster than a zipper." Political editor Trevor Kavanagh wrote: "If he has any sense he won't wait for impeachment. He will gather the last shreds of dignity and resign."

Not all commentators, though, were ready to write off Clinton.

"As a long-time Clinton watcher, I would not count out the possibility that he will admit the Lewinsky affair, deny the obstruction of justice and try to brazen it out," wrote Barbara Amiel of *The Daily Telegraph* in London.

U.S. Gives Communists In China Free Rein— November 1998.

The current U.S. President has openly referred to a "strategic partnership" with China. Ideologically, institutionally, socially and politically the U.S. and China have nothing in common to justify a partnership. They do not yet have visibly common interests that could lead to a confrontation.

The volume of trade between China and the United States is estimated at about $60 billion. The U.S. is the target of one-third of all Chinese imports, with the balance of trade heavily in China's favor. However, while a concerted effort was made by U.S. presidents to bring the imbalance of trade with Japan to politically acceptable proportions, China seems to be getting off scot-free.

There is a real fear that any change in the Sino-U.S. status quo will lead to economic slow-down in China, consequently affecting the American economy. Analyses of the Foreign Policy Research Institute and the Center for the Study of American Business suggest that this is nonsense designed only to ensure the profits of companies, which have invested in China.

Perhaps at some stage in the thought mechanism that condones China's spurious business practices, attitude to child labor, persecution of Christians and general repression, there is a desire to put an underdeveloped country on its feet so it can kick the free world. Perhaps. The doubt can be addressed by examining who really benefits in China from a one-sided business relationship with the west.

The French establishment daily *Le Monde* has baptized the Chinese People's Liberation Army (PLA) as "PLA Inc.". Over the last two decades, the PLA has become the center of an economic octopus. "Soldiers" are involved in the industrial production of items ranging from missiles to bras to condoms to sex aids! Directly or indirectly, 20,000 companies and the army are interdependent. And this is no military-industrial complex like the one in the U.S. Divisions of soldiers are employed in industrial production, and a host of illegal operations ranging from piracy of intellectual property to piracy on the high seas and alleged drug smuggling are protected by the PLA.

Chiang Kai-shek's Kuomintang was accused of Triad gang connections by the communists: the PLA is now the biggest Triad itself. Despite the success of its flood relief operations in September, the PLA remains a discredited institution going through an identity crisis. The recent death of General Yang Shangkun, the last of Mao's old guard, has reopened the debate on the role of the PLA. One faction supports Jiang Zemin as the first civilian to preside over the Central Military Commission. The lobby opposing him resents his absence from the communist party between 1947-49, and would like to maintain the PLA in its chosen role of legitimized bush guerrillas going to seed professionally, while prospering financially.

PLA equipment is obsolete, and training is still based on the doctrine of human waves. With the money earned from manufacturing bras, condoms and sex aids, the PLA has acquired sophisticated military equipment from the ex-USSR countries. Obviously no match for the U.S., who is this equipment intended to threaten, and why?

The reason can be found within China itself. Two years ago Britain's weekly *The Economist* estimated that China's economy had reached a watershed. It is now slowing down, and the Yen is poised on the edge of what could be a collapse. Economic disparity of alarming proportions threatens the unity of China's provinces. China will, as it has since the end of World War II, divert domestic crises outwards. Faced with a domestic crisis, China decided on the Korean adventure. When the Great Leap Forward resulted in sprains, China attacked India in 1962. As the Cultural Revolution degenerated into barbarism, the Chinese fomented tension on the Sino-Russian border in 1969.

Politically, economically and militarily China is on a weak footing at this time. Unfortunately, the White House is too pre-occupied with the presidential soap opera to take any advantage of the Chinese situation. The easy way out is to conclude that China threatens the oil sources of the South China Sea, its strategic lanes, and has its eye on Central Asian oil. If this is so obvious to everybody, then this is what the Chinese want them to think. In that case, the South China Sea and Central Asian oil are not priority targets—they act as a diversion. Ideologically, economically and militarily, after the acquisition of Hong Kong, the feather in the Chinese cap would be Taiwan

General Tao Hangzhang, senior advisor to the Beijing Institute for International Strategic Studies, published *Sun Tzu's Art of War: a Modern Interpretation* in 1987. Explaining Sun Tzu's terms "void" and "actuality", he explains: "sometimes there is real action in void, but most of the actions are deceptive…to deceive and trap the enemy" (p. 45). China's posturing in relation to the South China Sea and Central Asia is the "real action in void". The actuality is to neutralize India and take Taiwan. It is in the strongest interests of the West to pre-empt China from a fait accompli in either direction, failing which it might be impossible to avoid a collision course between the two. The reality of the Cold War never disappeared—it just moved house to Beijing.

Russia & China Pose Grave Challenge To U.S.—June 1999.

Russia and China have been engaged in the past few weeks in intense manic-depressive foreign policy moves. These moves represent the process of great powers going into opposition to a superpower. Both nations are well on their way to formalizing an anti-American, anti-Western alliance.

Right after the bombing of Kosovo began, Russia went ballistic, even threatening the United States with nuclear war. China remained sullen, but relatively quiet. Then Russia turned mellow, trying to work with the West while China went ballistic over the bombing of their embassy in Belgrade along with a host of other issues. The intense mood swings are, of course, calculated to have rational goals. Russia and China, individually, are trying to achieve three things.

First, both countries want to get the attention of the United States and major allies like Germany and Japan.

Second, they want to generate a substantial level of concern within the United States regarding the direction of relations with each of them. Russia and China both hope to increase their leverage within the relationship and, ideally, extract political and, more important, financial concessions from a concerned U.S. that is hoping to appease them and thus avoid a new cold war.

Finally, they hope to create serious fear among U.S. allies concerning trends in American foreign policy. This move is designed to split the Western alliance and weaken the United States.

From time to time, both Russia and China generate major confrontations with the U.S. projecting that a catastrophic collision is about to occur. Then, they allow themselves to be placated by the U.S. and its allies, extracting economic concessions in return for political and military quiescence. They recreate the image of the Cold War as a reminder of the "bad old days." The Russian announcement regarding its Black Sea Fleet and mobs of Chinese hurling stones at the U.S. embassy in Beijing all serve to remind everyone how bad things could get. That set the stage for the next phase that was bargaining on the price for not letting things get that bad.

No matter how much money the West provides, Russia cannot recover from its problems since these problems are deeply rooted structural and cultural defects in the Russian system. Money sent to Russia remains money to be spent on imported luxuries, used to bribe opposition politicians, or stolen. It does not create economic growth. Thus, the maneuvering gets the West's attention, followed by ineffective assistance and a return to the crisis stage.

In the case of China, several bilateral meetings were fruitless. In addition, criticism from the U.S. on human rights, the investigation of Chinese financial aid to President Clinton and the espionage scandal, have all contributed to a chill in relations. The Chinese see the bombing of their embassy as a marvellous opportunity to redefine their relations with the United States. Taking a page from Moscow's book, they recreated the world prior to Deng Xiao Ping, complete with howling mobs and resolutions condemning American hegemony. That got the U.S.' attention, but as with Russia, it was not clear what the Chinese wanted that the U.S. and the West could give them. Everyone rushed forward to see what could be done about World Trade Organization membership for China. However, given the structural dynamics of 1999 as opposed to 1995, and given China's unofficial economic crisis, it is not clear what WTO membership would do for China. It is also unclear what else could be rationally offered.

The real danger is that during these periodic ritual chest-thumping episodes, the situation might generally get out of hand. Yeltsin skilfully reined in the anti-Western forces he helped unleash. He cannot do this indefinitely. The same is true in China. The leadership can whip up anti-

U.S. frenzy on demand—it is not clear they will always be able to control it. Both Russia and China are well on their way to forming an anti-U.S. alliance while the U.S. looks on as a spectator rather than a player.

SECTION TWO—NATO

NATO Summit Ends With Hollow Warning To Serbs—September 1994.

The 13th summit in NATO's 43 years concluded with its sixteen members looking sheepish. The four Visegrad countries of MittelEuropa—Hungary, Poland, Slovakia and the Czech Republic, with little Lithuania hopefully peeping over their shoulders—will have to content themselves with article 4 of the NATO charter. In case of attack, they may ask NATO leaders to convene, and no more. They would have preferred article 5, according to which an attack on one member means an attack against the Alliance. Lech Walesa, Poland's redoubtable anticommunist warrior had dismissed Partnership for Peace, coined by the lustreless Les Aspin, as "short-sighted and irresponsible". The joint military exercises and training, development of common military doctrine and standardization of equipment offered to the Visegrad countries are nothing new. Two years ago, the North Atlantic Cooperation Council had offered them as much, and NATO today remains Warren Christopher's "meritocracy" so that the Ukraine can dismantle its 1700 nuclear weapons, gleefully count the three billion U.S. dollars in exchange, and chuckle over its influence on U.S policy.

The NATO summit suitably threatened the Serbs besieging Sarajevo, with aerial bombardment. Resolution 836 of the UNO had promised no less in August 1993. The NATO summit faithfully reiterated the UN resolution—down to the absence of a timetable. The Serbs impudently responded with increased shelling of Sarajevo, and Mr. Clinton blithely blew his own saxophone.

The weekly *European* had jeered at Partnership for Peace as "redolent of Clintonian New Age Cuddliness" in an article titled "Cuddly Clinton and

Tale of Two Bears". On the 7th of January, speaking in Milwaukee, Vice President Al Gore observed that the security of the MittelEuropa states affects the security of the U.S. The U.S. administration has tried to accommodate this reality within the traditional nostrum of Democratic Party Liberalism: keenness on multilateral intervention, use of the UNO, a shared burden of world leadership and timidity in the use of force to compel policy choices. The stature achieved for the U.S. by its brilliant military commanders in the Gulf has been compromised by the hiccups in Somalia, Haiti and Bosnia.

Sam Nunn, Chairman of the Senate Armed Services Committee, writing in *The Washington Post*, affirmed: "Russian military's traditional subordination to political leadership apart, it remains a politically potent force, more so in the light of the Yeltsin-Zhirinovsky power tussle. A poll of Russian officers of different ages and ranks reveals that two-thirds of them do not regard NATO with suspicion. There is no apprehension about the Visegrad countries joining NATO. In fact, the younger officers, impressed with the outstanding success of the Land-Air Warfare doctrine in the Gulf War, are quite looking forward to either joint exercises with NATO, or full membership".

The obstacles to a redefinition of NATO do not lie in Europe. A revision of the treaty cannot be proposed by a U.S. government without the two-thirds approval of the U.S. senate.

The Rusian army is seriously concerned about a restless Islam in their immediate neighbourhood. Kazakhstan and Pakistan are nuclear powers. Iran aspires to join the club, and conflicts rage from Ajerbaijan to Uzbekistan. Turmoil further afield (India, Myanmar, East Timor, Malaysia, Indonesia, Philippines, Nigeria, Sudan, Somalia, Mali, North Africa and the Middle East) provokes equal concern among the western economies regardless of their military alliance. There is no evidence to link terrorist acts inspired by Islamic fundamentalism with nuclear proliferation. However, the goals of sponsor countries are remarkably similar.

The geographical dispersion of Islamic ambition needs a well-knit alliance to curtail it, and the infusion of new blood cannot undermine its strength. Helping Pakistan, Algeria and Iran with nuclear technology, the Chinese are continuing communism's flirtation with Islam in an effort to undermine the West. A strong NATO encourages the liberal elements in Islamic countries.

The U.S. Armed Forces constitute NATO's center of gravity until the emergence of a European Army. A disengaged United States, unmindful of security threats in the post-cold war era, could nudge Europe towards military cooperation with the Russian army.

Weakening NATO denies it a post-war role, allows Russian hardliners to dictate U.S. policy, and shackles the American ability to bring about change.

EU Fighting Forces Become Volunteer Pros— May 1996.

On February 22, 1996, the French president, Jacques Chirac announced his government's decision to phase-out national service in favor of an all-volunteer army. He is aiming for "more efficient, more modern, and if possible, more cost-effective" armed forces, believing the present set-up to be "unsuitable". Their current strength is 500,000, which breaks down to about 300,000 professionals and roughly 201,000 conscripts. Conscription is to be phased-out by the year 2001, while 50,000 career soldiers will be added to the present number of professionals. This would give France a professional army of 350,000, and allow it to rapidly deploy a force of 60,000 where and when appropriate to French policy. A land-based system of nuclear deterrence -"force de frappe"—is to give way to a more mobile nuclear defense. Although Napoleon used a "national army" to devastating effect, it is no longer esteemed relevant to today's needs.

The principle of a mobile, well-equipped force of professionals capable of expressing French foreign policy beyond its borders is welcomed by left and right wing political opinion, and has public support. Critics of an all-volunteer army see it as "mercenary", a criticism based on second-hand interpretations of Machiavelli. This criticism represents a deep-rooted fear of a coup d'état—memories of the "colonel's putsch" during the Algerian war are still alive.

Retention of some form of national service is deemed essential to the inculcation of national values in a country where schools are state-run secular institutions with a reserved attitude to flag, country and prayer. A national public service has been suggested by the government. Conscripts would serve in the police, fire departments, education and health services.

The sense of national involvement is considered important for young people, especially alienated members of ethnic minorities.

France's allies in Europe approve of the French decision to professionalize its army, and are working on the same lines. Germany plans to have a professional rapid-action force of 50,000 by the year 2000, and reportedly might phase out its "citizens' army". Holland plans to replace national service by an all-volunteer army. In 1993, Belgium announced the professionalization of its 80,000 strong national service army by 1998, which would be reduced to 40,000. At the moment, Britain is the only EU country to maintain a professional army. If continental Europeans have nothing to match it, projection of EU foreign policy risks becoming hostage to British intransigence.

There are also economic considerations. According to NATO figures quoted by the French *Le Monde*, in 1995 the defense expenditures of France, the U.S., Britain and Germany came to 2.5 percent, 3.9 percent, 3.1 percent and 1.7 percent of GDP respectively. The emphasis is now on lean, keen and mean, with high-tech equipment the order of the day: fewer soldiers, better equipment, lower cost and increased efficiency. Britain, France's ally and historic rival, has already put out a $2 billion contract to digitalize its communications equipment, and 23 universities and industries are reportedly involved in developing the Mobile Advanced Robotics Defense Initiative, which translates as robots replacing men on the battlefield. The moral argument for this approach is sound, but not elastic enough to cover rising unemployment.

Over the past 10 years, defense industry jobs in Western Europe have shrunk by one-third, from 1.5 million to 1 million. The defense industry mergers in the United States leading to more streamlined business management, have inspired Western European defense industries to merge within and across borders, fuelling unemployment figures for profit and efficiency. The French president announced that his government would pursue "two new poles of excellence"—aerospace and electronics. Strategically, this leads to more mobile tactics, in accordance with de Gaulle's vision in his book *The*

Army of the Future, liberally praised by former U.S. President Richard Nixon in *Leaders.* However, if no new jobs are created to offset the unemployment that will certainly result from the new army reforms, it would be that much more difficult for Mr. Chirac to be reelected.

A creative arms export policy is likely to be expected as an alternative to decreased employment. Once the EU armies are "digitalized", their governments will be seeking markets for the replaced equipment which will still be of high quality and relevant to countries with regional interests. With China's aggressive naval maneuvers off Taiwan giving Asian countries the jitters, they are a ripe market for such materiel—perhaps a subject of unofficial discussion during the March 1996 Euro-Asian summit in Bangkok.

The implementation of army reforms should enable the EU to project a common foreign policy without undue reliance on American help, and be more self-reliant in the event of a resurgent Russia unwilling to abandon its historical appetites.

NATO Expansion A Double-Edged Sword—May & June 1998.

The North Atlantic Treaty Organization (NATO) and the Western European Union (WEU) are military alliances that cooperate and at times compete to maintain peace in Europe. While the United States of America and Canada are members of NATO, they do not form part of the WEU. Since the middle of this decade, the focus of the competition has been centered on the operational control of NATO's Southern Command and the Alliance's eastward expansion, while the profile of the Soviet Union's successor as a potential threat remains obscure. Military alliances are structured as a response to a future enemy, and not for other reasons.

Starting from the five-nation Brussels Treaty of 1948, NATO was founded by the U.S., Canada and 12 European Allies in April 1949. Subsequent to its creation, NATO continued enlarging: Greece and Turkey in 1951, West Germany in 1955 and Spain in 1982. There are now a total of 16 members.

In 1955, France, Germany, Britain, Italy, Spain, Portugal and the Benelux countries created the WEU to promote European integration, collective defense and security. All WEU countries are NATO members, whereas all NATO members are not part of the WEU. The geographical dispersion of the WEU member countries explains their keen interest in maintaining a decision-making capacity relevant to the Mediterranean Basin under the aegis of NATO or the WEU. The NATO southern command based in Naples is crucial to the Mediterranean basin, the North African side of which is a possible source of military threat or target of military intervention, taking into account the range of Libya's missiles and the excitability of Algerian fundamentalists. The WEU forces all have a commitment to NATO, and NATO, of course, offers resources vastly superior to those of the WEU, especially in logistics, intelligence, communication and transport. Of 36 satellites used to monitor events in Bosnia, 35 are American. The 36th, Helios, a French, German, Italian and Spanish venture, only functions in good weather. The combined defense budgets of the EU countries are estimated at about half of the U.S. defense budget. Ideally, the WEU leadership would like the luxury of NATO resources to implement a Mediterranean policy. The North Americans, however, appear disinclined to commit their resources to a decision-making process in which their participation is disproportionate to their contribution. The creation of a Rapid Action Force of French, Italian and Spanish contingents with British naval support is on offer to NATO for deployment in the event of a Mediterranean crisis. However, NATO's reaction to this offer remains lukewarm (*National Educator*, Nov '94). NATO's Southern Command based in Naples has assumed a status crucial to the definition of cross-Atlantic relations.

Currently, the NATO southern command is American. The WEU, and most of its members within NATO, have been actively lobbying for a European commander, with little success and much friction. British participation in the move to having a European Commander for Southern Command has been unenthusiastic, revealing no change in their fundamental approach to EU interests.

In 1989, the Berlin Wall came down, and the Soviet Union imploded. Since then, the WEU has been aspiring to increase Europe's decision-making capacity, whilst searching for venues to convert the European Union (EU)'s economic power into political and diplomatic influence. Its limited success has not deterred NATO's efforts to redefine itself in the post cold war period. Redefining potential threats and reassessing the number of NATO members has maintained momentum since the organization's creation. In 1993, a bewildered American foreign policy team under the "lusterless" Les Aspin (*National Educator* Sep '94) proposed something called Partnership for Peace. Selected ex-members of the Soviet Union would be offered NATO's security umbrella without being admitted as full-fledged members. Which in effect means we don't accept the obligation of assuming your problems, but if you behave yourselves and listen to us, we might give you a hand provided we don't have to go out of our way. That is a message for imbeciles, and East Europeans are far from being that! In 1994, Lech Walesa dismissed Partnership for Peace as "short-sighted and irresponsible". The weekly *European* had found it "redolent of Clintonian New Age Cuddliness" (*National Educator* Sep '94). However, lacking a better alternative, there was and still is, a respectable queue to receive Washington's benevolence.

The road to hell being paved with good intentions, the nobility of this decision stops at the intention. Entrance to NATO has become the big lolly over which East Europe scrabbles, Western Europe chuckles, Russia flourishes and the United States appears to flounder. The offer introduces a structural weakness within NATO, inherent to a double-tiered imperative.

The question is, which of the East European countries can slide into NATO, buff up their credentials for joining the European Union, tweak the Russians' nose and then call for help across the Atlantic? Washington shows itself incapable of setting clear standards for NATO membership. Its diplomatic hubris shows it up to the EU diplomats. Russia and the appeasement lobby on both sides of the Atlantic play up to fears of Russian reaction to the inclusion of countries that Russia would still like to consider within its sphere of influence. The erstwhile Campaign for Nuclear Disarmament (CND) based its hysteria on a similar fear. Perhaps the eminently experienced conductors of the CND lent their expertise to orchestrating this second sequence of Russian policy.

Russia's demand from observer status to participant in NATO decisions has become a subject of serious consideration, without taking into account the pitfalls inherent to including a historical adversary within the confines of military decision-making.

Since June 1993, NATO has been moving towards eastward expansion and structural changes. Just like Mr. Clinton's Africa tour in March was, among other things, designed to secure the African-American vote for his party, eastward expansion, with Poland top of the list, hopes to massage voters of Polish descent. The second motive is to neutralize German, French and Russian ambitions in East Europe. Poland, Hungary and the Czech Republic are members of the old Habsburg Empire. Their treatment at German hands fifty years ago notwithstanding, they still seek to "fleet their time carelessly" in the golden age of the Habsburg Empire. Germany, compared with all the other EU countries, is the single biggest trading partner of Poland, Hungary, and the Czech Republic. This relationship concerns the United States and France, as they both compete for a share of the market, hearts and minds of these countries. In the tussle for East Europe, whoever succeeds in taking credit for admitting new members to NATO will always exert a decisive influence on these countries.

On the eve of the Second World War, France held East Europe in a series of balanced alliances in pursuit of its well-known strategy of *Alliance de Revers*, similar to the Kautilyan mandalas. In 1936, the outbreak of the Spanish Civil War and Hitler's subsequent rapprochement with Mussolini seriously weakened these alliances. Hitler's invasion of Poland in 1939 is a classic case of a treaty rendered worthless by gun-barrels unless its signatories are willing to shed their blood to enforce it—at the right time. Just as the French are keen to regain ground lost over half a century ago, the Germans are only now recovering their old sphere of influence: the Habsburg empire bound these countries under the influence of a Teutonic Reich for over a thousand years (*National Educator*, Mar '96). Russia is content to wait for a similar opportunity. If Poland, Hungary and the Czech Republic seek French class, German butter and American guns, then Russian bayonets might one day relieve them of their burden.

At the 1996 summit in Lisbon, there was a hue and cry over "new dividing lines" liable to aggravate Russia, were Poland, Hungary, and the Czech

Republic to be included in NATO. The opposition declared by Russia at that time has become a fundamental necessity of Russian policy. Bowing to the pressure, the U.S. acceded to Russian demands that they be partners in NATO's decision-making process. The Russians have a permanent mission in Lisbon, whereas NATO maintains one in Moscow. The "radical reforms" of the Russian army being touted as liberalization by the pro-Russia EU lobby will only result in a leaner, keener and meaner military.

The structural reform of NATO underlies a good part of the U.S.-EU relationship. European defense comes under the aegis of the Western European Union (WEU), which is supposed to ensure strategic and political command of a NATO operation relevant to the EU, "borrowing" NATO resources. This translates as American equipment and European blood. In 1996, France and the United States had both taken unyielding stances over the operational control of NATO's southern sub-command, headquartered in Naples. The French interest was to be able to ensure the security of its Mediterranean flank. According to the French weekly *l'Express*, (5 Dec '96) President Chirac had written twice to President Clinton expressing his wish for NATO's two regional commands in Europe to be under EU control. The British weekly *The Economist* went so far as to title an article "War over Naples" (30 Nov '96). In the end, Naples was retained under American command.

Subject to other requirements completed by the three East European countries (Poland, Hungary and the Czech Republic) 1999 has been set as the date of their entry into NATO. Parliaments of the 16-member states need to ratify this entry, and the countries themselves need further preparation.

Insofar as its intention remains unrealized, Partnership For Peace was a failure. Everybody is scrabbling around, with the Russians looking smug. A dangerous game of piece-meal is being played by people who do not always understand the consequence of their little computer war games and scenarios. Not content with the achievements of their predecessors, they are determined to violate every known principle of strategy espoused by thinkers from Kautilya to Bismarck to Fuller and Liddell Hart. While NATO expansion will maintain the fecundity of the arms industry, it will not help to draw a clear profile of NATO's adversary, indispensable to the *raison d'être* of a military alliance.

The common threat to NATO comes from China and fundamentalist Islam. China's military expansion, economic watershed and acquisition of Hong Kong's resources encourage its "lost territory" policy. Any part of the world ever visited by the Imperial Chinese Navy is considered "lost territory", but only claimed as such in proportion to China's military capability. As this capability develops, it will lead China to "discover" more "lost territories". In the meantime, applying the Chinese proverb "my enemy's enemy is my friend", the Chinese actively aid countries hostile to the U.S. and its allies whose reaction of appeasement serves to wish China Godspeed in its ventures.

Fundamentalist Islam's antagonism towards the west has never been couched in diplomatic-speak. However, apart from a few rogue countries, fundamentalist Islam lacks statehood, remaining a revolutionary force dispersed in different countries. Unable to be localized as a state, an alliance of states like NATO is unable to treat it within its domain. After all, generals fight enemy forces on defined terrain, whereas propagandists, diplomats and the IMF help unstable regimes to contain what is considered no more than a destabilizing force within individual countries. Yet a close study of Antoine Sfeir's gripping book *Allah's Networks* (*"Les Reseaux d'Allah", Plon, France, 1997) reveals the existence of a well-organized, supra national Islamic force on another collision course with the west.*

Identifying China and this other force as potential threats upsets the political comfort of many of NATO members' leadership, keeping the Alliance poised between illusion and reality.

NATO Expansion Redefining Role Of Alliance— April 1999.

The inclusion of Poland, Hungary and the Czech Republic into NATO creates certain serious strategic problems that must be dealt with if NATO is going to be a military alliance as well as a moral project.

Last month's NATO expansion means that the mutual guarantees of assistance in time of war are now extended to the three new members as well. If any of them is attacked, it is the legal and moral obligation of all NATO members to come to its assistance. This dramatically increases both the responsibilities and vulnerabilities of NATO. The expansion may also increase the opportunities that need to be considered carefully.

NATO has become defined in two ways: first, along with the European Union as an alliance among democratic states. The assumption is that membership in NATO and the EU is so attractive that the former socialist states now freed from Soviet control would be motivated to reconstruct their political, social and economic systems in order to be permitted to join. Membership appears to have been given as a reward to three countries that have gone farthest in evolving into democratic polities with market economies.

The second role that NATO has defined for itself derives from the first. If NATO is a club for democratic, capitalist countries, and if its purpose is to motivate countries to be democratic and capitalist, then it follows that NATO should also punish countries that are not democratic and capitalist. One punishment is exclusion. Slovakia and Romania, for example, both wanted to join NATO, but were rejected for membership for not living up to NATO's standards. Since rejection, both have been trying to reform their internal systems in order to be eligible in the next round of expansion. There is another punishment. In extreme cases where the anti-democratic, anti-free market behaviour of states goes beyond certain limits, NATO is seen as an instrument of rectification, imposing penalties on the transgressor, including military penalties. Serbia has become the exemplar of this treatment.

NATO has, in other words, transformed itself from a defensive alliance against the Soviet Union into a system of relations designed to regulate the internal political, economic and social relations of not only member countries, but also of nonmembers on the periphery of the NATO alliance.

Deep and pressing strategic issues face NATO. The fate of Kosovo may be morally pressing but it is not strategically significant. It is not that moral issues are frivolous, but they always carry a price. That price can sometimes be paid, sometimes not. The price for Kosovo is not a military price, but an intellectual challenge.

Do NATO planners have the ability to ask broad geopolitical and strategic questions about NATO's expansion? Put differently, the expansion of the alliance may compel the Russians to begin acting strategically again. That development will compel NATO to respond to, rather than control, events.

SECTION THREE—THE EUROPEAN UNION

Politics Blocks Military Solution To Balkan Crisis—October 1993.

The sixteen month old fratricidal war in the former Yugoslav republic of Bosnia-Herzegovina has claimed 200,000 casualties. The religious lines that define this conflict involve the concern of non-European countries. The Islamic world lobbies this conflict to the non-Islamic third world on a North-South basis. This used to be the Soviet argument to rally third world "have-nots" against the forces of capitalism. The implosion of the USSR allows the Islamic world to continue this argument.

The morality of political decision is based on raison d'état. Thus the Islamic criticism of the West's umpiring the Balkan ball game on a moral basis has limited effect. At the same time, the necessity of decisive western action is vital to credible leadership.

The United Nations organization does not have an inherent leadership built into its framework. Leadership comes from countries such as the U.S. and France. The administrative setup of the UN legitimises military action for humanitarian and democratic principles. Third World member states have contributed troops for UN actions. Irrespective of their level of military skills, regional armies are out of their depth on global missions.

This leaves the onus of responsibility on the western alliance. The U.S. Armed Forces are the largest and best equipped. Yet this attribute becomes a drawback for a democratic government under the constant scrutiny of a critical press sceptical of unilateral action.

The other members of the western alliance are also wary of unilateral action. It could upset the balance of authority within NATO.

NATO member states under the aegis or shield of the European Community tried to defuse the Balkan crisis. They failed because they lacked a single political will and the means to express it. Since the beginning of the Balkan crisis, the lack of a European political will has been compounded by the hiccups of the European exchange rate mechanism. While the credentials of the EC as an economic entity are intact, its credibility as a political entity is under threat.

The EC's lack of enthusiasm over U.S. unilateral action in the European backyard is at odds with the EC's inability to act. This is further compounded by the listless domestic support in the U.S. of unilateral action in the Balkans, involving the commitment of ground forces. Public support in the U.S. for air action is, however, positive.

As the decision to send U.S. Special Forces to track down the recalcitrant Farah Aidid in Somalia reveals, small actions dictate their own logic despite the casualty figures and brevity of the Gulf War. In conflicts like the Balkans and Somalia, ground forces will need to pull their weight with only limited air support. The choice of another Army general rather than an Air Force appointee to be the new Chairman of the Joint Chiefs of Staff appears to reflect recognition of this reality.

Solutions to the Balkan crisis echo across the Atlantic. The U.S. and the EC do agree on the advantages of multilateral intervention. They also value the continuity of NATO in a post-communist world.

The only alternative to unilateral U.S. action is equal participation by the EC. This would be cost effective for all the actors. While the EC has yet to prove its political cohesion, its members have professional, globally oriented forces. Since the late 1970s, the French FAR (Force d'Action Rapide) has been honed in action ranging from demanding bush wars to the high-tech Gulf War. The French Foreign Legion is the mainstay of the FAR, and is mainly composed of foreigners from all parts of the world. This makes the Legion a truly multinational force of battle-tested professionals, which the French have successfully recruited, trained and led for over 163 years. Expansion of this force with the ethos on European recruits is a ready-made formula for a European Force that would allow NATO to redefine its role as an instrument of world peace.

Turkey Seeks Entrance In EC But Its Credentials Are Spotty—June 1994.

The removal of customs barriers between Turkey and the EC are scheduled for 1995. Procedural details are being worked out between Ankara and Brussels. Eventually, Turkey aspires to full EC membership.

Since the Islamized Byzantines' besieging of Vienna in 1529 and 1683, to the Sick Man of Europe kicked into life by Kemal Pasha Attaturk's 1922 revolution, Turkey has been rattling the European gates. Taking advantage of Europe's liberal immigration policies, Turks are already well represented in menial jobs all over the continent. Fulfilling Kemal Pahsa's scheme, Turkey even has a woman Prime Minister, the mediagenic Tansu Ciller. In January this year, she gave an interview to *The Independent, Le Monde* and *De Standaart*. The Prime Minister cited the challenge posed to the Turkish economy by her country's application to remove EC customs barriers. She alluded to the EC aid granted to Greece, Portugal and Spain to cushion their entry into the EC. Insinuations of unfair EC aid distribution from an official source, only question Turkey's status as a self reliant, mature regional power. The results of Turkey's municipal elections in April have blurred Turkey's image of itself as part of the West. With 19 percent of the vote going to the fundamentalist Islamic Welfare Party— compared with only 21.7 percent for Mrs. Ciller's True Path Party— Istanbul's Town Council is in the Islamic grip. The fierce declaration "Istanbul is the capital of the world", is provocative. As such, Turkey's credentials to join the EC have further sunk.

In Mrs. Ciller's eyes, Turkey's credentials to enter the EC are considerable: two billion dollars in aid to countries of "the region", wheat and medicine to Christian Armenia, and a love for democracy and human rights. Mrs. Ciller understandably ignored the selective application of human rights in Turkey, its five billion dollar defense budget and nearly 60 billion dollar debt. However, Mrs. Ciller soothingly reassured European newspaper readers that unlike Russia, Turkey has no ambitions of seeking its old frontiers. This comparison of Russian and Turkish appetites evokes the Crimean War (1853-1856) alliance of Turkey, France, Britain and Sardinia. Then, as now, Turkey lacked the muscle to match Russian ambition.

While Russia is pressuring member countries of the Commonwealth of Independent States (CIS) to sign bilateral accords, Turkey has chosen a more enlightened approach to renewing relations with its ex-colonies. "We would like to enter the game," (referring to Russian resurgence) declared Mrs. Ciller.

Turkey has a full agenda of Kiplingesque Games. In the days of SEATO and CENTO, Turkey, Iran and Pakistan formed RCD (Regional Cooperation for Development), which covered close military cooperation and survived the Shah's overthrow. In 1985, RCD became Economic Cooperation Organization (ECO), with headquarters in Teheran and a Pakistani General secretary, Shamshad Ahmed. In November 1992, ECO embraced Azerbaijan, Kazakhstan, Kirghistan, Uzbekistan, Tajikistan, Turkestan and Afghanistan—all ex-Soviet Islamic countries and, along with Pakistan, part of the old Turkish Qarakhani and Ghaznavid empires. Turkey's interests are locked into an organisation headquartered in the capital of the most venomously anti-western country. The General Secretary of this organization represents a country that missed its place on Mr. Bush's list of terrorist states by a hair's breadth. Writing about the ECO in the conservative Le Figaro of France, Hélène Carrere d'Encousse unambiguously remarkd "Is this not an Islamic common market?"

And if the Chinese Prime Minister, Li Peng, has his way, Istanbul and Beijing would be linked by a transcontinental rail line over the old Silk Route. In the last week of April, Li Peng touted this idea on his 12-day, five-nation visit of Central Asia to promote a "silk road".

Ottoman interests ranged over the Black Sea basin where Turk dynasties ruled between the 3d and 13th centuries. The 11-member Black Sea Economic Cooperation Zone in which Turkey and Russia jockey for leadership indicates another priority of Turkish foreign policy. As the Ottoman Caliphate included the Middle East, Turkey's construction of the Attaturk Dam on the Euphrates provides strategic leverage over Syria and Iraq (see Muazzam Gill's analysis in *The National Educator*, May 1992). Some 97 percent of Turkey's sovereign territory today is Asian. Taken together, the ECO, the Black Sea Economic Cooperation Zone and the part of the Middle East affected by the Attaturk Dam echo the Ottoman Caliphate. Turkey's desire to enter the EC is a response to the abortive siege of Vienna.

So far, Turkey has shown a commitment to Europe in word, but to the Islamic world in deed. It is also mindful of the fundamentals of Byzantine foreign policy. Between 394 and 491 AD, the Byzantine emperors astutely diverted the attention of Barbarians, Huns and Ostrogoths westwards. Will the energy of ECO citizens take a westward impulse? There are no barriers to intermarriage between ECO citizens. Naturalized Turks roaming at will across EC pastures will aggravate the native population. Isaie Garcia, construction supervisor with worldwide experience, demands— "If Turkey is given member status within the EC, why not Morocco?"

Turkey's foreign policy commitments are already disproportionate to its resources. Moving closer to the EC will overburden them. Faced with the stress of its obligations to the ECO and the Black Sea Economic Cooperation Zone, Turkey would be entitled to an EC bailout. The EC might find itself unwittingly financing Turkey's chosen responsibilities outside the EC. Turkey would also become a conduit for the liberal entry of cheap goods into the EC manufactured in the ECO and the Black Sea Economic Cooperation Zone, as well as Chinese goods brought over Li Peng's Beijing-Istanbul "Silk Road". The EC will end up divided against itself.

Western Europeans have the political maturity to understand this eventuality and the cultural sophistication to guard against it. A Turkey unencumbered by conflict of interest is an asset to the EC.

Until Turkey can provide suitable guarantees, European attention will stay closely focused on its political structure, human rights record and intricate foreign policy.

Anti-Corruption Broom Sweeping Europe—December 1994.

It started in Milan, Italy, in February 1992. Nearly a half-century of Christian Democratic and Socialist monopoly on power was swept away by what the press dubbed operation "Mani Pulite" (Clean Hands). Some 4600 preventive detention warrants and 2500 notices of judicial inquiries were issued. Recently, the brother of Silvio Berlusconi, the Prime Minister of Italy, was arrested twice. In pre-emptive defiance, the Prime Minister has declared that if he received a notice of judicial inquiry, he would not resign. Antonio di Pietro who started it all, has now published a best selling book.

In Spain, Felipe Gonzalez's socialist government has been confronted with its most serious crisis yet. In parliament, the opposition leader put it bluntly: "… off you go, Senor Gonzales." For a Prime Minister who contested an election on a sanctimonious "halt corruption" platform, Gonzalez's government has been offering corruption scandals. Its anti-corruption measures announced in May of this year were followed by a series of resignations by cabinet and parliamentary members accused of corruption.

Staid old Britain has had its own share of trouble, going beyond an overrun of libido and avant-garde sexual practices that have been fuelling tabloid circulation. The bathos of the royal family's philandering has been overtaken by the resignation of two cabinet members over corruption charges and the alleged involvement of Mark Thatcher in a financial scandal. Margaret Thatcher's son is under investigation for bribes reportedly extorted in the $26 billion Al Yamamah arms contract while mum was in power. As the Tories gathered for their annual conference in Bournemouth, a Gallup poll quoted by the British weekly *The Economist* "showed that a remarkable 61 percent of the electorate believed the gov-ernemnt to be very sleazy and disreputable."

The broom has now started sweeping France. *The Times* of London observes: "After a flurry of scandals in the 1980's involving the socialists, leaving party Secretary Henri Emanuelli still under investigation (this year has seen an) eruption of judicial inquiries around the Gaullists and center right.' The ministers of Defense and Enterprises are "the subject of intense scrutiny," the Industry minister has resigned, and the Communications Minister, Alain Carrignon, who is also the mayor of Grenoble resigned his cabinet post. On 14 October he was arrested and, at the time of writing, is still under police remand. He has been charged with having accepted gifts to the tune of $4 million. If convicted, he could be sentenced for ten years. Since the founding of the Fifth Republic in 1958, no serving or for-mer minister has been jailed. The Carrignon case has left France aghast. *Le Figaro*, the conservative daily, darkly hinted of a putsch if the political classes were discredited. The weekly *Le Point* loftily observed, "Justice is brandishing its sword and striking".

Gerald Dulac, Grenoble councilman, believed that "in the absence of the mayor, the town council should choose one of several solutions." Jacky Machu, National Front member of the Regional parliament, comments: "Corruption is known to have existed, but the judicial system had been held in check." Jean-Christophe Leveque, a Gaullist college teacher, remarks: "The European political apparatus is in line for an overhaul."

With the presidential election only eight weeks away, neither pole of the political spectrum can afford a scandal. Following socialist squabbles, public bickering over the presidential candidacy has now broken out among the right-wing coalition. If Mr. Mitterand scents blood, he could bow out in January, paving the way for a socialist ride on Jaques Delors' back. Writing for *The Times* of London, Charles Brenneur maliciously predicts: "Scandals dogging the ruling Gaullists are likely to boost social-ist chances of holding onto the French presidency, especially if they can persuade Jaques Delors to run."

Mr. Alain Carrignon's misfortune has become the focus of national attention to debate several issues. While France waits with bated breath for the inevitable outcome, it is also determined to avoid an Italian-style unravelling of its socio-political fabric. And as cronyism comes under attack across Western Europe, the leadership of the European Union is focused on France.

Industrial Giant Recommends Having No Army—July 1995.

Alessandro Bennetton is typical of the new breed of international Euro-business leader: young, U.S.-educated, vibrant, and almost a man with a vision. At thirty, he already heads a fast-growing international conglomerate. Dapper and well groomed, his opinions combine the endearing idealism of youth and the pragmatism of maturity, taking into account history, political realities and economic necessities. It is this writer's opinion that he is a man to be watched. In the coming decade, whatever its form, the process of Europeanization will have stabilized, and Alessandro Bennetton will be among the handful of Europeans who were part of the process. At about that time, the North American and East Asian trading zones will be rearing up on their hind legs. Their leaders will certainly face Alessandro Bennetton across a negotiating table, if their political counterparts have not already had to test their mettle against him and his peers.

Italy's United Colors of Bennetton are synonymous with sports and leisure at 700 outlets in 120 countries. Bennetton's controversial advertisements actually affirm the Bennetton leadership's grip on the expectations of today's youth culture. Bennetton are now turning towards product diversification, with an emphasis on sport systems. Thirty-year old Alessandro Bennetton, former financial analyst at London's Goldman Sachs International, is president of Bennetton Sportsystem. In 1991, he graduated with honors from Harvard Business School. He now directs Bennetton's diversification strategy that includes Movenpic hotels, Rollerblade and Nordica skis. Bennetton Sportsystem employ 2400 people worldwide, with 55 percent of their fast growing market in the U.S. and a turnover of nearly 100 million dollars a year.

The writer wishes to thank Msrs Panel and Guitton for their invaluable help in arranging the interview. The interview was conducted during a symposium arranged by Grenoble University's Department of Administration and Management and the Grenoble Chamber of Commerce.

A. Gill: *What is the guiding force in Bennetton's continued growth?*

A. Bennetton: (it's) a little bit like reading history. You can read Napoleon on Waterloo in about the '80's and you get a certain feedback. Diversification for us has been a natural, evolutionary process of a family that has been very successful in its own business...lucky to be able to maintain and keep on financing it own business and still have extra resources to allocate. Some families choose to allocate these resources outside of work. Others keep on challenging themselves. I think we are a family that likes challenges. We give companies the freedom to start challenging themselves. Bennetton's influence will be the mental attitude toward exploring new ways of doing business.

A. Gill: *How do you see the future of the European Union?*

A. Bennetton: I think...a more united Europe—there's no question in my mind. The question is always how long it will take—what steps need to be taken in order to get there. The question is how fast we'll get there, and what should be done in order to get there safe and quickly. I still see a lot of problems with Europe. From an economic point of view there's still too much imbalance. Talking about the monetary union and the difficulties that you have. Growth rates are different for different countries. You do not know how much money should cost to the borrowers. Objectively, there is no easy solution. Politically, there's a lot of instability. The lowering of frontier barriers in Europe needs to be done full time, and with the right balance.

A. Gill: *Do you feel the future would be determined by force?*

A. Bennetton: The direction is having no military. We should aim at having no army—nowhere in the world—not even in Japan, and not in Europe.

A. Gill: *What is the guiding force in Bennetton's continued growth?*
A. Bennetton: Probably not (but) that should be the goal. There is a clear indication that the culture of the world is towards interaction. It's a long process, but eventually we go there. The transition is very hard, because already people have invested. Certain balances need to be maintained and because of course there are some economic interests, because some people are living out of these industries.

Waves Of Balkan Refugees Swarm Continent— October 1995.

The new wave of Balkan refugees seems to be overwhelming European governments. In tackling the problem, their policies betray a lack of coherence and initiative. Hatred between Muslims and Christians, and rivalry between the Orthodox and Catholic churches further compounds a human tragedy.

The presence of the current refugee wave disturbs the European landscape less than the non-European immigrants of the preceding few decades with their quest for civility, responding to European employers' search for cheap labor. The war in former Yugoslavia has caused four and a half million refugees so far. The Croatian blitzkrieg in August inspired the United Nations to appeal to over thirty nations worldwide to accept Balkan refugees. That such an appeal was considered necessary bespeaks ill of our economic and moral health.

France has recently expelled illegal immigrants to their home country by charter flight, shocking liberal sentiment. However, these expulsions only included refugees whose asylum appeals had been rejected. The European Human Rights Commission only forbids mass expulsions of refugees whose asylum demands are pending. The means of transport used is not at issue, but underlines the defeatism of the "charter flight" approach. Obviously, existing frontier controls are considered inadequate to filter refugees back to their home country by normal means of transport. The refugees themselves artfully tend to "lose" their passports at the first inkling of a rejection of their asylum application, leading the French government to consider illegal immigration worthy of diplomatic processing. In 1993, a secret agreement to control illegal immigration was signed between the Algerian and French governments, not respected since Algerian Islamists hijacked a French plane last Christmas. In fact, the present government is so busy trying to steal a march on Mr. Le Pen's national front that it has no time to work out a coherent long-term policy.

By virtue of having accepted 80 percent (or 400,000) of the refugees from former Yugoslavia, Germany's moral flag flutters in the European breeze. Manfred Kanther, the German Interior Minister, declared in August "we have done our duty" Without actually saying it won't accept more refugees, Germany is urging other EU countries to accept more of them. The German daily *Bild* reports that Germany's foreign and interior ministers have called on EU countries to accept a quota system to take in war zone refugees. What is unsaid is what happens when the number of applicants exceeds the number allotted in the quota.

And there is an offbeat note to Germany's strident moral drum: discreetly reported by *The European* the EU has just awarded Germany an aid package of 72 million ECU to develop its eastern frontiers in the fields of environmental protection and transport. It is beyond Germany's eastern frontiers that its historical sphere of influence lies—the historical MittelEurope of the Hanseatic League, the Teutonic Knights and the Second Reich of Frederick the Great. Last time, this Mittel Europe was the spawn of German sweat, ingenuity and dynamism. This time Germany's historical ambition might be helped along by EU financing.

Britain is vainly trying a preventive approach before the next wave of refugees puts British civility to the test. Michael Howard, Britain's Home Secretary, announced that employees who hired illegal immigrants would have to pay a substantial fine. Although this policy has had some success in the U.S., Britain is structurally ill-prepared to institute such a measure since it is based on national insurance numbers, depressingly easy to fake. Unless Howard's Measure is backed up by the continental system of identity cards, it remains a blurp of hot air for the forthcoming election balloon. It is reported by the conservative Daily *Telegraph* that British officialdom is seriously considering the continental system of identity cards.

With British civility evolving backwards, and the erstwhile American "cousins" shying away from less fortunate relatives, Britain's solutions lie not across the Atlantic but under the channel.

In 1993 and 1994, Italy sent back boatloads of Albanians in violation of the European Human Rights Commission, and was faced with riots in refugee camps. The reaction to asylum seekers in Sweden is seen in the rise of Viking Skinheads and the inability of sociologists or the authorities to muzzle them: the City of Oslo has now decided to give them free board and lodging so that they may "express themselves"!

Despite the $1.2 billion in trade between Morocco and Spain last year, the Afro-Tunnel (28 kilometers or three-quarters the length of the Chunnel, 400 meters below sea-level, estimated cost $8 billion) which was signed 16 years ago between the Kings of Spain and Morocco, is in the doldrums. Spaniards welcome closer economic ties with North Africa without having to socialize with that lot. The British establishment weekly *The Economist* remarks: "a lot of Spaniards, edgy about the old French adage that 'Africa begins in the Pyrenees' and mindful of their ancestors' long struggle with the Moors, think there are quite enough Moroccans in Spain already".

France is still looking for coherence, Germany has inverted the principle of a quota system, redefining the roles of seeker and giver, Britain is in the process of redefining its concept of civil liberty, Sweden is confused, Italy pragmatic, and Spain wary. Ethnology and economic realities appear to pervade the problem of war-zone European refugees.

In actual fact, European Union press reports indicate that asylum applications across Europe have been falling: from 500,000 in 1993 to 300,000 in 1994. Waves of cheap labor entering Europe after the Second World War were treated with a measure of civility for which there is no historical precedent. Moral principle demanded it, and the old wallet agreed. Moral principle still demands it, but the wallet says no.

Bad sums, misguided principles, employers' greed and unscrupulous fake refugees from exotic corners of the globe have left barren fields for the

Balkan Diaspora. The Muslim clergy grinding the Middle East's axe in former Yugoslavia, and the Orthodox and Roman Catholic churches bickering (notwithstanding the Orthodox patriarch's Vatican visit), leaves the refuges with the dubious dignity of pawns.

European refugee policy is the accumulation of reaction to each new human tide. The initiative, thus, has never been wrested from the refugees. Administrative procedures are out of step with the principles, and moral principles have a very minor role to play in national policy. Political and economic realities take precedence over morality.

Anti-Abortion—The Issue Binding Vatican, Muslims—November 1995.

As NATO bombing runs sought to bring Bosnian Serbs to their senses, the Vatican unleashed EurHope, a mediagenic peace blitz reminiscent of Woodstock. At Lorette, on the banks of the Adriatic and one of the sites of the Virgin's apparition, Catholic youth clap-hopped and sang for peace in former Yugoslavia. The Pope was there in person backed by a dozen cardinals and fifty bishops. So were TV cameras that linked EurHope with six major towns, allowing young Europeans to share their ideals with the Pope. The brainchild of the Pope, the event has been taking place every other year since 1989, the year the Berlin wall came down. This is the fourth and the biggest, with messages pouring in from all over the world across the Internet in support of the Vatican's stand on Bosnia.

Taking the side of Bosnian Muslims against the Orthodox Serbs reflects the continuity of theological warfare between Byzantine and Rome. Many of Europe's eminent analysts believe that John Paul II joined Reagan to battle the Evil Empire to save spiritually hungry East Europeans from a communist-controlled Orthodox church. The collapse of the Soviet Empire might have been the end of a war for the Reagan team, but only the end of a battle for the Vatican. The incontestability of condemning genocide apart, support for Bosnian Muslims allows the Islamic world to view the Vatican as an ally in its world ambitions. At last year's UN women's conference in Cairo, Catholics, Protestants and Muslims united on the anti-Abortion issue. This year was no different. And while the conference was in full swing in Peking, posters of the Virgin Mary and the Baby Jesus proliferated in Teheran with full official backing. Iran is optimistically hoping that a single-issue alliance with the Vatican can lead to diplomatic successes in other domains—forgetting that the Vatican is Not Available for ambitions beyond the scope of the Vatican's own policy.

Russia, without exercising any disapproval of EurHope, is unambiguously disapproving of the NATO air raids against the Bosnian Serbs, fellow-Orthodox Christians. Relations between Moscow and the West are at their lowest since the 1980s. The Duma, Russia's lower house of parliament, does not feel that Russian condemnation of NATO raids and consequent support for the Serbs is vigorous enough. By a vote of 258 to 2, the Duma called for the foreign minister to be sacked, the lifting of UN sanctions against Serbia, and the suspension of Partnership for Peace.

It is not Russia's belligerence over the Serbs that worries NATO, but it's attitude to NATO's development. After a respectable period of ritual posturing, the Russians are now party to Partnership for Peace. A NATO document regarding the rights and duties of new members is being drafted. Russia has reportedly hinted that it would not contest Poland's membership of NATO in return for greater flexibility in deploying forces along its southern and northern borders with Europe. According to the terms of the Conventional Forces in Europe treaty, the Russians are due to reduce troops in Europe by November. At a recent meeting, representatives of Russia, Belorussia, Ukraine and Kazakhstan were doubtful of being able to meet the November deadline—a typically Russian way of oblique diplomacy. In other words, unless they are given more of a say in NATO, and moved up from observer to participant status in the Group of Seven, they will continue to exercise belligerent support in favor of the Bosnian Serbs.

Mr. Holbroke would be well advised to ignore Russian din, feel encouraged by Mr. Kissinger's praise of his "ability", and continue the realpolitik stroked into motion by the energy of the French president on behalf of the European Union. Russia's current stance over Yugoslavia does not indicate policy change, but an intensification of policy on a series of issues stacked up like a set of Russian dolls. The Slav doll, the Greek Orthodox doll, the NATO doll and the G7 doll—all mask the last doll—the cereal doll. Since

1990, Russian population has been growing, but the wheat crop decreasing. The1995 crop is expected to be smaller than even the 1987 crop. Since the days of communism, faced with the prospect of a deficient wheat crop, the Kremlin has diverted the attention a hungry peasantry by renewed hostility towards the west. More often than not, events have conspired to help the Old Men of the Kremlin. The war in Yugoslavia being no exception, it might sustain them until the December elections.

The divisions in the Balkan conflict are religious and not ethnic. The war has provoked the concern of Russia, NATO, the European Union, the Vatican, the Orthodox Church, and the Islamic world. Apart from the Vatican, the other mediators only react to each new escalation, leaving the initiative with the combatants. The U.S. administration is absent in its influence and vocal in its reaction, vainly trying to substitute a platform of international consensus as a substitute for foreign policy. The Vatican is displaying centuries of sophistication with a record of more successes than failures.

The Pope is only too aware of how the original Woodstock festivals of the 60s celebrated the release of hitherto dormant forces harnessed by powers that have since then waned. The forces of the Woodstock phenomenon in Europe would now appear to be in the hands of the Pope. How he handles these forces to swing the Balkan crisis in his favor will affect the ultimate resolution of the age-old tussle between Rome, Byzantium and the Caliphate.

Europe And U.S. Headed For Showdown Over Entertainment—April 1996.

The next World Trade Summit is liable to see a face-off of American and European Union negotiators over Hollywood's lead in purveying fable, myth and legend. The word legend comes from the Latin legenda, meaning things to be read. In monastic refectories in the 13th and 14th centuries, the narratives of saints were read out, especially in the sense of a "marvelous story", a meaning that came to predominate middle English and old French. Didactic stories carrying a moral are fables, and ancient fictitious stories dealing with gods and heroes are myths. Any culture worth its salt is defined by its storehouse of marvelous stories, heroes and morals. Sound psychology, high technology, brilliant marketing and an entrenched distribution system enable Hollywood to relate marvelous stories of gods, heroes and morality, allowing a worldwide audience to synthesize historical perspective and cultural tradition.

George Washington, Kit Carson, Andy Jackson, Davy Crockett, Paul Bunyan, Johnny Appleseed, Chisholm, the Earp brothers, Patton, MacArthur and a host of others are dyed in the wool American legends. Myths have been woven around them, leading to fable handed down as lore. Hollywood has captured imaginations from New York to Calcutta to Nairobi to Panama to Paris. Billions of people the world over claim identity with these legends, easing the way for MacDonald's.

So far, the ethos of American culture has been determined by America's European—and namely Anglo-Saxon—roots. Hollywood has thus, where appropriate, taken its inspiration from Kipling, Dumas, Robin Hood and King Arthur. Even in politics, late U.S. President Kennedy anointed himself King Arthur to his Democratic Party's Camelot.

Professor Bloom in *The Closing of the American Mind* (1987) regrets the pressure of what is called "political correctness" prevalent on campuses, withering away Euro-American literary and philosophical roots. Saul Bellow in the preface to Bloom's book (both Professors at Chicago University) remarks "What no one was able to foresee was that all civilized countries were destined to descend to a common cosmopolitanism...a concealed benefit of decline". In *Democratic Vistas* (1871-92), Walt Whitman, giving body to Ralph Waldo Emerson's vision of American literature independent of Old World constraints, remarked: "I hail with joy the oceanic, variegated, intense practical energy, the demand for facts, even the business materialism of the current age, our States".

Hollywood boldly evokes claim to its European heritage of legend and myth, Americanizes it, and then exports the legend to the rest of the world. It has succeeded in bringing the benefits of legend to ordinary people, freeing them from the constraints of history and culture while making full use of "business materialism".

The Robin Hood legend makes an interesting study. The Disney cartoon has American-accented sixties' biker's slang inspiring successive generations of British children to play Robin Hood in biker's cant rather than the *olde englishe* of *merrye Englande*! When film characters such as Robin Hood, Lancelot, Amadeus and the Three Musketeers speak with an American accent, and the films are hugely successful in Britain, Emerson and Whitman's vision of independent American literature enlarges its dimension to actually influence British English. Although international politics and movies both carry traces of cross Atlantic power shifts, Hollywood's playing upto political correctness at the expense of universal beliefs does not help its institutional popularity.

Take the movie *Robin Hood, Prince of Thieves* (1991). Not just a worldwide legend converted into popular entertainment by Hollywood's technology and business acumen, but politically most correct. Kevin Costner is sweet and winsome, unthreatening to modern feminism and Maid Marian meets the expectations of today's woman. There is no Moor, black or

Muslim in the Robin Hood legend. In one stroke of genius, Hollywood managed to please Muslims and non-whites. Audiences from Egypt to Indonesia are reported to have cheered when the film illustrates that Europeans were primitive compared with the technologically advanced Muslims of the Middle East with their telescopes and compasses.

Thanks to Hollywood, Robin Hood has become bigger business in Britain than it ever was: Robin Hood junk proliferates in Nottingham, and Yorkshire has challenged Nottingham for claim to the Robin Hood legend. Ironically, the New World's "variegated, intense practical energy" has wrested the legend from provincial England for the rest of the world.

Legends today are more seen than read, with consumer verdict measured by box-office sales. The resentment of European intellectuals on this issue influences EU policies protecting the European film industry against Hollywood's relentless efficiency as a purveyor of entertainment and historical and political perspective.

Founding legends and myths define a culture. Sacrificing them to the intellectually bankrupt inheritors of Kennedy's Camelot chasing Mark Twain and William Faulkner off university syllabi is equivalent to Abraham slitting Isaac's throat. To recreate the past is to regress: a trap the historian Gibbs warned against. The next World Trade Summit will see if the EU can successfully meet the pragmatic demands of today's high-tech information- age economics without compromising cultural traditions.

Communist Resurgence In Europe—August-September 1996.

Leftist parties, rebuilt on the ruins of their communist predecessors, retain power in Romania and Bulgaria. Poland reveals a steady rise in the popularity of Olesky's Democratic Left Alliance. Forty percent of the Russian, and 30 percent of the Italian parliament consists of communists under different names. On April 21, 1996, the left-of-center Olive Tree Coalition won 157 out of 284 seats in the Italian senate. In the Chamber of Deputies, which wields real legislative power, they retain 284 out of 630 seats.

The Olive Tree Coalition includes the PDS (Social Democratic Party) that won 21 percent seats in the lower house. The PDS is the soft center of the old communist party with a new name. The hard-core of the old communist party now calls itself Refounded Communists, who hold 9 percent seats in the lower house. The ranks of the PDS and Refounded Communists are made up of the old communist party members in a semantic sleight of hand. Between the two new parties, the ex-communists and communists hold 30 percent seats in parliament putting them at the gravitational center of Italy's coalition government.

A conservative coalition could only have been built on an alliance of mainstream conservatives with neo-fascists and separatists. The neo-fascists' anti-democratic stance, and the Northern League's separatist stance make any such alliance impossible. On the other hand, exclusion by mainstream conservatism influenced Umberto Bossi, head of the Northern League, to launch an outright Declaration of Secession from Montue, the Parliament of the North, on May 6, 1996. Bossi baptized his future state Padonia, a region comprising the Po plain, Piedmont, Venetia and Lombardy, historically opposed to a unified Europe since the 12th century, and today, perhaps by some standards, the richest area of Europe. According to the French daily *Le Monde*, Bossi's declarations "demand to be taken seriously", especially since the Savoy League in the Savoy region of France, bordering Italy, has also evoked the idea of secession.

The British weekly *The Economist* tactfully interpreted the Italian election results as both a rejection of the right and a victory for the left. Whatever hidden meaning the eminent weekly might have wished to couch in this non-statement, their victory has earned communists the legitimacy and credibility they never had during the hammer and sickle days. *The Financial Times* reported that the left-wing victory raised the prospect of the lira entering the European Exchange Rate Mechanism (ERM), a slim prospect anyway, considering a public debt amounting to "25 percent of GNP", servicing which takes up a fifth of the budget.

In 1981, the socialist victory in France provoked capital flight, the franc fell, the Paris stock exchange turned bearish, and the United States was alarmed. Today, *The Financial Times* concludes that a left-wing victory based on 30 percent communist support is good financial news. With the link between communism and the Soviet Union severed, the link between Russian and European communist parties goes unperceived.

In July 1996, Boris Yeltsin's victory against Gennady Zyuganov in Russia was reported as a triumph of pro-western forces against communist up-lash. The Italian liberal daily, *Corrierre della Serra*, referred to a "corporate sigh of relief" at Yeltsin's victory of 53%. The Dutch daily *De Folksland* went further, referring to Yeltsin as a "living corpse", and speculating on his possible death by October, followed by an election which would carry Alexander Lebed into the Kremlin. Michael Kay, news analyst for the BBC World Service drew analogies of Yeltsin's health with Lenin and Brezhnev. Spain's ABC wrote in terms of "the end of an era", clearly not seeing very many years ahead for Yeltsin, whereas the Basque *El Coreo* was of the opinion that Yeltsin's health reflects the state of Russia's economic and political health.

Allied with Alexander Lebed, following his daughter's advice to fire key cronies, putting forward the election date and dancing before the Russian populace to confirm his virility, Boris Yeltsin heroically managed to steer his party to victory. Yet, it is the terms of the communist defeat that merit scrutiny. According to figures given out by the Russian Central Election Commission, Gennady Zyuganov's communists won 32 percent in the first round, and 40.4 percent in the second round. A Kremlin advisor is reported to have said: "We can send the communists to hell". Actually, Russian communists can sit like complacent moles on their 40 percent seats before going to hell. History shows that lack of opportunity rather than legislative constraints contain communists. With their record for overturning the democratic process, their capacity for legislative mischief should not be underestimated. Their current comeback in Russia is a direct consequence of insecurity about the future stemming from lawlessness, disorder and poor economic conditions.

Italy, in terms of private income and property ownership, is ahead of Germany and France in Western Europe: yet the communists hold the key to power. In France, the rise in membership is linked with the rise in unemployment. The communists, then, take opportunities as and when they offer themselves.

In Italy, they changed the party name, and convinced non-communist writers like Leonardo Sciascia that "only communists can save culture" (French weekly *Nouvel Observateur*). *The European* reports that Massima d'Alema, leader of the ex-communist PDS, plans to launch a new movement in June 1997. Called the *Sinistra Democrata* or Democratic Left, it will be an Italian version of Germany's Social Democrat party embracing "a series of lay, Catholic, liberal, socialist and environmental parties". Public memories will be effectively erased as the communists, under different names, implement their program from within.

The political landscape of Europe is a kaleidoscope of right, center and left-wing coalitions. As the Spanish daily *El Mundo* reported Mr. Aznar's triumphant victory in Spain on May 13, Spain became, along with

France, Britain, Germany and Luxembourg, the fifth EU country with conservatives holding power without a coalition. Socialists under different names are in power in Portugal, Greece, Sweden and Denmark, and parts of coalition governments in Austria, Ireland, Italy and Finland.

Do European and Asian communists (China and North Korea not to be discounted, and communist unrest in Indonesia notwithstanding), interpret the Soviet implosion as the "end of history"—the title and ethos of Fukuyama's article in 1989—or a hiccup? If the latter, then communist resurgence in Italy, Russia, Romania, Bulgaria, Poland and other parts of Europe does not reflect unrelated phenomena: communists have realized the value of working from within the western capitalist institutions to good effect.

Keynesian Or Liberal Policy? One Issue Remains As Europe Eyes Single Currency— November 1996.

As the 1999 deadline for a single European currency looms on the horizon, European governments oscillate between liberal and Keynesian policies. The Keynesian approach encourages state intervention: stiff taxes on high income and redistribution of revenue designed to churn the economy, enhancing the purchasing power of consumers. The Liberal approach, attributed to Chicago University and successfully practiced by Ronald Reagan and Margaret Thatcher, advises reduced state intervention and lower taxes to encourage investment, generating the economy and improving living standards.

Creaking budget deficits and an electorate restless over high unemployment have been influencing European Union politicians to choose campaign boosters over fundamental solutions. Raising or lowering taxes can cause almost equal discontent since low taxes are invariably balanced by indirect taxation. It is interesting to see the percentage of income tax taken off workers' salaries and how it contributes to the Gross National Product (GNP) in Germany, France, Britain, Italy and Spain, and how it compares with the United States.

EU governments seem to be stepping on the brake and accelerator at the same time. Following a recent tax increase Chancellor Helmut Kohl of Germany has announced that, by 1999, Germany will further increase its Value Added Tax (VAT) to reach the 15 percent level maintained by most EU members. Income tax will go up to 26 percent, whereas the tax ceiling will change from 53 percent to 40 percent. Tax breaks are to be withdrawn, although no details have been announced yet. With the next election in two years time, both left and right are anxious for voter approval.

Although Spain and Italy, having held elections this year, should have no immediate election worries, their fears are parallel to Germany's. José Maria Aznar, Spain's new conservative Prime Minister, has offered a series of tax breaks to small and medium companies which contribute to 80 percent of Spain's industrial fabric. Shortly after lowering capital gains tax by 95 percent for family-owned companies and announcing a crusade against tax evaders, Aznar's government raised taxes on alcohol, tobacco, and petrol, and is expected to announce a tax on medicines. The continued support of nationalists in the rich province of Catalan is crucial to Aznar's government. The Catalans are anxious about the budget deficit, but unwilling to renegotiate the percentage of income tax (30 percent) that the central government redistributes to Spain's 17 provinces. A water tax and tollgates on Spain's freeways are in the air.

Prodi's communist-propped government seeks to pull Italy out of a bureaucratic labyrinth that encourages fraud. Tax returns are to be simplified, tax evaders hunted down. Existing taxes deducted at source are to be replaced by one single tax on income. Employers will be offered a 20 percent tax cut, and tax breaks if they set up operations in one of Italy's "special zones". The new income tax will be collected by the central government but managed by the provinces. Prodi's government hopes this might cool down secessionist sentiment in the north of Italy.

John Major's government has lowered income tax but instituted heavy indirect taxation, further increasing the Labor party's chances of success in the next general election due in 1997.

In 1995, France saw a rise in VAT along with a tax hike on petrol, alcohol and tobacco. This was followed by certain low interest loans and tax breaks, seen more as creative accounting by the French electorate than a fundamental solution to the budget deficit. Local taxes remain high. These measures hope to decrease the budget deficit and high unemployment in time for the parliamentary elections of 1997, but it appears that success in the parliamentary elections will have to be based on something more dramatic than "creative accounting". President Chirac's approval is down to 31 percent.

In Europe, as in the United States, right and left wing politicians stroke the electorate in response to polls. The EU politicians are playing ping-pong with the electorate using the approaching single European currency in 1999 as a shield. Media proliferation has resulted in a better-informed electorate than ever before. Political leaders would be well advised not to under-estimate their electorate, if the institutions we all cherish are to retain a modicum of credibility.

World Trade Organisation Summits Set To Pit European Union Against Cairns Group- December 1996.

Dr Daniel Haber, one of Europe's foremost authorities on China, Japan and the European Union (EU) is a Professor of International Trade at the Higher Institute of Trade in Paris, President of France-Pacific Consultants, Vice-President of the European Confederation of International Companies and Consultant to the French finance ministry. Dr Haber is one of Europe's foremost authorities on Japan and China. Invited by the Management Department (GEA,IUT II) of Grenoble University to give a lecture on international trade and the World Trade Organization, Dr Haber granted our European correspondent, Dr. Azam Gill, an exclusive interview in Grenoble, France, sharing his views in fluent English on a spectrum of issues encompassing East Asia, the European Union and the United States.

GILL: *What is the possible outcome of China's desire to be accepted into the world trade organization (WTO)?*

The Chinese are in a good trading position. Business with the U.S. is brisk, despite contention over balance of trade and charges of counterfeiting intellectual property. The U.S. position over the Chinese naval exercises using live ammunition off Taiwan just prior to the Taiwanese election, and the U.S. position over the Sprattley straits, is posturing. Both countries are satisfied with the business relationship as it is. As far as entering the WTO is concerned, there will be opposition from the U.S..

GILL: *And the EU's position?*

The strength of the Chinese trading position obliges the EU to lend some form of support to the Chinese demand to enter the WTO. However, China understands that the EU also has its interests with the U.S. to take into account. And there are other ways of acknowledging China's business strength. Cathay Pacific, a British holding company, just shed 10 percent of its shares to enable the Chinese to acquire stock in the airline.

GILL: *How strongly are the Chinese lobbying to enter the WTO?*

The Chinese are realists. They know they will not be able to get WTO membership this year. There are also internal political problems they have to resolve. China is a communist country, and no communist country has a stable system of succession. Deng Xiaoping is a dying man, and the possible instability that might result from his succession worries the Chinese leadership. It also worries the rest of the world.

GILL: *Was the $2 billion Airbus contract designed to enlist EU support?*

I doubt it. The Chinese are already equipped by Boeing, and this was an effort to diversify their dependence in technology.

GILL: *What does China's interest in buying Fokker indicate?*

Fokker is a bankrupt subsidiary of DASA (Daimler-Benz), a majority stakeholder in Airbus. Fokker needs a bailout, and the Chinese need aviation technology. The big question of the 21st century in Asia is—who will build planes?

GILL: *Who will build planes?*

The Japanese, maybe the Koreans.

GILL: *And the Chinese?*

China will be the biggest market.

GILL: *On the subject of ethics and trade, the Euro-Asian summit in Bangkok separated human rights and trade relations. How does this affect the west's moral leadership versus the rise of neo-Confucianism?*

Badly. The concept of a universal interpretation of human rights is under challenge from neo-Confucianism.

GILL: *When there is a choice between fairness and national interest, what takes precedence?*

Most of the time, the question is in the head. Trade is conducted between corporations and not nations. Corporations pursue corporate interests and follow corporate ethics. "What is good for Ford " etc etc.

GILL: *And in a case of conflict of interest between the national and corporate interest?*

U.S. corporations expect national interest to be in step with corporate interest. Corporate competition on national lines within the EU goes against the EU's larger interest.

GILL: *How?*

Intra-EU competition creates outside alliances.

GILL: *What does the EU hope to achieve at the WTO conference in December?*

Nothing dramatic. The WTO is just beginning its life. It's like a judicial court. To be honest, the Europeans will not be insisting on anything. They are, like the Japanese, happy with things. The Cairns Group (about a dozen cereal producing countries, notably Australia, Canada, Argentine and New Zealand) will be pushing for a change in the status quo. This will pit the EU and the Cairns Group against each other in the years to come, and keep the WTO arbitrators busy.

EU Running With Hares, Hunting With Hounds—August 1998.

While Mr. Clinton was using his nine-day China trip in June to bolster his standing with U.S. voters and legislators, the European Union (EU) was not to be outdone. By accident or design, the EU foreign ministers met in Luxembourg to approve the new dimensions of the European Commission's China policy. Although the rhetoric includes the politically correct semantics of human rights and rule of law, it also incorporates the pragmatics of mutual self-interest. When the EU claims to reassess its China policy, it is reminding China not to ignore Europe despite the attractiveness of the American orbit. China's liberty to trade with Europe is a privilege and not a right. At the same time, the EU's China policy seeks to "reflect China's growing economic and political importance in the world"—a thinly veiled attempt at flattery and a concrete offer of trade benefits.

The EU also intends to support China's "economic integration into the world economy", a broad hint to endorse China's entry into the World Trade Organization. Suitable plaudits to "encourage" China in its development towards a more open society based on the rule of law lend the required padding to an optimistic attempt at realpolitik in a bid to decrease unemployment.

The EU unemployment rate is alarmingly high: around 12 percent in its leading countries. The situation is a political time bomb for the current EU leadership. Scrapping Europe's Social Charter and encouraging foreign investment could stimulate the job situation. However, the first option is likely to inspire Europe's powerful trade unions to topple governments, whereas the second option offers a choice between American and Asian investment. There is concern within EU circles that American investment comes at the expense of European economic sovereignty. This worry influences a search for alternatives. With Asia still in the throes of a financial crisis, and Hong Kong's economic future uncertain, the EU is now betting on China. China cannot inject a massive dose of investment to ease the job situation, but by opening up its market to EU products, it can allow the EU to breathe easier. In return, China will position its assets to gain access to technology with no overt military applications. This exchange will also be in line with the EU's policy of offering the world a choice between U.S. and EU hegemony.

Lacking the pre-requisite cohesion or brawn to project a unified foreign policy, the EU leadership does not let any opportunity go by to remind the world of alternatives to U.S. power. Trans-Atlantic rivalry is a fact of the Atlantic Alliance, just as intra-alliance competition is a fundamental of all alliances. While the United States and China are both Pacific powers, the EU is limited to the Atlantic basin. The range of the U.S.' global interests does not always include the EU's ambitions. There is anxiety that if the EU presence on the world stage fades, the Atlantic basin will recede into irrelevance. Europe will slide into decline, with the European Union a vain exercise. The influence of this thinking on long-term strategy is no secret, and China is fully aware of its advantageous position. In the aftermath of India's surprise nuclear tests, inducting China to contain India emerged as the only option available to Western politicians. Active partnership in nuclear non-proliferation diplomacy has lent a new status to a totalitarian and repressive regime, but it is temporary and of short duration.

There should be no illusions that China supports the west out of altruism. China's policy is crafted to serve only its own interests. Militarily, China suffers from an antiquated system that relies (like Iraq) on the overwhelming capacity of human waves in conventional warfare. Much of its matériel is considered "obsolete". Economically, its banking system is shaky, growth is said to be slowing, and economic disparity galloping. Well aware of its weaknesses, China hopes to softly-softly waltz with the U.S. and the EU until it can bare its teeth.

Even though the EU knows it is playing with fire, its leadership has failed to find an alternative to the dual policy of running with the hares and hunting with the hounds. Offering more investment opportunities to the U.S. would ease the employment situation, but introduce a sharp-taloned eagle that defies caging and hunts on its own terms. Courting China, the EU leadership pretends it is only inviting a cuddly panda into the parlor. Yet, if one day the panda transforms into a fire-spitting dragon, there might be no Saint George conveniently on call. Alas, politicians often find it hard to think beyond their immediate electoral concerns without recourse to a dose of aspirin.

Socialists Make Substantial Gains In Europe—December 1998.

Nine years after the demolition of the Berlin wall, the European Union is looking up to socialism for answers. Thirteen of the European Union (EU)'s fifteen member states are now led by left-wing governments. While Mr. Clinton complacently talked of a "new era" and the "third way" at New York University's conference of world leaders, Germany's election result and the change in Italy finally confirmed Europe's rejection of the American model. With France and Britain already led by left-wing governments, the EU political leadership is headed towards the implementation of socialist policies.

Only three years ago, Jacques Chirac's right-wing victory in France had fired the imaginations of the young and unemployed. Figures showed an economic recovery, and optimism soared. It plummeted when economic growth refused to be translated into more jobs. The message was clear. Growth only meant more lay-offs for the employed, fewer opportunities for job seekers and more profits for employers and shareholders. Only a year after his triumph, Chirac's government was hemmed in by charges of lofty high-handedness. He called a snap general election, and suddenly the socialists under Lionel Jospin were merrily "cohabiting with conservatives, much like Messrs Chirac and Mitterand a few years earlier.

Then in Britain last year, Mr. Blair led Labor to victory. Although the content of Tony Blair's rhetoric in stagnant Britain only promised his people a future as the world's entertainers and jugglers, it convinced the electorate.

In the same year, Italians opted for a coalition of socialists, communists, ex-communists and environmentalists. Germany wanted a promise of stability and a change after sixteen years of Helmut Kohl's conservatives. In October this year, Gerhard Schroeder and his socialists swept into power in Germany with promises of a "new center"! In the same month, budgetary squabbles engendered Italy's 56th government since the Second World War. It is led by Mr. Massimo D'Alema, an ex-communist, who holds power on the basis of support from a Catholic group! *L'Avennir* the Italian Episcopalian Conference daily, has claimed, however, that D'Alema retains the reflexes of a communist!

Although informed circles are murmuring alarm, the consideration of two factors should reduce fears of a return to the pre-1989 period.

Firstly, the mainstream left and right-wing programs show convergence. After traversing their wilderness, the left wing have realized that they cannot sit in the halls of power by regularly spending other people's money on spectacular social and cultural programs. The right-wingers will now learn that the injustices of past centuries linger on in the memories of an expensively educated (or mis-educated) electorate. Conservative and progressive forces are both learning to balance economic realities with their ideological commitments. Both need to thoroughly revise Plato's *Republic,* and follow it up with a long walk in the woods comforted by a volume of Robert Frost's poems. If they do their homework, the future will see a harmony of programs but a contrast in electoral rhetoric. This will not encumber the democratic process. On the contrary, the voter will measure the result of program management and pronounce sentence on the inefficient.

And that is the second parameter to take into account. The convergence of left and right wing programs has focused attention on management and style. The "touchy-feely" Britain revealed in Lady Diana's death now fits the European voter's profile. This psyche is different from the American voter's.

The indifference of the American voter to the deterioration of their highest and noblest institution—the Presidency—has inspired revulsion in Europe. This has re-drawn attention to America's islands of inner-city poverty, its homeless people, and the precariousness of employment. Europeans (except for Britain, which cannot let go of Uncle Sam's coat-tails) know they need to look for European solutions. Captives of this logic, they will also accept that the EU's eastward expansion needs further reflection. They will thus support their leaders' attempts to exploit intra-European market opportunities, especially if this is seen to ease the double-digit unemployment. France and Germany—the EU leaders—suffer from. All this translates as a restricted trading market for the U.S., and increased trade relations between the EU and Asia. Chinese President Jiang Zemin, is already "planning trips to up to six European countries next year" (see Willy Wo-Lap Lam, *National Educator*", November 1998 issue). Dark hints of protectionism are in the air.

If the U.S. economy slows down, Europe will be forced to take protectionist measures to "create" jobs and contain discontent. Trade Unionists are watching the new left (or Schroeder's self-proclaimed "new center" as the case may be) like hawks. As the EU enters the European Monetary Union, there are fears concerning the integrity of salary scales. In that case, the strikes expected by French trade unionists after the Christmas celebrations might spill across the borders of France.

This has been a year of eventful changes in Europe. It is hoped that in the coming year the fruit of this harvest does not taste bitter.

Unified Europe Far From Being A Reality—
January 1999.

The single European currency, the Euro, has stopped looming over the horizon. It has now been implemented, and speculation laid to rest. However, soul-searching questions on the economic, social and political consequences of the Euro on the 374 million citizens of the European Union (EU)'s member states remain to be answered.

Economically, the Euro is expected to have an equalizing effect similar to Colonel Colt's Peacemaker. In the medium term, this prediction of analysts such as Erik Israelewicz appears doubtful. Countries of Southern and Mediterranean Europe have been pumping money into their economies to meet the criteria set for acceptance into the Euro mechanism. Once having entered this mechanism, they would have no reason to maintain a false economy. Western EU countries with strong economies could suddenly find themselves facing a nice big bill. Among these countries, Germany is expected to under-write the consequences of other people's creative accountancy. If Germany feels that it is being arm-twisted into a gunpoint bailout, it is liable to rear its head. History reveals that when Germany feels edged in, Europe suffers destabilization. Thus, even if the possibility of destabilization by war is remote, economic instability cannot be discounted.

Socially, the idea of a minimum wage has taken force. Although Britain is still being finicky about it, Oskar Lafontaine, the new German finance minister, would like to see the emergence of common salary scales within the EU. Trade unions in almost all European countries are lobbying hard for legislative acceptance of the idea. They are also keeping a close watch on their governments and industrial leaders to ensure that conversion to the Euro does not lead to reduction of purchasing power or social benefits.

Politically, with people of the stature of Vaclav Havel of the Czech Republic openly saying that "EU expansion is fundamental", the concept of the EU as a tidy little neighbourhood of decent folk is vulnerable to several forces. While federalism might be one answer, the chances that it would ever be realized are open to speculation. European citizenship cannot be defined until such time as the European citizen is profiled. What is of more pragmatic value in the immediate future is to unify immigration policy and, consequently, policy on citizenship. Citizenship as a right has two bases: by blood or by presence on national soil

Different European countries maintain different standards. The Scandinavian countries distinguish between citizen and national. A citizen is a foreign resident with voting rights in local elections. A national is a full-fledged citizen by birth or ancestry. Immigrants to Portugal, Britain and Spain from their former colonies may be granted citizenship by right of blood. Germany applies the right of blood received, whereas France, its lock-step partner in EU leadership, applies the right of soil. In 1992, Roger Brubaker, sociologist at UCLA wrote about "Citizenship and Nation-hood in France and Germany". He observed that France was heading towards the right of blood, whereas Germany seemed headed towards citizenship by presence on soil. On November 30, 1998, Gerhard Schroeder, the new Chancellor of Germany, was interviewed by French anchorwoman Anne Sinclair for channel 1 of French TV. He confirmed Brubaker's observation by declaring that Germany would accept the right of citizenship by presence on soil. In France and Britain, the right of blood has an added aspect, but only the French seem to at least want to discuss it.

Further to the question of blood received by ancestry, is the moral issue of blood spilled for service rendered to the state. France has its famed Foreign Legion, and Britain its Gurkhas. Neither country accepts their classification as mercenaries, and both render exemplary services beyond the call of duty. Yet, whereas after fifteen years of color service, a Gurkha has no right to settle in Britain, French Foreign Legionnaires have the contractual right to apply for citizenship after five years service. However, since the first few years of the contract are under a "declared identity", there is a difference between how a Legionnaire might have understood the terms of his contract and how it is actually applied by the state. After the Indo-China war, a popular song referred to legionnaires as "French by blood spilled", but it is not yet a statutory clause. In fact, when the President of the National Foundation of Former Legionnaires, General Coullon, approached the current government to beseech that at least every legionnaire injured in combat be issued with a card bearing the stamp "French by blood spilled", his submission was refused. A significant decrease in membership in former legionnaires' associations has lately been the object of open concern.

It is not in the intra-EU economic and social changes that the EU will search for its soul, but in the definition of European. Whether the myth of Europa, daughter of Cadmus seduced by Zeus in the guise of a white bull still holds true, or whether political and social consciousness has seen a fundamental metamorphosis will determine the duration of the age of enlightenment. This year might hold the answer to this troubling question.

Euro's Effect On International Market Unclear— February 1999.

Former British Prime Minister Baroness Margaret Thatcher does not expect the new unified monetary system known as the Euro to last more than three years. For French left-wing cabinet minister Jean-Pierre Chevenement, life with the Euro is like sailing on the Titanic! American Economist Martin Feldstein believes it could possibly lead to war between the European Union (EU) members or between the EU and the United States. The British *Financial Times* called it the "most far-reaching development since the fall of the Berlin wall". The French daily *Le Monde's* headline gloated on the Euro's challenge to the "hegemony" of the U.S. dollar. Former German Chancellor and one of the architects of the monetary union, Helmut Kohl, referred to the new European currency as a "once-in-a-lifetime event". All this high-powered intellectual energy is being brought to bear on a currency that is still only "virtual".

Nobody will actually see or touch a Euro before the year 2002, even though trading has been brisk since its launch on January 1, 1999. Membership of the Euro club is limited to 11 of the EU's 15 countries. Greece is excluded because it failed to meet EU fiscal standards, whereas Britain, Sweden and Denmark are still unsure whether their interest lies with the dollar, the Euro, or playing one against the other. Britain is certainly competent at this game, and its intentions are no nobler than any other country obsessed with a self-interest, disproportionate to its resources. London must tread with care if it is to maintain its hold on international currency trading.

In most world bourses, there was a clear drop in dollar investments and a sharp interest in the Euro. States like China followed suit. Up until the end of last year, 62 percent of China's foreign currency reserves had been maintained in dollars. It is now expected that this holding will go down to 50 percent, with the slack made up by investing in the Euro. From private investors to states, nobody is sure which way the Euro will turn. At this stage, the only certainty is its potential for mischief and potential for good.

Positively speaking, the Euro could propel the world economy into a new cycle of growth. After all, the capital market of the 11 members of Euro-club is as deep as the U.S.'. With a powerful central bank behind it, the Euro would be the first alternative to the U.S. dollar since World War II. And that is where the mischief factor would come into play. It would pit the European Central Bank against the American Federal Reserve. Both reserve banks will seek to control stability by raising and lowering interest rates. The world economy will become a yo-yo with two opposing strings. This bipolar financial world order is liable to create a new cold war, with the pawns being the countries having to choose between the dollar and the Euro as their foreign currency reserves. Those lacking the power and/or sagacity to juggle the two will risk going under. Members of the Euro club themselves might be faced with a problem that has not been foreseen in any of the procedures. If the economy of one member country goes into a downslide, and the solution is to pull out of the Euro, there is no existing procedure to accommodate such a decision. The imaginable chaos in any of the preceding scenarios of doom has no real precedent on the basis of which a solution might be inferred.

Viewed optimistically, the Euro would allow the EU to decrease dependence on American patronization. Financially, and in the world markets, monetary responsibility would be shared between the American Federal Reserve Bank and the European Central Bank. With the impulsion of added resources, world trading would benefit from increased stability and growth. At some time in the future, the balance of decision-making in NATO itself might undergo a change in proportion to the EU's ability to streamline its military cooperation and infuse adequate high-technology into its defense forces. A new Atlantic partnership could successfully neutralize the Asian side of the Pacific Basin without any risk to the United States economy. It would also allow the global economy to benefit from the positive aspects of a bi-polar World.

Prophets of hope and gloom both appear to have impeccable credentials. Many of the parameters they take into consideration can be analyzed by computers, but analyzing the fundamentals of human nature remains beyond the reach of microprocessors. After all, mere mortals are going to decide which way the Euro turns. Is man born noble, or is nobility invested in him by God's grace and his own humility? Man is a composite of good and evil. The ratio of this opposition in individuals, and the interaction of differing ratios among groups constitute this variable element. Eventually, the effect of the Euro will be based on the ratio of evil to good among the Atlantic leaders. Over the next three years, the wisdom of most cross-Atlantic gurus is set to be severely tested.

Voter Apathy Apparent In European Elections— July 1999.

Seven months ago, the European Union electorate was euphoric about its single currency, the Euro. Subsequently, polls indicated that the European electorate in all fifteen EU countries favored increased European integration. The European Parliament was given enhanced legislative powers. Yet, elections to the European Parliament in mid-June this year were a flop. In 1994, voter turnout had been 56.8 percent. This time it was 49 percent. Despite a majority of left-wing governments in power in the EU member countries, the conservatives grouped as the Popular European Party won hands down, winning 224 of the 626 seats. Britain's Prime Minister Tony Blair of Great Britain cut a rather lonely figure: at 23 percent, Britain had the lowest voter turnout, with Tories clearly trouncing Labor! Belgium, Italy, Greece and Spain had the highest voter turnout, in that order. Only in France, with the conservatives still in disarray, did the left wing gain a clear victory. The European voter choosing a left-wing government at national level and conservative leadership at EU level is not a paradox. The average European welcomes socialist promises, privileges and job security, but is unwilling to give up centuries of nation-hood.

The European Union Parliamentary elections refocused attention on the issue of a federal Europe at some future stage. Different opinions overlapping conventional right and left wing political stances were offered by different parties. The overlap can be explained by two central issues of concern to political parties and the electorate. The first is for Europe to redefine its identity in a unipolar world dominated by the United States. The second is the status of the nation-state within a European federation.

Spin-doctors will remain busy for a long time adding new meanings to known semantic values.

The pro-federal hard sell seeks to tackle U.S. power on eight main points. By the use of creative semantics, the slogan is of a "Europe of nations", maintaining the national rhetoric at the heart of the issue. Since it is believed that no single European state can match U.S. influence in the world, unity on the basis of a common threat is a rallying call. France and Germany, the European leaders, hope that a larger number of states will provide a greater following. Britain, knowing its claims to leadership are based on its usefulness to the United States, can only hope that its Prime Minister did not overplay his hand in the Balkan war by his saber rattling. The vision of a greater Europe is not new: Charlemagne, Frederick of Prussia, the Kaiser and Hitler, all shared the same vision, with different methods of achieving it. They also failed. Lately, when Charles de Gaulle was excluded from the 1945 Yalta conference, he offered a vision of Europe "from the Atlantic to the Urals". Imaginations have remained fired ever since, and the difference of opinion is over who runs this vast empire, and not the empire itself.

It is also considered that since closed frontiers are only a barrier to decent citizens and not to terrorists or smugglers of every hue, they might as well be kept open. Security concerns should be at a higher level of European defense and projection of influence. An intra-European defense industry with emphasis on a star wars type space shield covering electronic intelligence would decrease dependence on the U.S. A nation, it is suggested, is a state of mind, and if the corresponding geographical entity outstrips the mindset, such an abstraction is under no threat.

This is a red rag to the nationalist bulls, who abhor the idea of European federal agencies trampling over their fields to regulate mad-cow disease and genetically engineered agricultural products. They fear that a federal EU would be an unmanageable giant tripping over its own feet, to end up as the 51st state of the U.S. Their logic goes further to draw analogies with the USSR and its demise. Recognizing the reality of national feelings, they remind the electorate that when such feelings are yoked into an international identity against the will of peoples, they don't just vanish into thin air—they simmer, boil and then boil over into a USSR-style implosion, leaving Balkan-type messes to be mopped up by foreign elements. The EU has already gone further than it should have. After all, the Euro is not proving to be as successful it was supposed to be, and open frontiers are only porous. Thus, a system of alliances and treaties is considered a preferable alternative, within which a common defense industry, space shield, electronic intelligence and the projection of power are supposed to fit.

All these issues were vigorously present in the campaign rhetoric of the parties during the European parliamentary elections. What was missing was the desired number of voters to give body to the semantic reinventions of both opinions. This lack-luster reaction to crucial issues implies that Europeans, like their American counterparts, do not really care beyond their wallets. European leaders are bickering to push an issue rather than represent their electorates. If nature is left to run its course, in time it will decide if and when the EU should go beyond its present organization. The combination of an apathetic electorate and lofty politicians is paving the way for too much government. In a nation with solid traditions, that is bad enough, but in a state that yokes together disparate peoples of conflicting traditions and ambitions, it can spell disaster. The promised utopia is based on what the world "should" be like. The "Europe of regions" being touted by Britain's Blair and Germany's Gerhard Schroeder is a de facto scenario for the break-up of nation-states. The devolution of power to Scottish and Welsh parliaments is the first step in the Balkanization of Western Europe just as Mr. Blair invests so much energy in trying to de-Balkanize the Balkans.

The climate within which to achieve a federal Europe is evasive. Until that time, European greatness needs to be realized by tried and tested methods to achieve its destined success, and not Prince Charles' royal dreams of "honest cottagers" weaving Gandhian homespun in architecturally correct villages dotting the European landscape!

EU May Provide New Markets For South America—August 1999.

The stakes of the Great Game defined by Rudyard Kipling have now moved to the Latin American pitch with new players. On June 27 and 28, some 48 heads of state met in Rio de Janeiro at a cost of over $15 million to the Brazilian government. At the close of the Rio summit, the French establishment daily *Le Monde* declared: "EU was looking for space to face up to the U.S.," adding that the Americans worry about Mercosur and the EU getting too cozy. The Brazilian Foreign Minister, Mr. Lampreia, spoke of rivalry in Latin America, with the U.S. coming out on top, but the EU in hot pursuit for the past 20 years.Mercosur is the Latin American trading zone comprising Brazil, Argentina, Paraguay and Uruguay: the European Union, and Caribbean nations hoped to increase trade and commerce with it. The French President Jacques Chirac had launched the idea in March 1997 in an interview with Brazil's daily *O Estado* during the June summit. President Chirac stated the aim of the gathering as a strategic union of economic and commercial relations between the EU and Latin America. He further emphasized that ties between NAFTA and Mercosur were not detrimental to relations between Mercosur and the EU, evoking the need to construct a multipolar world.

This need had become more apparent in 1996 with the death of Alain Focart in France and the rise to power of ex-communist Laurent Kabila in the Congo. Monsieur Focart had almost single-handedly built up a network of relations with heads of Francophone African states, maintaining a desired level of French influence in Africa. Laurent Kabila came to power with American support and U.S.-led calls for a Pan-African peace force were seen as a direct challenge to French influence in Africa, thus engendering the need for a "multipolar" world.

While the June summit suitably took a sideways swipe at the Helms-Burton law aimed to prevent trade relations between Castro's Cuba and the international community, the participants' greatest accomplishment was to schedule talks of free trade in November. However, since no date for the completion of the talks was set, the United States can proceed with its plans for the World Trade Organization conference in November. Although Mercosur claimed the Europeans dominated the proceedings because they were much better prepared for Rio, the inclusion of agricultural products in the November agenda is to its advantage.

Latin America is an agricultural powerhouse, and the EU has subsidized farmers. The issue is political dynamite in most EU countries. Were a French government, for example, to allow the free import of agricultural products, farmers would just fold up, and the government would be liable to lose tenure. Spain and Portugal are probably the only two competitive agricultural producers in the EU. Appropriately so, a week before the Rio summit, Spain took a unilateral decision to reach an agreement on agricultural trade with Mercosur countries. In spite of, or perhaps due to this move, the two-day summit was permeated by a flurry of bilateral discussions between the EU and Mercosur heads of state.

In concrete terms, this means that the EU member countries have once again proved themselves incapable of acting as a single entity. The French President's idea was supported so that apparently the EU countries could cut their own private deals while clamouring about EU unity and U.S. hegemony.

If the current trend to world trade is not disrupted, Standard and Poor estimates that it will reach $11.5 billion by 2005. The leading actor in this scenario will obviously be the United States, and the EU has no intention of being a bystander. The EU subscribes to Fred Bergsten's view that regionalism and multilateralism are not contradictory.

Mercosur countries still live under the spectre of banana republics in which United Fruit was king. While seeking to distance themselves from that past, they do not see the EU as a replacement in the same sort of relationship but a parameter in a new equation. The test will be which trading zone provides Latin America with an outlet for its agricultural production. The United States is another competitive agricultural dynamo. When the chips are down, with the United States being unable to throttle its farming industry to the profit of investment speculators, Mercosur will look for solutions within the framework of its cultural heritage on the old continent. If, at that stage, the EU countries are still involved in cutting bilateral deals with individual Mercosur countries, and unwilling to decrease its farm subsidies to accommodate agricultural imports, Mercosur will find itself in a very forceful position. From the position of strength, it might well be tempted to look towards the Caribbean and horizons beyond it. Yet, as Francis Fukuyama now says, the end of history does not spell the end of technology. The future of bio engineered agricultural products and an expanding world population will structure the dynamics of this game.

SECTION FOUR —FRANCE

Resentment Grows Over France's Refugee Policy—January 1994.

When Julius Caesar's Roman eagle fluttered over most of Europe, present day France was an ungovernable land peopled by bellicose tribes under strong-willed chiefs. They loved battle, respected the weak and granted succor with grace. Eventually, these warring groups surrendered their tribal independence to a stable monarchy which legitimized succor. The catholicising of France confirmed this tradition in canonical law. In 1789, a bloody revolution, which reverberated across Europe, replaced the monarchy with a republic. This revolution studiously separated church from state. The right to succor was expressed as political asylum. Four years later, the abolition act was passed. Other European countries followed suit: political asylum and abolition were liberally supported all over the continent.

France found itself at the forefront of European liberalism, but the torch kept passing across the Atlantic to other abolitionists, to the Muckrakers and Prohibitionists and then to the anti-colonialists straddling the Atlantic.

In the period after World War II, colonial structures were hastily dismantled: the dust has still not settled. In 1946, the right to political asylum was unanimously voted into the French constitution. In 1968, restless students overthrew President Charles De Gaulle without a single loss of life. Unable to stop the Vietnam War, these forces expressed solidarity with the casualties of American bombing by flinging open the gates of Europe to the have-nots of the Third World.

Political refugees and immigrants came in droves, packing the gates of the Ministries of Labor and Political Refugees of Western Europe. In their haste to process applications, harried clerks, prodded by naïve politicians blurred the line between economic immigrants and political refugees.

The overall atmosphere of bureaucratic laxity and political myopia emboldened terrorists of every hue to travel first class across Europe, arrogantly flitting from one deluxe hotel to another about their nefarious business. German unification, the Schengen Accords, economic recession and the Gulf War have made us look a little harder around us. Not an identifiable political refugee in sight!

With unemployment rising due to a badly misunderstood second industrial revolution, the most vocal expression of resentful native Europeans comes from the extreme right. German skinheads seig heiling their fists into the faces of defenceless immigrants in a surge of national pride, caused Msrs Mitterand and Kohl to accelerate the ratification of the Maastricht treaty, which blew up in their faces.

The most expedient response to the forces of fascism is a clear redefinition of political asylum. The tribal tradition of succor has become untenable as an umbrella for immigration. European governments need to rescue this heritage from its comic opera status. France has taken a bold, though controversial action in amending its constitution to accommodate the application of the Schengen accord. The findings would be uncontested by other European countries.

Left-wing politicians oppose the application of the Schengen accords because it threatens the Gallic tradition of tribal succor. They would also like to ensure against any miscarriage of justice. Gerald Dulac, management consultant, university professor and parliamentary candidate of Grenoble (techno pole with a population of 400,000), adds: "Ill-defined political goals risk alienating the populace and provoke discord".

Right-wing leaders are equally concerned about the European tradition of succor. "France will always be hospitable to victims of oppression", proudly declared Jean-Christophe Leveque, a free market economist, consultant and college teacher. Republicans are determined to restore credibili-

ty to the political refugee, reduce their constituents' resentment against foreigners and contain the extreme right.

This consensus on principle and discord on procedure is today's
European dichotomy. With NAFTA a reality amid the trans-Atlantic din
of GATT, Europe's heartbeat flutters to keep its soul.

Realignment Of Major Players Causes France To Rethink Options—6 November 1994.

For the first time since Charles de Gaulle withdrew France from NATO's integrated command structure 28 years ago, a French defense Minister has attended a NATO meeting. Sixteen defense ministers met in Seville to discuss curative action on Bosnia, preventive action on Islamic militancy in the Mediterranean, a Mediterranean Rapid Action Force, and to elect a new secretary general.

France has a socialist president and a Gaullist majority prime minister. The left and right wings are united on a single-issue platform: no return to integrated NATO command. With the presidential election due in 1995, the Gaullists dare not appear to be distancing themselves from de Gaulle's ideas of an independent France. Neither can the socialists compromise their stance of an independent defense.

Francois Mitterand took the opportunity of deflecting criticism of his wartime associations with the Vichy government. In an interview to the conservative French daily *Le Figaro*, the left-wing French President, Mr. François Mitterand, in his 13th year of presidency, questioned the Gaullist's commitment to an independent defense. He drove home the point that he had categorically forbidden the Chairman Joint Chiefs of Staff to attend the meeting in Seville. The President declared himself "formally hostile" to a return to NATO command. In fact, the French Catholic daily *La Croix* reports that last April, when Mr. Mitterand was visiting Uzbekistan, Admiral Lanxade—Chairman French Joint Chiefs of Staff—nipped over to Brussels to talk about Bosnia, Mr. Mitterand summarily ordered him home.

In an article in *Le Figaro*, Francois Leotard, the Defense Minister, explained the defense imperatives which compelled a French presence in Seville. Europe, he says, is incapable of defending itself. Russia is still powerful, and Europeans are aware of it. Only NATO, with the ethos on American participation, can defend Europe against a massive "hypothetical" invasion from the east. The French Defense Minister has declared himself in favor of giving body to the American idea of Partnership for Peace with West Europe, an idea to which Russia is at best lukewarm.

On 27 September, receiving Boris Yeltsin for a two-day summit, Bill Clinton talked of Russia and the United States being "partners in a quest for a more prosperous and peaceful planet."

The Times of London commented that "… U.S. and Russian interests now coincided far more often than they collided."

In Seville, the French and Americans saw eye to eye on major issues. From Bosnia to Partnership for Peace, Britain and the U.S. disagreed on most issues. Francois Leotard mostly put France in a mediating role.

Despite senators Sam Nunn and Richard Luger's doubts over Willy Claes' competence, the Belgian foreign minister was approved Secretary General, to the satisfaction of his Franco-Spanish backers. NATO enthusiasm for a Mediterranean Rapid Action Force of France, Italy and Spain, however, remained muted. NATO is surely uniting for a pledge that in wartime, the Mediterranean Rapid Action Force, like Eurocorps, would come under its command.

In January 1994, the Western European Union accepted that European troops could intervene on peacekeeping missions using NATO logistics. Since then, the idea of NATO as the UN's peacekeeping instrument has been taking stronger hold. In that case, France cannot afford to be excluded.

United nations peacekeeping based on Russo-American cooperation would make Western Europe uneasy, whence the French support for Partnership for Peace.

At the same time, the U.S. cannot ignore the Mediterranean powder keg, part of the worldwide Islamic threat. Although France is the western keystone to containing Islamic militancy in the Mediterranean, the degree of U.S.-NATO support for the Mediterranean Rapid Action Force will be in proportion to its commitment to NATO command.

The post-cold war world has not changed fundamental principles of defense, cooperation and sovereignty. What has evolved is the role of the principal players. Compromising the realities of today with principles of the past requires boldness and agility.

Will France Turn To National Front?—
September 1995.

Jacky Machu, math lecturer at Grenoble University, is the National Front Regional Councilman of the Rhone-Alpes Region, of which Lyons is the capital. The National Front party won 15% of the vote in the first round of the presidential elections, and Rhone-Alpes is a region comprising 43,700 square kilometers, with a population of 5.5 million. In 1994, the average turnover of the region came to about 80 billion dollars. The regional council has taxation powers, and oversees rural transport and high schools. Jacky Machu, member of a political minority, retired colonel who was in Algeria at the time of the "paratrooper's revolt" against de Gaulle, shares his views on Values and Education, History, the European Community, and The United States in an exclusive interview to *The National Educator*. Questions by The National Educator are in bold type.

THE NATIONAL FRONT IS VARIOUSLY DESCRIBED BY THE PRESS AS "EXTREME RIGHT-WING", "XENOPHOBIC" OR "ULTRA-NATIONALIST". WHICH OF THESE DESCRIPTIONS DO YOU AGREE WITH?
"Ultra-nationalists", because we take pride in our patriotism, and cherish it as a value. Calling us xenophobic is politically immature, and there *is* an extreme right in France which represents 0.4 percent of the electorate.

WHAT DREW YOU TO THE NATIONAL FRONT?
Nationalism, integrity and uprightness.

HAS THE NATIONAL FRONT BEEN ABLE TO MAINTAIN THESE PRINCIPLES?

Our members have a proven record of probity. I do admit that honesty is a natural attribute of those not in power. We will now come under public scrutiny. The presence of the odd black sheep notwithstanding, I feel sure we will hold up better than other parties.

WHEN WAS THE NATIONAL FRONT FOUNDED?

Twenty years ago, by Mr. Jean-Marie Le Pen.

IN 1984 THE NATIONAL FRONT'S ELECTORAL SCORE JUMPED FROM 1%TO 10%, WITH A RECORD 15% IN THE FIRST ROUND OF THE RECENT PRESIDENTIAL ELECTIONS. WHAT CATALYSED THE DRAMATIC CHANGE OF FIGURES IN 1984?

An institutional change in the electoral system finally introduced the procedure of proportional representation, allowing the French people to legitimately air their political views. We emerged as a sizeable and fast growing minority.

TYPICALLY, WHO ARE YOUR SUPPORTERS?

Blue-collar, hard working patriots looking for decency and civility.

WHAT ARE THE IDEOLOGICAL ROOTS OF THE NATIONAL FRONT?

Nationalist sentiments after the Second World War. Patriots hurt by the extremism of anti-war activists during the Indo-China war. War is decided by politicians and not soldiers, but extremists used to throw stones at soldiers.

THE NATIONAL FRONT IS ALSO SEEN AS OWING ITS ROOTS TO MARSHALL PETAIN, HEAD OF THE VICHY GOVERNMENT THAT DECIDED TO CAPITULATE TO THE NAZIS IN WORLD WAR II.

The values of Work, Family and Nation have always been dear to the French. Field Marshall Petain espoused them, and so do we.

THE SCHENGEN ACCORDS NOW ALLOW OTHER EUROPEAN POLICE FORCES TO MAKE AN ARREST ON FRENCH SOIL. WHAT IS YOUR POSITION ON THE ISSUE?

Such arrests are tantamount to meddling. There have always been international accords on extradition, and then there is Interpol. We are not against a federation of European states with common values, but sovereignty ensures our identity. Inasmuch as the economic entity of the European Union does not encroach upon the sovereign tradition of individual nations, benefits member countries. Advocates of World Government backed by monopolists banded together as Freemasons are a threat to nations.

WHAT CONSEQUENCES DO YOU SEE OF THE WORLD DEMO-GRAPHICS?

Developed countries will come under aggression from the birthrate of unassimilated communities. If world population continues at the current rate, we will face more calamities and epidemics like AIDS.

ANY OTHER CONSEQUENCES?

Natural disasters, calamities, and epidemics like AIDS.

THE NATIONAL FRONT TALKS OF "NATIONAL PREFERENCE" IN TERMS OF JOBS AND SOCIAL BENEFITS. WHAT DOES THE TERM MEAN?

It does not exclude people of foreign birth, people who are French by choice. Take the example of "harkis". They were Algerians who fought on the French side during the Algerian war. Hundreds of thousands were massacred after Algerian independence. Hundreds of thousands were sheltered in France, but they have stayed in marginalized conditions.

HOW CAN A NATION RETAIN ITS IDENTITY AND ROOTS?
Enlightenment without roots is a vacuum. A people's identity is linked with their history. Heroes are links in the chain of continuity. They should not be reviled but revered as models to define our own behavior.

ARE YOU THEN SATISFIED WITH THE TEACHING IN FRENCH SCHOOLS?
In schools, pride in history should be pivotal. Civics should be taken seriously. Unfortunately, this is far from being satisfactory. There is an insidious orientation towards replacing French as the language of national unity by languages representing unassimilated communities within us.

ARE YOU AGAINST THE TEACHING OF FOREIGN LANGUAGES?
Not at all. France cannot shut the world out. As a university professor I realize the necessity and value of openness, in which knowledge of other cultures and their languages plays an important part.

HOW DO YOU ASSESS THE CHIRAC GOVERNMENT's MEASURES TO REDUCE THE BUDGET DEFICIT?
Mr. Chirac's government has addressed the problem by indirect taxation—raising value added tax from 18.5 percent to 20 percent . We need measures to create additional revenues. It should be done in accordance with the legalities of legislative procedure.

WHAT WOULD YOU SUGGEST?
Encourage the market economy, and reassess the option of income tax.

WHAT IS YOUR POSITION ON TAXES, THE FREE MARKET, AND GOVERNMENT INTERFERENCE?

No government can function without revenues, and no overtaxed economy can realize its potential. Government intervention limited to individual cases maintains the balance between meddling and duty.

AND ON THE RIGHT TO BEAR ARMS?

In the U.S., it is a symbol of individual liberty. In France, defense of the individual is a state responsibility. If the law enforcement agencies lack the strength to protect citizens, their resources should be augmented. State duties should not be divested to individual citizens.

IF YOU HAD A MESSAGE FOR THE UNITED STATES, WHAT WOULD IT BE?

Since the American Revolution, France and the U.S. have been close allies. I admire the American way of doing things, but this approach is not relevant to the French, who have their own history and culture, and consequently, their own way reasoning. There are good and bad things on both sides. Message? Trust in God and love your country.

French President Gambles To Redefine Nation's Identity—October 1996.

From October 19 to October 24, the French President's Middle East tour took him to Syria, Israel (including Ramallah), Jordan, Egypt and Lebanon. On the eve of his visit to Israel to address the Israeli parliament, Jacques Chirac, the French President, attended an official banquet in Damascus, the Syrian capital. He chose this moment to suggest the European Union (EU) as a co-sponsor with the United States in bringing about the realization of a Palestinian state. The French left-leaning *l'Evenement du Jeudi* decried Chirac's speech as a "rhetorical scud missile". The right-wing *l'Express* called it a "mistake", whereas the Gaullist *Le Figaro* mitigated it to a "plea". The French President's Middle East tour caused concern in Washington and diplomatic sparks to fly between Jerusalem and Paris. The Arab countries applauded Chirac's initiative, Israel was indignant, the United States reticent, and the European Union surprised.

Chirac's basis was dictated by old-fashioned Gaullist pragmatism. The European Union is the Middle East's biggest trading partner, its largest aid donor, shares the Mediterranean basin, and includes front-line states on the terrorist battle-ground.

The French President is actually seeking to restore France's position in the Arab world, perceived to be in decline since the Gulf War, thereby improving his standing in the polls which is at an all-time low. The French share of reconstruction contracts in Kuwait was in proportion to its military participation, which came as a rude shock. The Gaullists are determined to avoid a repeat performance. Before a Palestinian state assumes the mantle of reality, France wants to make sure its credentials are deposed in the right quarters. There is also Lebanon, where France already has lucrative contracts in telecommunications and power supply. With approximately 35,000 Syrian troops in Lebanon, Syria is still a power broker in the Levant, motivating the French President to choose Damascus as his venue of appeal. Syria also has a foreign debt of 22 billion dollars, France is one of the lenders, and French imports have slowed down of late. Chirac's appeal hoped to rejuvenate a Syrian interest in French imports, offer the Syrians an alternative power brokerage, and imply French leadership of the European Union with a well-planned *fait accompli.*

The question within the European Union is whether Chirac spoke for the Union or for France. The British *Daily Telegraph* reports Sir Leon Brittan, the EU Commission vice-president, as having "condemned" the action. An un-named British official was quoted in the same report: "it is an example of France taking a French position and trying to put a European label on it". The British press chose, either to ignore the event or give it second place to Britain's foreign secretary's denunciation of the European Court's ruling on value-added tax that "left the government facing a bill for hundreds of million pounds" German criticism was muted: in the wake of a Franco-German call to suppress EU member countries' power to veto acts of bilateral cooperation (leading, in effect, to a two-speed Europe), German hostility to France was effectively compromised!

Although Syrian Defense Minister Tlass understandably praised Chirac's courage compared with his socialist predecessor's "colorless" approach to the Palestinian problem, the Israeli reaction was unexpectedly strong.

Ovzi Landau, President of the Foreign Affairs Parliamentary Commission, boycotted Chirac's scheduled address to the Israeli parliament. David Levy, Israel's Foreign Minister, made a pointed reference to France's culinary tradition, warning the French not to "add another piece of ox-tail to the mid-East's simmering soup" (French daily *Le Monde*).

According to the French daily *Le Monde*, Israel trusts only the United States on the subject of Middle East peace. In a BBC World Service report, when President Chirac tried to visit the old city of Jerusalem, Security guards "hemmed him in". On October 23, Channel 1 of French TV showed Chirac, hemmed in by security guards and the press, complaining angrily in his heavily accented English, "No problem. This is provocation". Israel later apologized for the incident. From its headquarters in the Quai d'Orsay, the French foreign ministry complained that while the Israelis had allowed a Socialist president to address the parliament in 1988 and 1992, a Gaullist was denied the honor. The Israelis hotly denied the charge, citing Chirac's intention to address the Hebron Arab parliament without their official knowledge as a possible reason behind Mr. Landau's decision.

Four days after Chirac's speech in Damascus, Bill Clinton's speech in Detroit, (carried by Voice of America), evoked a "peaceful and undivided Europe" with NATO a "bedrock." When Clinton's speech is linked with the Franco-German communiqué calling on the European Commission (made just prior to Chirac's trip to the Middle East) to provide for a two-speed Europe, Bill Clinton's prudence about the EU's NATO-based status quo, and anxiety about the entry of East European countries into the EU, is a gentle rebuff to Chirac's offer of "co-sponsorship" and an attempt to solicit votes from the descendants of East European immigrants.

On the heels of Chirac's diplomatic Scud missile, Bill Clinton, in a report carried by *The Jerusalem Post* on October 28, phoned Benjamin Netanyahu and Yasser Arafat and "urged" them to finalize a "Hebron redeployment deal", confirming Washington's lack of interest in the French President's offer. Although *The Irish Times* in Dublin (the current presidency of the EU is held by the Irish Republic) declared Netanyahu to have been "castigated" by the international community, a CNN broadcast quoted Netanyahu's optimistic declaration of a "Hebron deal within reach."

In reaching out to the Arab world at the risk of diplomatic indiscretion, Jacques Chirac gambled on the French determination to retain a world position, hoping to move his popularity rating of 29 percent back to the 59 percent in May of this year. With unemployment at 12 percent, and economic growth below expectations, the French President courageously put himself in the line of fire to dymanise a people searching for a redefinition of their national identity. The next few months will show whether the risk was worth the effort.

France Being Drawn To National Front—April 1997.

The National Front's punchy solutions to pressing national issues of equal relevance to other European Union (EU) member-states, have once again been welcomed by the French. The town of Vitrolles (pop: 39,000), north of the port city of Marseilles became the focus of the European press at the beginning of February this year. In a by-election to the mayoralty, the National Front candidate docked smoothly into city hall with a comfortable 52.5 percent majority expressed by voters in a free and fair democratic election. *The Financial Times* of London, Italian *La Republica* and *La Stampa*, Spanish *ABC* and *El Pais* and the German *Berliner Morgenpost* set a strident moral tone for the rest of the European press, tripping over each other in their eagerness to apologize for the National Front success as a failure of the mainstream left and right-wing parties.

Read in plain terms, the National Front Vitrolles victory adds further legitimacy to their election manifesto. However, the emergence of "political correctness" has imposed the imperative of seeking a secure position against charges of intolerance. The overall position of the European press corps abides by this imperative. While the National Front itself has never made any effort to couch its manifesto within a "politically correct" framework, the mainstream political leadership is keen to disassociate itself from National Front terminology and solutions. There is a distinct ambition to prove that they and their supporters have the intellectual sophistication to measure up to current standards of tolerance. Last November Alain Juppé, the French Prime Minister, openly charged the National Front with being "racist". So what *did* happen in Vitrolles that had France and the rest of the EU a-buzz?

Bruno Megret, the 47-year old disenchanted ex-Gaullist, sometime speechwriter for de Gaulle, graduate of elite French academic institutions and Berkley, reputedly heads the "modernists" of the National Front. His mayoral candidacy for Vitrolles was rejected on the grounds that he had exceeded campaign spending. In a daring act of public loyalty, his wife Catherine, a Cambridge graduate, and mother of a three-year old son, decided to contest the election in place of her husband. At the outset, she made her position clear: "a woman's role is to bring up her children, run the home and support her husband". And support him she did, right up to the time of the election result when she delegated the physical taking over of city hall to her "special advisor"—Bruno Megret.

Megret fielded reporters' questions and promptly announced a 30 percent reduction in councilor's salaries. Two weeks later, Catherine Megret, in an interview with the German daily *Berliner Zeitung*, pledged to reduce the social benefits of immigrants.

The Vitrolles victory now brings to four the number of towns under outright National Front management, the other three being Orange, Marignane and Toulon. The National Front also gained 39 percent in Dreux, 40 percent in Gardanne, and 45 percent in a part of Nice, but found its way into the City Halls barred by hastily sprung left and right wing alliances.

The National Front has come a long way over the past 22 years. In the 1974 general elections, it showed 0.74 percent support. After 1984, its support was estimated at 10 to 14 percent. The 1995 presidential election confirmed a solid 15 percent standing with the public. A recent poll revealed 20 percent of the French public with a "favorable opinion" of the National Front. The National Front has now started organizing trade unions among prison warders, the police and transport workers. In the 1998 legislative elections, the National Front is estimated to capture 100 of the 577 seats.

By and large, a hostile French and European press denies the National Front any intrinsic credit to undermine the effectiveness of its political manifesto. The National Front espouses traditional values of family, flag and duty, believes in the nation-state, the abolition of income tax, expresses dissatisfaction with what it sees as a "weak" foreign policy, resents the dimensions of U.S. world power, and seeks to bring illegal immigration under the rule of law. Indeed, unemployment (at about 12.7 percent) and immigration are seen as directly linked. The bulk of the National Front support is based on Frederich Nietzsche's "morality of the common man". In fact, a new law passed by the Gaullists will devolve the power to curb illegal immigration to city councils and mayors. The National Front city halls will no doubt apply this law with fervor, adding to the credibility of their party and enhancing its chances of national power-brokership.

The issues addressed by the National Front, especially the potential conflict-of-interest situation in which unassimilated communities of dubious loyalty are liable to find themselves, are real and pressing in all EU member-states. The public is aware of these issues, ineffectively dealt with—if at all- by the parties in power. The solutions offered by the National Front shock the self-image of intellectual sophistication dear to the heart of every French and European Union citizen. But as support for the National Front increases, it evokes John Ruskin's questions: "Which of us is to do the hard and dirty work for the rest of us—and for what pay? Who is to do the pleasant and clean work, and for what pay?"

When Jean-Marie Le Pen Speaks, France Listens—May 1997.

Jean-Marie Le Pen, who founded France's National Front party in 1972, is one of the most interesting and vilified politicians in the world today. A sharp critic of immigration into France, he has been called a racist, fascist and worse. His party's vote total has risen from .74 percent in 1974 to 15 percent in 1995. With French President Jacques Chirac having called early parliamentary elections for May 25 and June 1, Mr. Le Pen's party will again be prominent in news coverage—thus this interview. Our exclusive interview was conducted in French by *The National Educator's* Europe Bureau Chief Azam Gill at Mr. Le Pen's villa in the Paris suburb of St. Cloud on April 16th. Here are some excerpts:

Due to the unprecedented scale of worldwide immigration, is national and cultural security of nation-states at risk?

This is the most vital question of our time. The demographic explosion in underdeveloped countries has caused devastating migratory pattern that threaten to destroy the judicial, political and cultural institutions of nations. I sincerely believe that the nation-state remains the beneficial, efficient means of insuring security, liberty, tranquillity and the identity of prosperity of a people. My party, the National Front, opposes unchecked immigration. Population transfers which refuse to adapt to the host culture create colonies with disastrous consequences. I believe a one-world order and mercantile ideologies conspire to create an international melting pot. I believe that the beauty of mankind lies in our diversity, not uniformity.

Will improved economic conditions in the emigrants' home countries reduce the flow of immigration?

You are right because mass immigration is motivated by socio-economic factors. Take France, for example: the government has to bear total responsibility for our immigration situation. I am accused of being xenophobic and anti-immigrant. That is a false charge. I am not anti-immigrant. I blame French politicians. In 1974 when unemployment was close to the million mark, French politicians continued their egalitarian ideology and played to the El Dorado dreams of immigrants. These French politicians have committed a crime against their own people as well as the immigrants from poor countries.

What effects will the economic competition coming from the Pacific Rim have on Europe?

In my book, *Law and Economic Democracy*, which I wrote in 1978, I made the case that the oil crisis did not result from economic, but from structural factors. I am convinced we need to undergo our own intellectual and moral revolution to confront legitimate competition from other countries. I cannot blame poor countries for becoming rich by intelligence and hard work. I can only admire them, and I do.

What will be the largest global challenge of the next century?

Food will be the biggest issue and challenge. We must do all we can to help poor countries achieve self-sufficiency in agriculture. Until the recent blockade on Iraq, that country had ignored its agricultural base by relying on cheap imports. I have now learned that Iraq has renewed its interest in agriculture. In the United States, the Black Muslim leader, Mr. Louis Farrahkan, rightly points out that due to social welfare programs, some African-Americans have not worked for four generations. I believe the welfare system is designed to enslave people. It is by hard work and traditional virtues (which are absent in state education) that true liberty can be achieved.

Who do you feel will hold the balance of power in the next century?

The United States, especially since the Soviet Union is no more. It is desirable that another power balance the U.S. It cannot be the European Union which has consciously placed itself politically, economically and culturally as a satellite to the United States. The U.S. is tempted to abuse its power since its power is absolute. Only a nationalist Russia can ever be capable of counterbalancing the United States.

Do you think China will remain communist?

I'm not sure about that since, like Russia, China is adopting the structure of a market economy. Earlier, I emphasized a nationalist Russia as a challenge to U.S. power because any nation entering a U.S.-dominated world order will have to do so at the expense of its national integrity.

How do you view the financial scandals besetting the U.S. President, Mr. Clinton?

I think Mr. Clinton's situation is worsening and he is heading toward impeachment. He may end up like President Richard Nixon did over the matter of electronic eavesdropping.

Should the U.S. have helped the British to prolong their control of Hong Kong?

No, I do not think that would have been wise. We are bound by our legal principles to respect our contracts.

Will Chinese control of Hong Kong change their official policy towards the island?

If China wisely preserves the status quo in Hong Kong, it can continue to be a bridge between China and the rest of the world. Hong Kong is the goose that lays the golden eggs. Twisting its neck would mean no more eggs. I think if China is involved in a confrontation, it is liable to be with Russia.

How do you interpret the rise of the British Labor party led by Tony Blair?

I think Tony Blair's personality gave the British Labor Party the same boost which the French Socialists received from the late Mr. Mitterand. Britain is a country where there has never been a Communist Party. So left- and extreme left-wing radicalism could only express itself through the Labor Party. I do believe Labor has displayed a more civilized behaviour lately.

France Co-Habits Again!—July 1997.

Although informed circles had been dropping dark hints for some time, the French public and a large number of politicians were caught unprepared by President Jacques Chirac's dramatic announcement in April. He dissolved the national assembly and called a snap election. Austerity measures and structural reforms designed to dock France into the European Union (EU)'s full monetary union (Euro) had caused unprecedented high unemployment. The Gaullists' popularity had plummeted. Further measures necessary to the achievement of Franco-German economic co-rule of the EU and containment of the dollar's bite could have led to massive public unrest. Feeling cornered, Jacques Chirac felt he needed to confirm electoral support before going further. He gambled, and lost.

For the third time in eleven years, a French President has to fulfill his term with a legislative minority and an opposition Prime Minister, known in France as "cohabitation". A conservative President has had to swallow his ideological gall and nominate a socialist Prime Minister hitching a ride with communists. The President retains his authority on foreign and defense policy while domestic affairs will be managed by the Prime Minister. Bickering starts in the domestic and foreign issues that over-lap. This time, the Prime Minister, 60-year old ex-college lecturer in economics, even has three communist ministers to hold on to.

Before Chirac's attempt at controlled demolition that blew up in his face, the Gaullists held 463 out of 577 seats. They now hold only 258, giving the champagne and caviar Socialists, their street-smart Communist bedfellows, Greens and a motley collection of other ageing left-wingers 319 seats. Due to France's two-round electoral system, although the National Front won 15 percent of the total vote polled in the first round, allowing 133 candidates to make it to the second round, only one was successful. The erstwhile left-wing minority has been struggling hard to reinvent itself on the British Labor Party model, but Lionel Jospin is a far cry from the wily Tony Blair. Jospin's economic outlook is classic Keynesian with a dash of Marxism. It is the caviar left's vain hope that this lethal mixture will allow them to run with the hares and hunt with the hounds. Pulling the reins on France's participation in the European Union's (EU) single currency Euro project will undermine Franco-German plans to co-rule Europe The socialists' promise of creating 700,000 jobs for youth is based on the faded tax and spend approach cold-bloodedly chucked by Blair's reinvented labor. In the short term the Left wing will reap the political benefits of decreased unemployment leaving the economic debris for the next government. The Jekyll and Hyde socialist-communist alliance is liable to spring leaks similar to the communist-propped Italian coalition in Italy, where Bernittoti of the Refounded Communists is prone to ram tidbits of communist legislation down Prodi's socialist throat. And professor Jospin, not known for his tap-dancing, will also have to nimbly sidestep well-aimed Gaullist flak, its accuracy sharpened following the near-certain shake-up of a tired Gaullist party.

Victims of their own success after the euphoric 1995 electoral landslide, the smug Gaullists had over-estimated their electoral support. France is grappling with the need for change. Old taboos are being challenged, and ghosts of the past rise up to haunt the French. The elite technocrats determinedly cling to the 17th century principles of Jean-Baptiste Colbert, minister of state to Louis XIV, the sun king: an interventionist state as the guarantor of a strong presence abroad and a content populace at home. The Gaullists tried to administer the bitter medicine of change, but when push came to shove, they backed down. Loss of credibility swiftly followed. It seems doubtful whether professor Jospin has the cunning and will to take on Colbert's inheritors. Failing that, Jospin will lead his party into the same marsh that bogged down the Gaullists, to the latter's obvious delight. After the statutory nine months granted to the new socialist-communist dominated legislature, the president can dissolve the parliament and call fresh elections! Expect the battle-hardened conservatives to exploit the slightest chink in left-wing armour.

The political landscape of the European Union is now dominated by left-wing governments. In Sweden, Portugal, Greece, Italy, Britain and France, the left are in a clear majority. In Holland, Denmark, Austria and Finland, they head coalition governments, while in Ireland, Luxembourg and Belgium, they form part of coalition governments. That leaves only Germany and Spain under conservative rule. While these left-wing governments are still a far cry from Britain's repackaged Labor, they rely less on Marxist solutions and respond more positively to the realities of their economic environment. In France, the new government has announced its support of Spain and Italy to enter the first stage of the Euro, and challenged the timetable promoted by Germany. Germany's rising unemployment, its Chancellor's promise to lower taxes, and the stranglehold of the Maastricht treaty's convergence criteria for the Euro have combined to lead Germany into the trap of creative accounting and desperate privatization bids. As the initial vision of the Euro recedes, so does the Franco-German dream to co-rule Europe. That is not bad news for the American dollar, since it means less fiscal competition and more market for the United States. Jean-Marie Le Pen, leader of the National Front known for his outspokenness on sensitive issues, declared in a public meeting on May 29 "France is in a state of war with the United States of America".

Just as conservatism is nourished by national sentiment, left-wing ideas thrive on joblessness and insecurity. Both left and right have had a nasty awakening to the realities of governing. The victorious Socialists are still carefully avoiding public signs of gloating. There is an undercurrent of public fear that France might just slip back to the ugly days when, only a few decades ago, weekends off were not a statutory right, and telephones and refrigerators were a rare luxury! "Never touch a Frenchman's wallet" is a street-wise adage ignored by the Gaullists. Chirac, however, is still President. As his Gaullists lick their wounds and gird up for the next battle, the left wing will be scrabbling hard to retain electoral support and ensure that the fading Franco-German dream of co-rule does not degenerate into rivalry and a polarized EU.

National Front Prospers—October 1997.

All political parties hold annual conventions. In France, they're called Summer Universities, and the atmosphere can get studious: earnest party members breaking up into work groups with notebooks and pencils. Accordingly, the French National Front held its annual convention from the 25th to 29th of August. The atmosphere on the last day was one of fierce optimism for the future. Between the National Front's outspoken President, his two seconds-in-command Bruno Golnisch and Bruno Megret, the ambitious program of the National Front was thoroughly covered. The National Educator was granted exclusive interviews by the two Brunos, both of whom have been described as "egg-heads" by *The Economist* (UK). Silver-haired Bruno Golnisch is a Paris University Law Professor, with a degree in Political Science. Fluent in Japanese and Malaysian, he is reckoned to be one of the sharpest Nipponologists in France. Bruno Megret, a spry and straight-backed engineer from France's most prestigious institution, also holds an M.Sc. in town planning from Berkley. They shared their world-view in two separate exclusive interviews covering the same subjects.

ON THE EFFICIENCY OF ECONOMIC BOYCOTTS IN GENERAL, AND THE BOYCOTT ON GOODS MANUFACTURED BY CHILDREN

GOLNISCH: The National Front itself has been victimized by boycotts at all levels. Boycotts may be efficient and immoral, or justified but inefficient. The ones against Franco's Spain, Cuba and Iraq were unsuccessful. The boycott on multinationals using child labor to manufacture cheap goods should be followed up by suing these companies.

MEGRET: Goods passing a frontier should be scrutinized by customs, to control unfair competition. The third world suffers from social ills, down to unacceptable exploitation of labor. Free trade devastates the third world environment

ON THE CHARGES AGAINST EXCESSES COMMITTED BY UN TROOPS IN SOMALIA

GOLNISCH: It goes well beyond "excesses" or misbehavior: it illustrates the inability of the UNO to apply its own charter. China abstained from the UN Security Council's decision to dispatch United Nations troops to Somalia. The UNO has a charter it neither respects nor applies, and in the resulting confusion, people get hurt.

MEGRET: The United Nations is guilty. Assigning fighting units a police role dumps on them a mission they are not oriented to.

ON THE ENLARGEMENT OF THE UNITED NATIONS' SECURITY COUNCIL

GOLNISCH: The balance of power within the Security Council is ensured by the veto of its permanent members. This same power has been a source of paralysis for United Nations action. Increase in the number of permanent members should further paralyze the United Nations. The gap between the UN charter and its application is already unsatisfying.

MEGRET: The United Nations allows the United States to play world policeman. The criterion, by which the United Nations chooses to intervene in, or ignore a situation meriting intervention, is an American criterion. Augmenting the number of permanent members of the Security Council will not decrease this tendency. As such, I do not feel that such a move is in the interest of the United Nations members. A new national order should balance the new world order.

WITH MOST EUROPEAN UNION GOVERNMENTS BEING LEFT-WING, THE FUTURE OF CONSERVATIVE FORCES IN THE EU

GOLNISCH: The left-wing argument is a spent force. Socialist governments in the EU have achieved legislative power by espousing right-wing policies! There used to be two main forces in Europe: the so-called progressives and the mainstream conservatives. Lately, the progressives have ceased to progress, and the conservatives have failed to conserve our values and traditions. This has resulted in a dissatisfied electorate that will respond to nationalism.

MEGRET: A change from the world order to a national order is only to be expected, and the choice of the Austrian electorate is a recent example. The world order and the national order are forces in collision.

ON TONY BLAIR's "NEW LABOUR" IN BRITAIN

GOLNISCH: The policies of the British Labor government are disparate and contradictory. They have suggested that EU countries adopt their electoral system, which is totally irrelevant to other European countries.

MEGRET: The Labor party in Britain makes a change for the voter! Left and right wing ideologies converge in the arguments of Mr. Blair, re-centering the traditional left-right cleft.

ON THE GENERAL FEELING WITHIN THE EU THAT BRITAIN IS THE UNITED STATES' TROJAN HORSE IN EUROPE

GOLNISCH: Yes, and its a pity.

MEGRET: Yes, and I regret that Britain does not choose to defend a European identity.

ON THE WORLD BALANCE OF POWER IN THE NEXT FEW DECADES

GOLNISCH: Communism was a monstrous system, leaving instability in its wake. People will not choose their destiny under the anonymous dictatorship of a world order based on an international caste system, which goes against the grain of all nations. These factors will decisively affect the balance of world power.

MEGRET: The new national order is taking root, and will grow. This will lead to bilateral accords between regions. Regional problems will be solved by regional efforts, unlike the approach to Yugoslavia. The implosion of the Soviet Union was not exactly the end of history, as Fukuyama had declared: the resulting instability is still teetering. An erstwhile bi-polar world will have to settle down to a multi-polar relationship.

France Makes Hay While U.S. Looks On—
March 1998.

Marshall McLuhan, the controversial media guru of the '60s, warned, "backward countries can learn from us how to beat us". Despite McLuhan's exaggerated fears, totalitarian regimes of "backward countries" are becoming proficient in manipulating western public opinion. Well-packaged and timed, Saddam Hussein's Iraq did very well with CNN during the 1991 Gulf War. More recently, Iraq's hereditary enemy, Iran, turned the same service to its advantage. On January 7, Iranian President Mohammed Khatami's handlers launched him on the American public as "the Iranian Gorbachev", via CNN's "carefully head-scarfed Christiane Amanpour". The ground, of course, had been prepared with unwitting help from the French, driven to distraction by a witless White House.

Caught up in its own wisdom, the American Administration had decided to dislocate French influence in Africa. France started looking eastward for greener pastures, from Russia to India to China, and eventually, the international pariah, Iran. Last year, the French oil company Total succeeded in obtaining an oil-exploration contract in Iran said to be worth billions. Subsequent to this deal, it was reported by *The European* in January that France intends to expand its Foreign Legion base in Djibouti on the Horn of Africa. A Rapid Reaction Force of eighty five thousand troops, 30 aircraft and an aircraft carrier, financed by the Gulf Cooperation Council, would thus be able to intervene in the Gulf to ensure the security of UAE oil fields. French interest in Central Asian oil fields is now a policy keystone. In any further oil exploration, Franco-Chinese cordiality is set to play a crucial role, just as it will mitigate Chinese adventurism in Central Asia.

Twisting the French tail in Africa has inserted the American administration between the devil and the deep sea: sanctions against Total will channel more Iranian business toward France and the European Union, strengthening French credentials in dealing with other Central Asian countries. With the credibility of the American government reduced to world-class comedy by the libidinal indiscretions of its President, not enforcing sanctions would raise it to the status of farce.

The Khatami interview provides the administration with a convenient escape-hatch. Since President Khatami is now coming across as an Iranian Gorbachev rather than a "mad mullah", the administration can save face and justify a semblance of normalized relations, without further deteriorating its relationship with France and the EU by imposing sanctions on Total.

Mr. Khatami's hard sell to the American electorate bespoke the professionalism of a resource-rich entrepreneur in search of corporate expansion. He expressed familiarity with the works of de Tocqueville, (one of France's most illustrious sons), praised America's mixture of "religion and liberty" and claimed to sense an "intellectual affinity" with the "essence" of American civilization. The last remark may be taken to mean that Mr. Khatami recognizes the content of American values, but their form does not merit his attention: an omission designed to reassure the anti-American lobby in his home constituency.

The neo-Confucianists of South East Asia, led by Malaysia's president, Mr. Mahathir Mohammed, do not even accept the "essence" of American values. They actually question the very foundations of western civilization, and openly sneer at it.

Indeed, writing for the Foreign Policy Research Institute (*America versus the West* October 1997), Professor James Kurth of Swarthmore College expresses concern for American ideology. The American academic elite, in deconstructing Western civilization, have made way for a multicultural ideology, replacing the modern idea of the west with "a disparate collection of post-modern, post-western ideas". This is now affecting the "body politic". Professor Kurth predicts the effect of this incoherence on the

NATO alliance, "opening up a new gap between the foreign policies of the American elite and the international convictions of the American people".

In 1987, Alan Bloom's *The Closing of the American Mind* had warned against the diversified fall-out likely to occur from an unqualified pursuit of multiculturalism. Just over a decade later, Professor Bloom's analyses have the ring of prophecy. The identity of a prankish adolescent assumed and projected by the United States, leaves the American people at the mercy of their economic dynamism. Heroes are conjured by Hollywood's dream merchants: a far cry from classical bards and poets.

These short-circuited currents, emanating from the United States' misguided elite, risk re-ordering the global mosaic of power, and threaten the vision of the Founding Fathers for succeeding generations.

SECTION FIVE—GERMANY

Germany's Central European Game—January 1996.

Decisiveness by the European Union (EU) leadership this year is crucial to the abortion of a disguised German MittelEuropa in Central Europe. Germany's involvement with Central Europe spans a millennium of history. In 962 AD, German kings launched their own Holy Roman Empire following the decline of Charlemagne's empire (800-925 AD). It included the five countries that constitute Central Europe today: the Czech Republic, Slovakia, Hungary, Poland and Slovenia, with a total population of 70 million. Conversion to Catholicism put these countries in the western camp, and they formed part of the Austro-Hungarian Empire led by the Habsburg dynasty until 1918. The institutions created, and the state of mind inculcated by their Teutonic masters over a thousand years, survived communism and allowed Central Europe to be better prepared for the post-communist world.

A couple of years back, they were known as the Visegrad Group, referring to their leaders' meeting in Visegrad, Hungary, in 1991. They have shed this appellation, and are busily disassociating themselves from the term "Eastern Europeans". The label, they feel, insensitively identifies them with the "vodka-guzzling" Slavs converted by the Orthodox Church. Within the East-West rivalry separating Rome and Byzantine, Central Europeans seek to confirm their western credentials and consequent membership of the EU and NATO to ensure a sunny future.

These countries are seeing healthy growth. Even though average living standards are one-third below the European Union average, trade with Germany is remarkably brisk. Over the past five years, the mass of Central Europe's trade has shifted from the former Soviet Union to Germany, the biggest foreign investor in Central Europe. Approximately half of EU imports are German, and half of Central Europe's exports go to Germany.

Germany now casts a bigger shadow in Central Europe than Russia. It is clearly shepherding Central Europe into the EU and NATO, coyly referring to itself as a "tutor" or "advocate"! Germans sees this as a duty second only to upgrading the former East Germany, an operation costing around $140 billion a year, four times the estimated cost to the EU of granting membership to Central Europe. And Germany's motives run deeper than a simple nostalgia for its Habsburg links with Central Europe, or the German Reich's MittelEuropa, which blurred the line between military and economic ambitions.

Integration of Central Europe within the EU provides Germany with a convenient market in the foreseeable future. NATO membership for these countries secures Germany's Eastern Frontiers, although German officialdom is said to be allergic to the term "buffer".

Helmut Kohl has reportedly promised Poland admission into the EU and NATO by the year 2000. This promise is usually taken to include the other four countries of Central Europe. Although Poland, on the surface, stands out as Germany's prime choice, the real favorites are—as they were for a millennium—the Czech Republic and Hungary. Poland has "buffer-value" and soothes German guilt about the Second World War, allowing its Central European ambitions to assume a moral dimension.

An additional motive of German interest in Central Europe is the Germans settled in Poland, and Czech Sudetenland. Germany's federal constitution is committed to granting them citizenship by virtue of their German ancestry. Germany wants to look after its own people, and also reassure the Czechs and Poles. An eventual grant of German citizenship to these "expatriate settlers" would neither subvert the loyalty of Czech and Polish citizens, nor would the fatherland use their presence as a pretext to invade them the way Hitler did.

Admitting Central Europe into the EU and NATO is a political decision. This year will see two important conferences—the EU summit, and the EU Inter-governmental Conference. The most important decision will be on the future of a single European currency. That in turn will influence the nature of Central Europe's entry into the EU, allowing other EU countries to broaden their economic ties with Central Europe, and check Germany's Central European hegemony. It is up to Germany and France to resolve the problem of a single European currency by1999. The time to achieve that is now, otherwise Kohl's promise to Central Europe will be compromised, leaving Germany with a conflict of interest vis a vis the EU. By curbing government spending even at the expense of domestic credibility, the French government is seeking to provide Germany with an option other than the creation of a de facto MittelEuropa disguised as a trading zone. The latter event would leave France with no choice but to create a similar entity with Italy, Spain, Portugal and Ireland, searching for horizons towards Latin America. It would also be a custom-built situation for a resurgent Russia to realize its historical ambition and supplant Rome with Byzantine. If the EU leadership fails to take steps now, it is liable to leave Europe a pawn of the very forces it unleashed.

Germany Again Moving Into A Decisive Role— February 1996.

No single member state of the European Union (EU) thinks it is a world power, but collectively the EU has world power potential. This potential can only be realized by a common currency and foreign policy. Power cannot be wielded on the basis of potential alone: there would be more superpowers than the world could cope with. Eurosceptics and Euroenthusiasts are at odds over the feasibility of the EU's so-called "sovereign" status. The Maastricht treaty of 1992, prematurely diffused to citizens, contains terms, which, if and when completely applied, amount to devolution of sovereign power by individual member states.

The Intergovernmental conference of EU members is due in a few weeks. It will seek to make the terms of the Maastricht treaty palatable. Since June 1995, a think tank headed by Carlos Westendrop, Spain's Secretary of State for European Affairs, has been studying ways of getting European Union citizens to support the Maastricht Treaty. The cornerstone of the treaty is neither open frontiers nor a common police force, but a single currency and a common foreign policy.

Since the EU Summit held in Madrid on November 23, Euro, the proposed German name for the hoped-for single currency, has been accepted. The Euro is supposed to be launched on January 1, 1999, and meant to take effect in 2002. Hard discipline is required to meet this timetable. The maximum acceptable budget deficit of a country adhering to the Euro has been fixed at 3 percent of its GNP. France has bitten the bullet by introducing stringent economic measures designed to contain its yawning budget deficit. It has consequently faced trade union rage in the form of paralyzing strikes by government employees over weeks, with losses not yet calculated, but definitely running into the billions. Britain has opted out of the single currency with Fred Astaire-like alacrity, but that is of no significance at the moment. When de Gaulle created the common market, it was meant to keep the British out. They wanted in, more so when they realized the Commonwealth leadership was not theirs by right. Once they got into the then European Community, characteristically, they wanted out—Mrs. Thatcher complained it was "not working" for the British! Just as the loss of Commonwealth leadership decreased British options, the end of the cold war and the loss of Hong Kong will leave them with even fewer, and at the last minute they will jump on the Euro-bandwagon.

On the issue of a common EU foreign policy—which pivots on a common defense—Britain hopes to be able to play a key role. The European Union makes firm claims of being able to come up with a foreign policy for Europe. The peace for ex-Yugoslavia brokered in Dayton is not a triumph of EU foreign policy, but a reminder of American indispensability in cleaning up the European backyard. The EU is also waiting to see if Mr. Clinton is capable of keeping the totality of his hyped-up promises concerning ex-Yugoslavia. That it will take U.S. troops to bring peace to Ireland is another bit of stark reality that haunts EU leaders. After all, a common foreign policy without a defense is verbiage. Mutually suspicious of each other, no EU state is willing to exchange the NATO umbrella for one which elevates another European state. France and Britain are the only nuclear powers in the European Union. There are rumors to the effect that Germany, seeking an alternative to a possible Franco-British nuclear umbrella, has been discreetly stroking a "special deal" with Washington, preparing for a time when it might need to recreate a MittelEuropa, dilute ties with the EU, slip from under NATO and cut a direct deal with Washington.

Since 1992, Britain and France have maintained a "nuclear dialogue", most of which remains shrouded in secrecy. In 1993 a Franco-British Commission was constituted to study deterrence, doctrine and advanced concepts. In 1994, the same commission worked on a "European dimension to deterrence", which plainly means "Life After NATO"! A common Franco-British delivery system is reportedly underway. A Joint Strategic Air Force Command already has a French general in command based in Britain. At the same time, 45,000 well-equipped troops of Eurocorps (France, Germany, Spain, Belgium and Luxembourg) are now ready for operations. Two separate European forces are being prepared for intervention solely in the Mediterranean.

Common currency and common foreign policy mean the Euro and a common defense. A U.S.-led NATO is less threatening to the sovereign status of EU members than one of their own invested with the same powers. The looming question is: if the Germans cut a deal with Washington, Washington cuts a deal with Moscow, and NATO ceases to be cost-effective to the Americans, where does that leave the rest of Europe?

Germans Busy Muckraking—March 2000.

Germany's historic reunion achieved by the conservative Christian Democratic Union (CDU) under Helmut Kohl is being undermined by the socialist Social Democrats now in power, in an effort to ensure their continuity in office. Charges of sleaze against Germany's former chancellor Helmut Kohl are now abetted by a grisly suicide and a shadowy French Connection.

French socialist President François Mitterand's government is alleged to have given Mr Kohl $16 million in state funds for the 1994 re-election. Excluding the French sum, the CDU has confessed to a total untraceable amount of $15 million in its coffers. In order to ensure its survival, the party's leader Wolfgang Schauble has now bared his fangs to Helmut Kohl. He reported to the Bundestag that during Mr Kohl's tenure, the law was often broken. The CDU's treasurer Matthias Wissman, said the party was unable to identify the source of $1 million, an amount admitted to by Mr Kohl, the source of which he refuses to disclose.

The question being debated is whether the French Connection influenced Germany's rapid integration into the European Union (EU). The French oil company Elf is said to have bought the East German oil refinery Leuna for $45 million in 1992. The purchase was apparently over-priced, and the difference was slipped into the CDU's coffers. These allegations were made public as a result of joint investigative reporting by Germany's ARD TV channel and French channel 2. Quoting a source in Mr. Mitterand's inner circle, it was "not a bribe, but a campaign contribution". Although the Prosecutor's office in Paris has not yet been able to confirm a link between Elf's acquisition of Leuna and illegal campaign contributions,

Volker Neuman, Social Democrat MP leading the parliamentary inquiry in Germany, said that his commission would "expand the focus of the inquiry."

Wolfgang Hullen, head of CDU's finance and budgetary office, was found hanged. The German daily *Berliner Zeitung* reported that a suicide note referred to the deceased's fear of investigation, and that the Berlin state prosecutor is connecting the suicide with embezzlement.

Mr Kohl denies the charges. He has resigned from the post of honorary chairman of the party, but retains his parliamentary seat that offers him immunity from prosecution, though not from public disgrace.

Even if the charges are unfounded, it refreshes memories of past left and right wing alliances based on mutual interest. Currently, a right-wing French President and his left-wing cabinet are further collaborating with left-wing EU governments to trash Mr Haider's extreme right wing party's legitimisation in the Austrian parliament. The late François Mitterand had himself initiated electoral reforms in France to the advantage of his socialist party, thereby allowing the extreme right-wing National Front to sit in parliament. Reaction was strong, but both the socialists and the National Front prospered. In Israel, former President Weismann has been questioned by police on the subject of misappropriation of funds whilst in office. Not so long ago, the European Commission had to resign en bloc under a cloud of corruption charges, and across the Atlantic, the U.S. President was impeached.

It is tempting, though far-fetched, to invoke a dark, third force at work in the western world, using an ethical broom to orchestrate the downfall of governments. However, a combination of naïve activism and zealous investigative reporting getting carried away by a belief in their own legend can always work to the advantage of those who think that true revolution escaped them in the sixties. Investigative reporters today are expected to conform to the standards of the Watergate reporting, and thus have to dig harder and amplify more to measure up. The inheritors of the defunct Temperance League have more causes than they ever did before: over-all political correctness, anti-smoking, anti-gun laws, pollution etc.

Misguided activists pushed for prohibition at the wrong time, allowing neighbourhood thugs to establish themselves as Al Capones.

The world has changed, and the *greatness* of *great men* who form pivots of history is being challenged. Nothing is being offered as a substitute, and the price of sparkling cleanliness risks becoming a veneration of mediocrity. The price of greatness must be carefully weighed before pronouncing judgement. What appears to be embezzlement today might just be yesterday's sloppy bookkeeping. Oversights of clerical procedure need not obscure the appreciation of historical accomplishment. Helmut Kohl reunited Germany, and that single accomplishment should be enough for the German public to ignore a few million dollars acquired towards achieving that aim. Instead, they have decided to peck at the flesh of the man who cut a few corners to give them a country Hitler had lost for them.

A people obsessed with flogging themselves for the sins of their fathers have now found a whipping boy in Mr Kohl, their benefactor. In seeking to exorcise their demons, they have chosen to become demoniacal. The Social Democrats are neither saints nor do they have a guarantee against political change: they are liable to fall short of their own exigent standards and find themselves at the mercy of the very forces they are now unleashing. And the influence of anti-septic expectations being fed to the German people might soon seep its way into the management of international relations. If that happens, the network of relationships built by Mr Kohl will no longer be able to serve Germany's interests, reducing it to the sole status of an economic powerhouse. History will then be even more unkind to Germans than they feel it is today.

German Military Reforms Inappropriate—July 2000.

Military reforms proposed by the Wëizsacker Commission in Germany have re-focused attention on the issue of values polarising right and left, while the German nation seeks to redefine itself within Europe, the western alliance and the international community. Conservatives favour a three-year national service as a means of infusing the nation's youth with patriotic values. The left-wing supports an all-volunteer army with training and logistics sub-contracted to civilians. Both envision the German military as an active partner in international crises management, and neither wishes to see an isolated force of professional warriors in the Junker tradition. The issue was brought to the forefront on 24 May by General Hans Peter von Kirbach's resignation in response to the Wëizsacker Report

General Kirbach, Inspector General of the German army—the Bundeswehr—had been nominated by former Chancellor Helmut Kohl, a conservative. Richard Scharping, Germany's current Socialist Defense Minister, initiated a commission under Herr Wëizsacker, former president of the Republic Christian Democratic Union, to assess the Bundeswehr's suitability to Germany's present needs. Germany seeks to maintain a well equipped, modern and cost-effective army adapted to the security needs of the country. The report observed that the Bundeswehr is "too heavy, badly organized and increasingly obsolete. In its present state, the Bundeswehr has no future".

The Commission proposes to reduce the overall number of personnel from 320,000 to 240,000 over ten years. The reduction will be in the number of conscripts—from 135,000 to 3000 for a ten-month period, with beefed-up salaries. The maximum number of military personnel liable to intervene internationally is estimated at 140,000, including troops earmarked for the 60,000 strong European Rapid Deployment Force due in three years time.

This reduction is only the first step towards the elimination of conscription by a Socialist government. The Commission esteems that the end of the cold war has laid a conventional threat to rest, with crisis management the new imperative. The Bundeswehr Generals and their left-wing Minister would like to retain the option of classic territorial defense, dependant on conscription. Citizens in uniform are also seen as a guarantee against threats to democracy.

The Commission recommends obtaining this guarantee by privatizing training and logistics. Thus, what the conservatives wish to accomplish by an extended period of conscription, the left-wing hope to obtain by making the military subservient to union power. Napoleon is reported to have said that "an army crawls on its stomach". If the left wing has its way, the Bundeswehr will creep to union policy, further subject to the intellectual prescriptions of the middle-aged men in power who fought in the streets in 1968. What Baader and Meinhoff were unable to gain by terrorism might now be achieved by a simple act of privatizing Bundeswehr logistics and training. And military training goes well beyond dissemination and acquisition of units of knowledge. It is when and where the groundwork for efficient soldiering is laid, and loyalties forged, incorporating troops into a brotherhood which eventually blossoms into an esprit de corps, giving one body of troops the advantage over another, despite a common training programme. Troops trained by civilians will either be incompetent, sub-standard mercenaries or hostage to an ideology of little use to a professional warrior. There is little doubt that this privatisation will function with cost-effective efficiency for long enough to inspire other European countries to lay themselves at the mercy of unions. Once a sufficient number of countries have been coerced into doing so, the unions will be able to decide which intervention they approve of and which intervention they disapprove of.

This means that over time, German peacekeeping ability within an international force would lose credibility.

German determination to have a world-class army on the same footing as its allies is understandable. Germany has no desire to be a mere economic giant like Singapore. Not powerful enough to take unilateral decisions in international crises, Germany has to keep in step with its European allies and the U.S.. Thus it is with Europeans under the NATO umbrella that Germany can maintain a self-gratifying image.

It was no accident that the publication of the Wëiszacker Report coincided with President Clinton's visit to Germany as part of his European tour. The Germans laid out a flattering welcome. Bill Clinton was the first U.S. President to receive the prestigious Charlemagne Prize at Aaschen. Charlemagne, the Frank Emperor of the first Reich, lies buried in the majestic cathedral (814 A.D.) that served as the backdrop for the ceremony, during which Schroeder repeatedly called his guest "dear Bill". He underlined the fact that a strong U.S.-European alliance remains essential, but also noted "We are also well on our way to realizing a common European security and defense policy. It will create the framework for swift and efficient action by the European Union in crises and thus represent an important contribution toward transatlantic burden-sharing". He also echoed European concerns about a new arms race possibly sparked by U.S. plans for a national missile defense system.

While Germany's political leadership worries about civilian control over a professional army that can ensure the status of its economic powerhouse, the Generals fret about the decreased influence of military service over national values, and subjugation of military values and operational mobility to union ideology. Barring the subcontracting of army training and logistics to civilians, the generals and the politicians should be able to come to terms over professionalisation and suppression of conscription. A balanced, self-confident Germany is in the interest of all its neighbours who have little desire to see a frustrated Germany redefine itself.

SECTION SIX—UNITED KINGDOM

Are We Seeing The Last Days Of Britain's Monarchy?—January 1995.

Great Britain's over 1000 year old monarchy has successfully chosen to add itself to the list of threatened species. Their power chipped away since 1688 by successive Whig governments, the royals adroitly managed to steer their throne into the 20th century. In 1917, shortly after H.G. Wells criticized his "alien and uninspiring court," George V of the Hanoverian Grieffs nimbly reinvented them as the House of Windsor.

The value of public relations has never been lost on the British royal family. From 1967 to about 1980, Neilson-McCarthy Ltd. of Mayfair discreetly handled Prince Charles—"a first class product" according to Nielsen, a New Zealander. The last few years have seen the product lose some of its class. Charles and Diana's undignified public squabbles are a godsend for Britain's unscrupulous press.

The royal futures depend on retention of the monarchy by the British people. According to royal biographer John Pearson, "the British are a matriarchal people," with a "public image of the British royal males …(as) dedicated and undemanding figures…family loving."

Opinion polls show 70 to 75 percent of the people in favor of retaining the monarchy. A decade ago, the figure was 85 to 90 percent. In 1990, 70 percent of the people believed Britain would still have a monarchy in 50 years time. Today, only 35 to 50 percent believe the same.

These are figures cited by *The Economist*, Britain's establishment weekly which has called for Britain to do the sensible thing and become a republic. From 1861 to 1877, Walter Bagehot served as editor of *The Economist*. In 1867 he published *The English Constitution*, still used as a guide by monarchs and parliamentarians. Bagehot believed the British needed a monarch because the vast majority were unfit "for an elective government. A better-educated populace", he held reluctantly, would not need "old world debris."

In October, the conservative *Daily Telegraph* quoted Prince Philip as saying that "a perfectly reasonable alternative" to a constitutional monarchy was a republic. The decline of Britain's institutions had been sensed by Rudyard Kipling as early as 1899. By publishing his poem "The White Man's Burden" in the U.S., he symbolically passed on the torch of Anglophone western civilization to the United States, conceding a British burnout. Following the First World War, Britain tied itself to America's apron strings while seesawing with the European continent. The end of the cold war decreased Britain's relevance to U.S. foreign policy, shifting Britain's vision from over the Atlantic to under the channel.

The British media often harp on the superiority of continental public services. Britain's postal service, water supply, funeral services, rails and roads and garbage disposal can best qualify as quaint. The press has itself sunk to questionable standards. Football, the blue collar institution, has been taken over by hooligans. The lack of adequate judicial safeguards has prompted many people to seek redress of grievances in the European Court in Strasbourg, and the police are now admittedly corrupt. Nearly two percent "brown Jews"—immigrants from the Indian subcontinent—reportedly own around 20 percent of Britain's wealth.

It is perhaps recognition of this new economic reality that prompted Prince Charles to declare that when (and if) he succeeded to the throne, he would renounce the title "defender of the faith" in favor of "defender of all faiths."

The British never had a French style revolution. Instead of standing up for themselves, the British working classes meekly accepted handouts trickling down from devolution of royal power. State education has allowed them to put their illiterate past behind them. Perhaps by Bagehot's law, they are now fit "for an elective government."

Britain is showing classic symptoms of an ungrateful peasantry willing to participate in a barbaric ritual of sharing royal carrion with today's Whigs. Led by the royal family, Britain has unwittingly decided to destroy its last remaining institution. The year 1995 will see institutional changes which cause Britain to take a keener look at itself.

Ideologically Bankrupt Labour Party Goes Conservative —June 1997.

Labor is back in power in Britain under Tony Blair After confining the British Labor party in the political wilderness for nearly two decades, British voters gave Labor a second lease of life, fittingly on Labor Day, with 419 seats representing 43.09 percent of the vote. Conservatives won 165 seats, or 30.6 percent of the vote, and the liberals managed 46 seats at 16.7 percent. Labor day is also known as Mayday, and serves as the international distress code. So whose Mayday was it on the 1st of May?

Since its creation in 1911, the fundamentals of the British Labor Party's election manifesto have expressed concern for the less privileged at the expense of the privileged.

Inspired by socialism, labor offered an interventionist state as a hedge against social exploitation. With state coffers clanging empty at the end of World War II, Clement Attlee's Labor government inopportunely decided to offer the British workman a sumptuous, over-ambitious National Health Service. The Bank of England and major industries were nationalized, and the Soviet nuclear threat was perceived as a response to capitalist policies. Consequently, the left-wing Campaign for Nuclear Disarmament projected the blissful vision that if only NATO renounced its nuclear weapons, the noble Soviets would immediately follow suit and we would all live under a pink sky.

Inspired by conservative values, Reaganomics and common sense, Lady Thatcher led the British Conservatives to a decisive victory in 1983. The British public had also, by then, seen through Labor's microeconomic approach: employ people to dig holes, and then employ other people to fill them up. Since Lady Thatcher's departure in 1990, privatization, reconciliation with the idea of the European Union and rising unemployment have given the Conservative Tories a rough ride. Internecine political struggles creating lethal rifts have also taken their toll. Despite a healthy economy, rising standards of living and social calm, the conservatives were denied re-election by cynical voters.

The death of functional conservatism within the British Tories allowed Labor to snatch the body and claim it for themselves. Five years ago, 43-year old Tony Blair, with his urbane looks, public school accent and Christian faith assumed the party leadership to replace Neil Kinnock, the "Welsh wind-bag". In a brilliant display of creative semantics, Tony Blair offered the British public what they wanted—a conservative program and a new look. As the Tories bickered and retreated into Euroscepticism bordering on xenophobia, Tony Blair abandoned Labor's traditional anti-EU stance. He seized leadership of the public and business class that sees close relations with the EU as opportunity rather than threat.

Labor's changed colors are colorfast and market-literate. Blair's blow-dried boys are eager to influence City finance and determined to replace the Tory hub.

Sheltered under the morally sound argument of bringing order to the City of London, Labor is liable to merge the Self-Regulatory Organizations into the Securities and Investments Board, lending it a structure similar to the U.S. SEC, and also set it up as a counter-weight to the Bank of England. This move would allow the Laborites to trade with Wall Street on mutually beneficial terms.

The British weekly *The European* referred to Labor's "repackaged" look. The British tabloid *The Sun*, a hitherto solid conservative Thatcherite supporter, chose to bet on Tony Blair as the winning horse. In private, Tony Blair is reported to have talked of a "Euro-club of the Big three—France, Germany and Britain". Lady Thatcher herself declared that there was "no fear for Britain under Blair"! The establishment weekly, *The Economist*, however, remains wary of Tony Blair's ability to follow word with deed.

Indeed, stripped of the politically correct semantics designed to satisfy voter expectations, Blair is acrobatically vague on how to achieve his noble goals. Serious doubts remain on Labor's competence in macroeconomics, while in microeconomics it is liable to reveal its old spots by signing the European Union's social charter that the British economic structure is ill equipped to implement without consequent social disorder.

The bankrupt ideology of the Labor party is dead. Like any business-man buying an ageing company with brand loyalty and a retail infra-structure, Blair's boys moved into the Labor party, reshuffled it, retained the name for what it was worth, along with the ward-bosses, and infused new life into conservative thinking. Ideologically, the labor party's victory confirms the singularity of conservative values and recites the last rites of Labor's socialist dialectics on Britain's political wasteland.

British Sun Sets At Last—August 1997.

Britain's conservative *Sunday Telegraph* referred to it as "the last sunset of the British Empire". At the stroke of midnight on June 30, 1997, Britain ceded Hong Kong to China after 156 years, shoring up its stiff upper lip by fanfare, highland jigs, and boisterous pub revelries. The Chinese quietly moved in 4000 crack troops in civilian transport six hours before they were due. Jiang Zemin, the President of China, made a speech, carrying enough reassurances to massage western liberals and a sufficient number of ambiguities to raise fears. While reiterating China's determination to maintain rule of law, direct elections and liberty of expression, he pointedly evoked the future of Taiwan. At the same time, he credited the ethnic Chinese and China itself for Hong Kong's financial success. It was left to Tung Chee Hwa, the new Chief Administrator of Hong Kong, to interpret "rule of law" and "liberty of expression" for Hong Kong's 6.2 million people. Public demonstrations will require official permission, local organizations will be denied foreign funding, "undue" references to British culture will be toned down and defacing the Chinese flag will entail three years imprisonment. This goes further than handwriting on the wall: it is a declaration of war.

The reaction in France, with a conservative president and socialist prime minister, was split down the line by ideology, and bound by the desire to uphold human rights, explore market opportunities and nurture relations with China. Public statements from Lionel Jospin, the socialist Prime Minister, and Jacques Chirac, the Gaullist president, were artfully crafted by their blow-dried speechwriters in creative diplomatic-speak.

All 7 TV channels in France covered the event. Accordingly, the major papers and magazines carried special features on the historic development.

The hammer-and-sickled mouthpiece of the French communist party stuck to its communist guns, its headline patronizingly gloating "Hong Kong back in the fold", and its editorial regretting the independence of Taiwan. The Catholic daily *La Croix*, pondered over individualism versus collectivism, wondering whether "Hong Kong's western values will influence China or vice versa"? The Gaullist daily *Le Figaro* was forthright, giving Hong Kong a good chance of converting China.

The French, like other Europeans, and many Americans, see the British departure from Hong Kong as "opportunity", believes chartered accountant Pierre Ahidzi. Despite French and German courtship, the U.S. is liable to emerge as Hong Kong's biggest trading partner, resented by EU countries.

There is a general feeling in France that the U.S. is poaching on French reserves. For instance, the last few months have shown an increased American presence in Francophone Africa. The unwritten agreement giving strategic natural resources to the Americans and law-enforcement to the French is being put to the test by the American insistence on a Pan-African force. The German economic magazine *Wirtschaftswoche* observed, "European capitals are increasingly irritated by the aggressiveness of U.S. foreign trade helped by its intelligence agencies". Peter Schraeder of Loyola University, Chicago, points out that after the cold war, there is now a cold peace, with every inch of market being hotly contested. James Lilly, the American ambassador in Beijing at the time of the Tiannemen massacre, gave an interview to the conservative French daily, *Le Figaro*. He referred to the U.S. as the sole guarantor of stability in East Asia.

In France, the U.S. desire for a pan-African peace-keeping force in Africa, and its offer to guarantee "stability" in East Asia are interpreted as a single policy: increased trade for the United States. Relieved by Britain's departure from Hong Kong, the European Union countries are scrabbling for a share of the market, while the Chinese laugh at western nations pitted against each other in a macabre yin-yang of which Sun Tzu would have heartily approved.

Tung Chee Hwa, son of a shipping magnate bailed out by Mainland China during a financial crisis in 1982, is the new strongman of Hong Kong. In a meeting with Asian Ministers and the Trade Minister of Canada, which excluded Taiwan, he reiterated the Chinese call for reunification with Taiwan on the one-country-two-systems basis. Taiwan responded by suggesting that Beijing adopt a multi-party system.

Although the acquisition of Hong Kong raised China's GNP by 20 percent overnight, Taiwan is the plum: the combined gold and foreign currency reserves of China, Hong Kong and Taiwan come to 267 billion dollars, much higher than Japan. Beijing is already estimated to hold about 20 percent of U.S. treasury bonds, and the U.S. Administration is falling over itself to grant them their Guantanamo Bay in the U.S. (*National Educator*, May and June 97 issues), significantly strengthening China's bargaining position in any trade negotiations. Theoretically, the Hong Kong dollar is independent of the Chinese yen, but in case of a monetary crisis in Beijing, could be maneuvered to prop up the Chinese yen. Conversely, in case of a crisis in Hong Kong, Beijing could force Hong Kong to open its gold reserves.

A monetary or other crisis may be expected, even if it does not resound with a thunderclap. In a survey of senior executives across 10 Asian countries, the *Far Eastern Economic Review* found that 70.5 percent expect an onslaught of corruption, and 61.4 percent believe a drop in financial status will follow. This may be helped by Beijing itself by bypassing Hong Kong in its trade links with the rest of the world, reducing Hong Kong to the status of Venice after Vasco de Gama navigated around the Cape of Good Hope in 1498.

Takeshi Hamashita, Director of the Institute of Oriental Studies at Tokyo University, and specializing in the Chinese Diaspora, believes otherwise. Asked to comment on the future of Hong Kong by Japan's *Asahi Shimbun*, he remarked that Hong Kong would shift its ethos from "the logic of the sea" to emerge as a creator of lateral relations and converging point for Asian nations.

In fact, China's decision to ban the inflow of foreign aid to non-governmental organizations reflects its own fretfulness. In 1911, Dr Sun Yat Sen fled to Hong Kong seeking help to overthrow the government in Beijing. The Beijing Dragon is fully aware of the repetitiveness of history and the eruptive potential of the prodigy it has drawn back into its womb.

Britain's New Prime Minister Smooth As Silk— November 1997.

Eighteenth century British parliamentarian Edmund Burke wrote of "the only infallible criterion of wisdom to vulgar minds—success". Had he been alive today, he would have doubtless dropped this pearl of wisdom onto the British Prime Minister's impeccably successful lap. Britain's Labor Prime Minister, Tony Blair's vision extends far and wide. He even has the intellectual humility to borrow a Chinese dictator's maxims to achieve success with his electorate. Just like the erstwhile Chinese leader Deng Xiaoping talked of "four modernizations", our friend Tony has pulled as many rabbits out of his political hat. The British public may thus rest assured that they are only one step behind China. The Blair modernizations promise a flexible economy, a modern welfare state, constitutional reform and a role for Britain in the world.

These modernizations tacitly admit that Britain's economy is rigid, its welfare state outdated, it desperately needs a constitution and that its grip on the United States' coat tails to define a world role for itself is slipping. Talk of a "new" Britain is exciting the British public. In 1964, the British Labor Party talked of a New Britain that was saved from disaster by the timely intervention of Dame Margaret Thatcher. Labor is now back at its game of ersatz.

Tony Blair certainly inspires confidence. Patterned on the American model, his blow-dried look carries a smile that could charm a nest of Arkansas rattlesnakes. Unlike the sheriff in old westerns, he doesn't wear a white hat—but his crisp white shirt does just as well. For a socialist, his French cuffs and expensive cuff links bespeak an aristocracy that is still dear to the heart of Britain's pageant-loving mobs. His tasteful ties, carefully chosen by wife Cherry, a high-powered lawyer, and approved by his handlers, are as well knotted as Bill Clinton's. But whereas Bill keeps his collar buttoned against the chill of Washington's investigative winds, Tony Blair, in his best-known billboard picture, has an unbuttoned collar over a loosened tie. Perhaps the weather in Britain has really become Mediterranean, and the island will never have to be towed away to the sunny Pacific. It is safer to conclude that the billboard message seeks to reassure the British public that although he is of the "right" stock, he wouldn't mind mixing with the plebes.

Taking into account the touchy-feely side of Britain that came to press attention following Lady Diana's tragic death. The British Prime Minister and his spin doctors know what they're about. Lady Diana was loved because she was a "people's princess". Tony might be headed towards being a "people's prince". He has already limited the membership of the House of Lords to life peers. The "constitutional reform" being touted might establish a "life monarchy" with an elected monarch. Failing that, if Prince Charles abdicates before his son William is of age, who will be the Regent? Lady Diana's brother, Lord "champagne Charlie" Spencer whose speech at his sister's funeral had mobs howling approval, or the institution of the Prime Minister itself?

In a contest for Regency, Tony Blair would win hands down. After all, he isn't stuffy and promises the British a New Britain But truth, as we all know, lies within an opposition, which is where the truth is encapsulated by Britain's labor party wordsmiths. You just have to cast a line in the semantic waves and hope to hook up the truth.

Accordingly, based on the proliferation of Britain's creative service industries consisting of pop music and clothes designers, Mr. Blair strokes the British into believing that their country could be the "biggest economic powerhouse of the world". The truth is, that he promises former empire builders and civilizers a rosy future as the world's tailors and entertainers. He promises a flexible economy that overrides job security, a modern welfare state based on privatization and a clear identity role which means all hype with no action. As long as beer is cheap and weekend soccer ensured, the British mobs will cheer him on.

With help from the U.S. Democrats' media midwives, the British Prime Minister is the child of image-smiths. His billboard smile could sell enough whole milk to reduce the European Union's notorious milk-lake. His truths would never open him to charges of deliberate falsehood. He is so beautiful, that he gives a new dimension to Keats' line from *Ode on a Grecian Urn* "Beauty is truth, truth beauty".

God save Britain.

Queen Elizabeth's Visit Diplomatic Disaster— December 1997.

The Queen's October visit to India was a shambles, provoking an undignified diplomatic row between India and Britain: the harvest of bad judgment, spite, strong reaction and bickering. This year, India and Pakistan celebrated their 50th independence anniversaries. It was also Queen Victoria's diamond jubilee. Accordingly, the Head of the Commonwealth, Queen Elizabeth II of Great Britain, visited India and Pakistan from 12 to 17 October on twin five-day visits planned two years ago. Her Majesty was accompanied by her consort, Prince Philip, Duke of Edinburgh, and Robin Cook, her government's Foreign Secretary. Pakistan was the first stop, a red carpet welcome replete with the heart-stirring pageantry of "mounted Pathan warriors" (British *Daily Telegraph*). Reportedly at Pakistan's behest, Mr. Cook offered to mediate in the 50-year-old Indo-Pakistan conflict over the Himalayan state of Kashmir.

The Indian Prime Minister, Inder Gujral, was in Egypt at that time. Misunderstanding the nobility of Mr. Cook's altruism, he declared Britain a "third-rate power", ill fitted to offer itself as mediator in what India regards as an internal matter. To reduce the resulting hue and cry in India, Mr. Cook hastily retracted his clumsy offer! The Indian Prime Minister promptly withdrew his remark. India's free press almost unanimously questioned British credentials in resolving internal conflicts in view of its track record over Ireland.

The Indian government's reaction was swift. The Queen's scheduled public address in Madras was cancelled. In response, the enraged British High Commissioner, Sir David Gore-Booth, is said to have called Indian officials "incompetent bunglers", and alleged to have been asked to leave

India for his "rude and arrogant" behavior. Prince Philip added his own masala spice to the curry pot. At a monument dedicated to the deaths of India's freedom fighters, he is said to have wondered whether the wounded were included in the figure! The insinuations of the remark reflect the dimensions of royal spite after a half-century. There was a ruckus at the airport during the Queen's departure. While the jittery British High Commissioner reportedly waved a newspaper in the Indian Prime Minister's face, the 71-year old monarch appeared forlorn: separated from her entourage, she was hemmed in by reporters. One, or more of her aids are said to have been jostled, perhaps even reduced to tears.

Earlier this year, the French President suffered a similar fate in Israel. In 1979, at Lusaka airport, Zambia, Lady Thatcher was "frog-marched" by reporters to a hangar, despite Lord Carrington, the foreign secretary's assurances that she would be greeted by dancing and waving crowds (*Inside the Foreign Office* by John Dickie). The legendary services responsible for informing their government of the conditions in the host country had failed. In the Indian affair, they failed deplorably, reducing their monarch to the "little old lady" in English stories.

Perhaps the Pakistanis *had* set up Robin Cook to blunder to their advantage. However, it is hard to believe that British diplomacy has now achieved the status of an oxymoron by allowing its government to be manipulated by an ex-colony that only just manages to get by. And the most puzzling aspect of this international comedy of errors is Prince Philip's lack of self-control at the Indian monument, leading the French daily *France Soir* to question his breeding.

Perhaps the princely remark would be more appropriate when the British finally decide to raise a monument honoring the over 1.5 million Indian warriors slain for their liege lords in the two world wars. (Philip Mason, *A Matter of Honour*). These figures remain conveniently submerged in the number of "British losses".

The absence of imperial phlegm is pardonable in view of Britain's strained circumstances resulting from the loss of what Churchill regarded as the "biggest jewel" in Britain's colonial crown. There is much wisdom in the observation by Britain's establishment weekly *The Economist* that "most Indians worry less about the colonial past than some Britons".

Actually, the gall over this loss rankles well beyond royal circles. In 1995, the Labor Party's National Executive said that Britain "has an imperial responsibility" to find a solution to the Kashmir dispute. The remark gained the Labor Party support from British voters of Kashmiri and Pakistani stock, but lost them India's good will. This time, by cold-heartedly using a distressed and elderly Queen in pursuit of their political well being, they have only drawn attention to their ideological bankruptcy and diplomatic immaturity. European Union countries are embarrassed by Britain's inefficiency, but gleeful at its bungling The United States cannot fail to note that diplomacy in the Commonwealth countries can no longer be subcontracted to the British.

Britain's erstwhile imperial status is only relevant to the British: they need to reason with themselves and the world around them to redefine their identity. The American President Lyndon B. Johnson's Biblical quote "come, let us reason together" has a strong inspirational value for Britain's foreign policy. Maturity comes from self-awareness, and the late French President, Charles de Gaulle, showed it when he defined France as a "middle-rate" power, pre-empting charges of being third-rate. Of course, this self-realization must be followed by act. The resulting dignity will be something for the British to cherish, and be proud of.

Britain Reaffirms Special Relationship With U.S.—April 1998.

The French daily *Le Monde* has predicted a "renewed special relationship" between the United States and Britain. In February, while President Saddam Hussein of Iraq escaped a humiliating bombing, President Clinton of The United States of America appeared to be weathering the Monica Lewinsky storm. In Bill Clinton's hour of embarrassment, the British Prime Minister, Tony Blair, flew to Washington on the weekend of February 7 to stand beside the American President and be counted. After all, they do have much in common: nifty first names, youth, disarming smiles, remarkable wives, a mastery of political semantics and a proven record of vote-getting. *Le Monde* also praised Mr. Blair as a "perfect gentleman", who expressed "confidence" and "pride" in his American mentor. Mr. Clinton, noblesse oblige, extolled Mr. Blair's virtues as an "international leader".

The extent to which this visit influenced American public opinion in the commendably Christian principle of pardoning their President rather than demanding justice, is un-clear. Yet the prolonged interest displayed in the U.S.A. over Lady Diana's death indicates a certain fascination with upper-class representatives of a culture that permeates American roots. Following the First World War, when the United States took over the torch of western civilization from Britain, there is said to have been an Oxbridge whisper behind every American decision-maker. The first turning point in this relationship came when, in 1941, Winston Churchill, visited the White House. He apparently let Franklin Roosevelt discover him naked in his bedroom: a crystal clear illustration of Britain's dependence on, and desire to build an intimate relationship with the U.S.!

The end of the Second World War saw the beginning of the Cold War: British expertise in certain areas was deemed indispensable to the Americans. At the same time, the illusion of a Commonwealth "second empire" had to be acknowledged. But Britain clung on grimly, until, in 1986, it had to face another reality. Some U.S. cartoonists depicted Dame Thatcher's trip to Moscow on President Reagan's behalf as a post person's errand. With the demise of the Soviet Union, Britain conveniently offered itself as the United States' Trojan Horse within the European Union.

Things might have continued thus, but fate took a hand. First Bill Clinton, and then across the Great Water, Tony Blair erupted into power. A new cross-Atlantic left wrested the advantage from conservative forces and used it against them with the consummate skill of judo masters. While Mr. Clinton, the former Oxonian and Rhodes scholar may thus be classed as "British-trained " (for whatever that is worth—a term dear to British hearts) Mr. Blair's team is certainly American-trained.

Two of Mr. Blair's most influential advisors, David Miliband and Geoff Mulgan, and the British Chancellor's closest aide, Ed Balls went to MIT and Harvard University for enlightenment in the late '80's. Larry Summers (U.S. Treasury), Lawrence Katz and David Reich (U.S. Labor Department) were at Harvard during the same period. At Harvard, Messrs Balls, Katz and Summers jointly wrote a paper titled "rational activism", a keystone of Mr. Blair's domestic policies. Ergo, long-term unemployment reflects mismatched skills and an absence of work culture.

Even the decision to grant the Bank of England independence by Mr. Brown, the British Chancellor of the Exchequer, is said to have been influenced by a series of conversations with Larry Summers and Alan Greenspan. As a consequence, these two banks will be able to take joint decisions. Since London's currency market is twice the size of New York's, perhaps at some stage the Americans could be served a slice of this pie.

Britain is also hard at work within the EU to confirm its "new special relationship" with the "cousins". It appears to be no accident that the German Chancellor, Helmut Kohl, was elected Honorary Freeman of the

City of London just after Tony Blair's return from Washington. Having decided to decline the ride on the first wave of the European Single Currency, the British are seeking to establish a bilateral relationship with the future European reserve bank, which is the Bundesbank in Frankfurt. If they succeed, The United States will be provided with a channel into the vaults of the European Union. This enticing morsel would help explain the Clinton-Blair strut-and-simper act in Washington. Britain's acrobatic expertise in reinventing itself seeks to revive phantoms of the past—even though the risk of being haunted by them cannot be discounted.

The Prince And The Prime Minister—May 1999.

In Shakespeare's *Hamlet,* the Prince of Denmark regrets that "The time is out of joint; O cursed spite, that ever I was born to set it right!" With socialists endorsing big business and Anglo-American policies threatening to create an alliance of France, Russia, China and India, it remains to the Prince of Great Britain to set things right. Prince Charles is going about it by resuscitating '60's communitarianism, to the annoyance of his mother's Prime Minister. Confident of his legislative majority, Britain's labor Prime Minister's socialist Fabian Society discourse betrays a total disregard for the consequences of genetic engineering and political brinkmanship in Euro-American relations. The only challenge to Mr. Blair's avarice comes from Prince Charles on the issue of genetically engineered agricultural products.

The Prince actually maintains a strident web site to oppose Monsanto and other companies that threaten the market of his organic farm products. His Highness has been heavily investing in this sector for several years, and has built little model villages expressing his notion of ideal architecture and town planning. The public discourse is built around holistic arguments of organic communitarianism with echoes of the good old sixties.

Between the two of them, Messrs Blair and Clinton now head left-wing governments applying conservative economic policies, whereas Prince Charles is becoming the spokesperson for a return to nature. The Blair-Clinton lockstep is understandable: after all, it was Mr. Clinton's 1992 election that showed Mr. Blair the path towards the centrist glade—similar to the compositional approach of a ghetto talent at a mixing table.

The Prince, heir to Britain's conservative establishment, is fuelling a hippie revival on his web site. Mr. Blair finds that threatening to Anglo-American relations. He is said to have asked his highness to close down his web side to avoid jeopardizing Britain's relations with Monsanto and Mr. Clinton. As usual, both sides are trumpeting on a moral base—more food for a growing world population—while doing quite well out of the whole business: Mr. Blair, to protect Mr. Clinton's deal with Monsanto, and the Prince to protect his bio-industry investments. Of the trio, Mr. Blair has certainly got the best deal so far, having astutely played on the sufferings of the people of Kosovo.

The results of a Gallup poll carried by Reuters reveal 67 percent support for Mr. Blair in Britain on the issue of the Balkan bombings—far higher than that achieved by Lady Thatcher during the Falklands war. That is understandable—Britain was the lone ranger in the Falklands, but this time Mr. Blair has allowed the British voter to feel a sense of partnership with the Americans, thus reviving their sense of being a super-power. This desire to be at par with the Americans comes out clearly in the autobiography of General Peter de la Porte de la Billiere, who commanded British troops during the Gulf War. He reassures the reader that "in the UK, we were able to show that we were not entirely subservient to the Americans", a recurring theme in his book prefaced by Prince Charles. It is this British "need" that drives Mr. Blair's irresponsible whisperings into the U.S. President's receptive ear.

After all, thanks to Mr. Clinton's decision to bomb Milosevic, Britain can once again feel like a world power, or at least consorting with the high and mighty. With his well-known absence of military aptitude or experience, Mr. Clinton cannot really be blamed for believing that air power, without commitment of ground troops, can solely bring the Serbs to heel. Gun-shy advisors of Mr. Clinton need a refresher course in the limits of air power. Its greatest accomplishment might just be to have spawned the Talibans' European headquarters. Messrs Blair and Clinton were both elected to look after the interests of their own people—are they doing that in the Balkans, are they just reliving their youth, or is there another game being played?

The ritual of the daily phone call between the American President and British Prime Minister is now well entrenched since the Balkan bombings. The financial interest of the peoples of NATO is unclear, but the political interest of their leaders' decisions is demisting. After the massacre of over a million Christians in Southern Sudan and East Timor, there is now a callous concern for "granting" them independence. A review of the events would suggest an argument running along the following lines: if the Muslims grant East Timor and Southern Sudan some sort of status, we will then bomb hell out of the Serbs to prove that our moral worth is nonpartisan. Yet the massacre of Christians under non-Christian regimes is surely a stand-alone issue, unneedful of the Balkan sacrifice letting loose a nest of Islamic fundamentalists scratching at Europe's jugular, brought to power by NATO gun-sights.

The tentacles of Britain's disjointed time are also reaching across the Atlantic and the English Channel to tickle the German war-machine into revival, as the Balkan bombing campaign attests to. Encouraging this renaissance in Europe is dangerous and shortsighted. The British did it in the 19th century, and then they had to beg for American help years later.

The U.S. needs to look at Europe through its own lenses, and not peer through a British monocle to recognize their true partners in Europe. If not, they will drive them into an alliance with Russia China and India, and the Prince's web site of return to the good old days of "honest" folk will have the value of a Constable print bought at a souvenir shop in Piccadilly.

Bureau Report—May 1999

Tony Blair's parliamentary devolution, resentment at the heady success of certain ethnic communities, the decline of working class decency manifest in hooliganism, and Britain's descent into the imperial has-beens club of Egypt, Greece Italy, India and others explain the impotent frustration expressed in the April bomb-blasts in Britain. A culprit was arrested, with Scotland Yard promptly declaring that these were individual acts, allowing the British to console themselves that they still live on a Churchillian island of "clipped hedges". This is based on the assumption that the British police are both efficient and honest. If the last decade's sordid revelations are taken into account, the British police are highly efficient because it takes a lot of efficiency for a corrupt organization to convince such a highly intelligent people that their legendary institution is honest!

The British have a good track record of tying up politically explosive cases which then blow up in their face. Over twenty years ago, six innocent Irish people were arrested and convicted for a crime they did not commit, but which needed to be solved rapidly in "the public interest"— the now infamous case of the "Birmingham 6". James Morton's book, "Bent Coppers" (1993), makes it eminently clear that Scotland Yard officers, by wining and dining Fleet Street journalists, convinced the British of their integrity, questioned by the author. The entire serious crimes squad of the Midlands was suspended for corruption some years ago…The April bombs could very well be the act of an individual, which would then suit all parties. However, if it is part of a planned effort to disrupt law and order, it could be the genesis of the next century's Baader-Meinhof gang—British efficiency adroitly replacing German thoroughness. In the latter case, the speed of a police conclusion and press acceptance of it, could be the consequence of a 'D' notice—an understated euphemism for press censorship in a democracy.

SECTION SEVEN—RUSSIA

Russia's Interest In Chechnya—Oil And Islam—March 1995.

The Cehchnya conflict has focused close attention on the fragility of Russian liberalization. On 27 December 1994, Boris Yeltsin declared that the Russian Army had been ordered into Chechnya to maintain Russian federal unity and contain organized crime by Chechens. Actually, the Federation's integrity revealed no symptoms of ill health, and Chechen gangs were past their prime. The real reasons behind Russia's adventure were oil and Islam, and the Russian military's budgetary squabbles.

Russia is determined to keep oil rich Azerbaijan out of Iran or Turkey's orbit, thereby ensuring Moscow's control of the eastern Caucasus and oil reserves under the Caspian Sea. Oil from Azerbaijan's Daku oil field is piped across Chechnya to Novorossiisk on the Black Sea, in line with Moscow's policy. However, large scale, organized siphoning of oil from this pipeline (with Turkish blessing), had started enriching the Chechen mafia and enfeebling oil revenues. The Russian response to the organized sabotage was to reduce dependence on the pipeline and increase reliance on tankers through the Dardanelles. In July 1994, citing safety imperatives, Turkey tightened rules of passage for tankers carrying oil through the Dardanelles.

On September 3, 1994, Russia retaliated by blockading the export of Chechnya's own modest oil production. Shortly thereafter, Russia signed the passage of a pipeline with Bulgaria and Greece, which would allow its tankers to bypass the straits of Bosphorous and Hormuz. The move checkmated the Islamic hope of the pipeline crossing fundamentalist Iran or guerrilla infested Turkish Anatolia.

On September 20, 1994, Azerbaijan signed a fat oil contract with a consortium of western companies. The route of the pipeline from Gunechi, Tchirag and Azeri has not yet been stipulated. Russia hopes that its military muscle will encourage Azerbaijan to use the Chechnya pipeline all the way through Bulgaria to Greece.

The dispatch of troops to Chechnya pleased elements in the Russian military, led by Defense Minister Pavel Grachev. Certain Moscow circles firmly believe that the reduced military budget led to fears among the Grachev clique that the Interior Ministry and the Secret Services would hook into a disproportionately large share for themselves. A high suicide rate among conscripts, unpaid salaries, poor housing and outdated equipment have demoralized the Russian military. Corruption is rife: $65 million has reportedly been lost to the state by the military's illegal sale of property in Germany, and General Burkalov, the Deputy Defense Minister, has been dismissed.

Yeltsin's disapproval rating rose to 67 percent: it is generally believed that his grip has weakened. According to the ex-prosecutor general, "Korzhakov runs the Kremlin show." Korzhakov heads Yeltsin's security detail, and is a drinking and tennis partner.

The Chechnya crisis marks Boris Yeltsin's separation from the liberal intelligentsia. There are serious worries about the economic consequences of a prolonged conflict for an over-burdened economy whose inflation rate is a galloping 16 to 18 percent a month. There are already around 25,000 Russian troops committed in Muslim Tajikistan, where fundamentalist Afghanistan-based Badakhshan rebels launch raids on the Moscow propped Kulyab government. The toll so far is estimated to be 50,000 dead, a million homeless and near famine conditions for the almost five million Tajiks.

The Chechen crisis has been considered of enough interest to the United States for a meeting between Warren Christopher and Russian counterpart in Geneva. The Russian foreign minister declared Moscow's readiness to hold elections, whereas his American counterpart gave a statement recognizing Russia's territorial integrity, and expressing a concern for human lives.

The Russian government hopes to sanctify with elections what it sought to purify by fire, and the U.S. is not opposed to the democratic trimmings of the Russo-Turkish power play. Everything would seem to be neatly tied up, except for Chechen bellicosity, historical animosity and support from the Islamic world.

Crime Rampage Spreading From Ashes Of Soviet Union—May 1995.

The implosion of the Soviet Union has spawned organized crime as a major growth industry in the ex-empire's commonwealth. Its outflowing effects on Eastern Europe have started lapping at the shores of Western Europe, provoking consternation within the European Union.

Albanian gangs peddle drugs and lead protection rackets beyond their home frontiers. In Sofia, the capital of Bulgaria, the going rate for a contract hit is $10,000. Bribery is rampant in the Czech and Slovak republics at all levels: it takes $500 to get a phone connection. In Hungary, crime has doubled: Szeged is known as Mafia City where organized gangs openly conduct illegal deals to smuggle oil to Serbia in naked defiance of sanctions. Most of the one million companies registered in Hungary are reckoned to be fronts for tax dodging. In Poland, the national police chief had to resign when his force was proved to be an active participant in organized crime.

But the mother lode of all East European crime is Russia itself. The number of organized crime related deaths runs in the thousands. Fifty godfathers reportedly operate with impunity in Moscow alone and the going rate for buying bail from a judge is said to be around $10,000. Russian citizens are now reportedly arming themselves faster than any other nation in the world.

However, the Russian Mafia has attained center stage status because of its accessibility to nuclear and biological warfare material. The source of the sarin gas which was used by religious terrorists to create lethal havoc on the Tokyo subway on march 26th, is generally agreed to have originated from CIS stockpiles in which the Russian Mafia is known to trade illicitly.

Organized crime built around East European minorities settled in Western Europe is flourishing. Abolition of border checks within the EU will give further impetus to the dynamics of organized crime.

On March 21ˢᵗ, the 52 nation European conference on stability concluded in Paris. Apart from eventual membership of ex-soviet bloc countries into the EU and NATO, stability linked with minorities and frontiers was prominent on the agenda.

Foreseen by the Maastricht treaty, the European Police Force, known as Europol, set up shop in The Hague in January 1994 as the Europol Drugs Unit with 76 officers. Its functions are mainly analytical although it is also supposed to combat the smuggling of people, cars and drugs. Spain has suggested enlarging Europol's brief to include terrorism. France and Germany are expected to approve the Spanish suggestion, further burdening the 76 officers.

There is also wrangling over whether the unit should disseminate information to national police forces on a need to know basis or be given direct access. Europe's credibility is subject to a decrease in ritual Euro-bickering and an increase in resources.

The proliferation of fraud, tax evasion, stolen car rackets, drugs, illegal immigrants and terrorism are alarming western European opinion. Over the past three months, the extent of Islamic terrorist activity discovered by law enforcement agencies across Europe lends substance to the Spanish demand to add to Europol's agenda.

Insofar as political links allowed the mafia its success, there is no reason to doubt that East European organized crime thrives independent of political corruption. The impunity with which hereditary crime families from the Indian subcontinent operate in Britain alone confirms political and police corruption. The fecundity of clandestine cells maintained by Islamic extremists across the EU affirms their determination to use western European civil liberty to gain their theocratic objectives.

On March 26, as scheduled in the Schengen accords, France, Germany, Belgium, Holland, Luxembourg, Spain and Portugal ended passport controls across their frontiers. Although the abolition only applies to airports (excluding road and rail links for another three months), it is already the focus of political controversy.

Discordant notes emitted by Europe's political leadership reflect the dilemmas confronting the EU: retain passport barriers and risk stunting EU growth or abolish barriers and devolve national sovereignty to Brussels and a credible Europol. While the EU leadership skates on its own mosaic, Asian and American market forces lurk on its doorstep.

KGB Boss Controls Russia—October 1998.

Russia has a new Prime Minister—ex-communist Yevgeni Primakov. Boris Yeltsin had to bow to the power of the ex-communists in the Duma, which had twice rejected Victor Chernomyrdin's candidacy. A third rejection would have led to a new election and further chaos. Actually, Yevgeni Primakov is not a bad compromise for a Yeltsin denuded of options: or at least not in the immediate future. At 68, he is not too old for a Russian leader. In 1996, this ex-functionary of the dreaded KGB succeeded Andrei Kozyrev as Foreign Minister.

He is also, according to the French Catholic daily *La Croix*, known to be attached to the "ancient diplomatic links of his country". As Foreign Minister, he was keen to restore Russia's erstwhile great power status. During his tenure, there was an attempt to revive the old relationships with China and India from the good old days of the non-aligned movement. Seeing Central Asian oil from the old republics of the ex-USSR being piped through Afghanistan and Pakistan cannot bring joy to Primakov's heart. Further destabilization of Pakistan and Afghanistan leading to abandonment or postponement of the pipeline project may be expected some time after the Russian crisis returns to its normal dimensions.

That the Russians actually survived this long without the economic crisis attaining the dimensions it did in August is a surprise indeed. The Russians have always lacked a system of common law, allowing the Cossack spirit of pillage to permeate all social, economic and political sectors. Under the Czars, it was plunder by the nobility. Under the communists, it was plunder by the *nomenklatura, which afforded protection to or participated in the activities of organized crime. The dismantlement of the*

Soviet Union only offered further opportunities to a Mafia that had always been an integral part of the Russian culture.

The post-Soviet economic reforms in Russia have only worked to the advantage of plunderers and looters. When nearly one hundred and fifty million Russians shook off the communist yoke, there were hopes that a well-educated labor force would lead to a stable, productive economy whose dynamics would be of equal benefit to Russia and the West. Today, the economy of this vast country of eleven time zones and a rich cultural heritage is compared in quality with Spain's and, in quantitative size rated two-thirds the size of Indonesia! Organized crime, corruption and warlords with private armies following spurious ideologies abound. And from the midst of these frightening enough parameters, Russia's nuclear potential of poorly secured facilities manned by corrupt personnel rears its ugly head. More nuclear materials and know-how in the hands of rogue states is a nightmare scenario.

The average Russian never had a chance under the communists, and his condition has not much improved since. Primakov, by all accounts, will try to restore the national economy by taking protectionist measures and instituting state intervention for industries in trouble—a thinly disguised attempt to return to a command economy. That means that tariff barriers will be instituted to protect local products. Western exporters will be faced with a choice: either pay the state more for the entry of goods, or pay the local Mafia. While American prohibition produced one Al Capone, Primakov's mixed-economy reforms are liable to sow them into the ground like the mythical dragon's teeth.

The European Union states are worried by the situation in Russia. The EU would like to be as free of American dependence as it is possible to be, without risking a historical eastward threat. An unstable Russia threatens this ambition. A strong, stable Russia, challenging the United States on the economic front, puts the EU in an excellent bargaining position. Based on that hope, the EU, like American investors, tried to penetrate Russia. They have lost, and will lose even more. Economic competition with Russia will only succeed when the playing field is outside Russia. These investors thought they could succeed financially where Napoleon and Hitler had failed militarily.

A weakened Russia, struggling to reinvent itself in the wake of the recent crisis will get little help from Primakov's mixed-economy reforms, which have had a deplorable record of success in the past fifty years. The EU fears that Russia might divert its population by military adventurism within the Commonwealth of Independent States. Investors are wary, and politicians are desperately hoping that they do not need to evoke Washington's security umbrella. At the same time, there is as much worry in Europe as in the United States concerning the security of Russia's nuclear missile sites. The logical solution would appear to be another IMF bailout to protect existing western investment at the least, but the Group of 7 are clamoring for reforms in Russia while the IMF has put further lending subject to these reforms.

Russia is within the devil and the deep sea. Only a miracle can save it from slipping to the status of a genuine third world nuclear power. Perhaps another Gorbachev needs to appear, unless it is time for Gorbachev himself to come in from the cold and once again save Russia from the communists.

Putin Seeks Russian Revival—May 2000.

Former Russian President Boris Yeltsin's protégé, Vladimir Putin, is ensconced in the Kremlin as the new President with the bitter determination of seeing a domestic and international revision of Russia's status. While Putin shares a KGB background with the leadership of Russian organized crime, he also adheres to a military brand of patriotism. He envisions a Russian renaissance based on an assertive international posture and return to fundamental values within Russian society, to be accomplished by remilitarization. Military training at schools, more or less abolished since 1989, has been revived, and the nuclear option re-defined.

Of eleven Presidential decrees during his term as acting President, six pertain to military reforms, including a reinterpretation of the doctrine of dissuasion. Putin's Russia has affirmed its right to resort to nuclear weapons in case of aggression if all other means either fail or have no effect. This assertion coincided with the start of Russian genocide in Chechnya, shortly after Boris Yeltsin had accepted that a deteriorated human rights situation in a country justified intervention by the comity of concerned nations. On January 27, a 50 percent increase in the military budget was announced, and on March 4, the French daily *Le Monde* reported that Russia's sole seaworthy aircraft carrier, the Admiral Kuznetsov would hold exercises and conduct battle drills with the rest of its fleet in the Mediterranean and "other unspecified parts of the world". A perusal of this year's issues of the authoritative British defense reviews *Jane's Defense Weekly* and *Jane's Intelligence Review*, reveals that Russian arms exports are on the increase, notably to China and India. Regiments, which obtained their best recruits by adopting orphans and children of single mothers, are being encouraged to do so again, and military cadet training is being enforced in schools.

These acts of commission give rise to disturbing thoughts. In the long term, will a resurgent Russia do a "Hitler" on Europe, or will it pursue strategic relationships with China, India, France and perhaps Brazil and Argentina in response to losing the cold war? In the short-term, when the Russian Foreign Minister was received by the EU foreign ministers in April, no mention was made of Chechnya, granting it the de facto status of a domestic problem—a fierce victory for Putin's government. However, Putin's omissions are more alarming than his commissions. Apart from firm statements on general law and order and banditry—a euphemistic reference to the Chechen rebellion—Vladimir Putin has not pronounced verdict on the *Mafyia, perhaps due to his background.*

Putin's devotion to duty is one of Russia's modern myths. In an interview with the Russian periodical *Kommersant,* Putin reveals that as a schoolboy, he visited the KGB headquarters for career advice! Recruited after his law degree, he spent two years at the KGB academy training to be an officer. As a counter-intelligence officer, he claims he was "disgusted by the persecution of artists". Courageous, his assessment report observed that he was liable to underestimate danger. Posted to foreign intelligence, he distinguished himself by efficient operations and hopeless inability at foreign languages. If all this is true, it draws the portrait of a KGB officer who would never wilfully betray his brother officers. Perhaps his sense of duty and loyalty restrain any firm statements on the *Mafyia,* perhaps the *Mafyia is the new structure within which the former KGB, officially dead, now operates. Similarities at all levels are alarming.*

The *Mafyia* network structure is a mimesis of intelligence organisations, whereas the Italian Mafia, Japanese Yakuza and Chinese Triads retain a strict hierarchy, initiation rites and cultural traditions going back to the time when they were a phenomenon of an oppressed minority gone underground. The Russian *Mafyia* is not a manifestation of repression, but a repressive tool looking to redefine itself. It is blatant reengineering of unemployed state terrorists, unless state terrorism itself has now assumed a change of appearance with a view to international operations.

The *Mafyia* is already known to operate in 60 to 65 countries. They have forged extensive links with South American drug cartels, but their main thrust is in East and Southeast Asia, where they seem to be having a merry time building a vast empire with Thai gangs, the Triads and the Yakuza. Their traffic in conventional arms is increasing, and their grip on the heroin trade tightening. Opium production in Khyrgistan alone has tripled in the last few years, and its export is a *Mafyia* monopoly. Hackers are an integral part of the *Mafyia*, and after the 1998 crash, there was a 30 percent increase in financial crimes in one year. It is tempting to wonder whether the recent NSA blackout and the ex-KGB led *Mafyia* hackers were linked. Russia itself is not immune to the spectre of the *Mafyia*.

According to a Kremlin report, the *Mafyia* controls 40 percent of the Russian economy, while 70 to 80 percent businesses pay 10 to 20 percent of their profits in protection. There are twelve to fifteen major *Mafyia* structures, compared with six for the Chinese Triads and four or five for the Italian Mafia. Drug use is in Russia is on the increase, with supply and distribution in *Mafyia* hands. The vast net thus cast from Russia to the U.S. to Japan and Europe would be impossible to sustain without a safe haven in the west and sure-shot money laundering conveniences. It is significant that the *Mafyia* has chosen London and the Channel islands over Switzerland or Luxembourg. The leadership has invested heavily in prime London property, and penetration of the hallowed lanes of the London City financial district is now considered complete. Pin-striped respectability of Britain's upper crust is added value to its money-laundering, and all *Mafyia* structures respect a gentleman's agreement to treat London as neutral territory, lending it the de facto status of the *Mafyia's* international headquarters right under the nostrils of their erstwhile adversaries of the British Secret Intelligence Service. Russian audacity and the pragmatism of Britain's financial institutions both deserve to be applauded.

Although the British will never refuse to enter a lucrative deal, they are not unaware of possible ricochets. Consequently, Keele University has started a flourishing Organized Russian and Eurasian Crime Research Unit. Its director, Dr. Mark Galeotti, believes that for the next ten years, the *Mafyia* will "remain a powerful, mercurial and dangerous constant of Russian life". Even though the basis for Dr. Galeotti's ten year calculation is unclear, and may be substituted by "the foreseeable future", the genocide in Chechnya is busy playing into the *Mafyia leadership's hands, by destroying its only real rivals—the Chechen mafia*. The scenario bears a macabre resemblance to Richard Condon's (of *The Manchurian Candidate and Prizzi's Honour* fame) thesis in his novel *Mile High*, in which prohibition was a conspiracy designed to project neighbourhood gangs to the status of national players masterminded by a genius. If Putin's troops succeed in Chechnya, the *Mafyia* will be elevated to confirmed international status, allowing it to serve the Russian national interest with perfect deniability for the Kremlin, and the Russian people to taste, once again, the grapes of wrath.

SECTION EIGHT—ASIA

China Orders Clinton: Clam Up On Human Rights—February 1994.

From 1966 to 1969, Mao Zedong's cultural revolution in communist China targeted the influence of western values and the lingering traces of Confucianism. The red guards' orgy of destruction was exhumed by the People's Liberation Army at Tiannamen Square in 1989. China's new policy of free enterprise within a communist political structure has released a new ally—Confucius.

Neo-Confucianism is the Asian Pacific's new clarion call, trumpeted by intellectuals in Singapore with their President (a Rhodes scholar)'s blessing. China finds it a convenient umbrella against the drizzle of human rights criticism from the west. The Chinese President Jiang Zemin laid down the law to Mr. Clinton at the APEC summit held on 27 November 1993 in Seattle: hands off the human rights issue. The value of western democracy was questioned but that of Confucianism and communism, which maintained China as a successful economic basket case for 2,500 years, was not. In China's case this is a stock communist stance against western capitalism.

In the case of Singapore, Taiwan, South Korea, Thailand, Indonesia and Malaysia, it is the greed of coattail economies who owe their prosperity to their Most Favored Nation (MFN) status with the United States. Muslims form the largest community in Malaysia, and Indonesia is predominantly Muslim. The Malaysian boycott of the APEC summit cannot be isolated from popular Muslim sentiment in Indonesia. Both countries are united in a dismal human rights record, and the Islamic bond explains their natural rejection of western democracy. Communism, neo-Confucianism and Islam can now cruise around the Pacific on a liner piloted by China.

Overlapping elements of these ideologies reject consensus through debate as discordant and weak. To government by edict and decree there are few ideological obstacles to postponing social welfare as the price of the GATT harvest.

Communism in China is no better than it was in the USSR. The first fissure in the Soviet Empire was Poland, brought about by the efforts of Solidarity and the Pope's visit in 1979. Tibet and the Dalai Lama are to China what Poland and the Pope were to the USSR.

The Dalai Lama visited France in November 1993. The itinerary of his visit to Grenoble was changed around at the last minute, indicating a possible security threat. Apart from the Chinese, the Dalai Lama's gentle smile intimidates nobody.

In 1910 the Chinese invaded Tibet. In 1950 they occupied it, and in 1959 they crushed a popular revolt. The Dalai Lama fled to India, was received as a head of state and has enjoyed that privilege ever since. Hundreds of thousands of Tibetan refugees followed in his wake.

The Indo-China war broke out in 1962 and, in the same year, by Prime Ministerial edict, India raised the 10,000-strong Special Frontier Force (SFF) composed entirely of Tibetan refugees. They come under the Home Ministry and not the Ministry of Defense.

These SFF commandos made highly classified forays to place sensors in the Himalayas to detect Chinese nuclear and missile tests. The Indo-Tibetan Border Police (ITBP) is another 10,000-strong force that patrols the Indo-Tibetan border.

For a country with a full economic agenda, India has maintained an elite force of Para-qualified commandos for the past 31 years. Clearly, the Indians, in the light of their successful interventions in Bangladesh (1971), Sikkim (1975), Sri Lanka (1987-1990) and the Maldives (1988) are biding their time for a crack to appear in the Chinese empire.

The split could come from two directions. The Chinese Economic Area (CEA) is an informal trading bloc of Hong Kong, Taiwan and Southern China, collectively accounting for 4.5 percent of world trade, equal to that of France or Britain. They already form a de facto economic entity, and the government in Hong Kong is not averse to the development. Chris Patten, Hong Kong's shrewd and discreet governor, used to be the head of Britain's Conservative Party.

The second way is Tibet, the Dalai Lama with western backing and 20,000 Tibetan Para-commandos sustained by India for over three decades.

There is only a thin red line between the economic reality of the Chinese Economic Area and its political reality. If Tibet plays Poland's role, the CEA continues to prosper, and the Indians have industriously done their homework from Sikkim to Sri Lanka, the de jeure independence of the Chinese provinces is a tenable scenario.

If the West has diligently studied the dissolution of the Soviet Empire, the liberty of the peoples of China need not be accomplished with Sinkiang an Islamic nuclear power. GATT's benefits should not be denied to the workers of the world, regardless of the hemisphere they occupy.

Asian Nations Quietly Building Up Naval, Air Forces—March 1994.

The APEC summit was held in Seattle on 27 November 1993. Malaysia boycotted it, and China had haughty eyes. The President of the United States meekly took in Jiang Zemin's 15-minute lecture on the irrelevance of western democracy. Handling China like a china doll has not affected the popularity of neo-Confucianism. In January 1994, a U.S. delegation blithely skipped over to Europe with Partnership for Peace, which, on the surface, allows the world's only super-power to realign resources and attention to the Pacific Basin. The French government's recognition of The People's Republic of China as the sole representative of the Chinese peoples is a clear signal that Europe is aware of Washington's reassessment of options.

America's new China card appears to have met with less success than the old one. It remains to be seen how snugly it fits up the European sleeve. In the meantime, a Japanese card seems to be on discreet offer. Since the Gulf War, our attention has been periodically focused on Japan's reluctance to commit itself to an active role in world affairs. After partially bank-rolling the Allied effort in the Gulf, the Japanese have successfully interacted in Mozambique and Cambodia. Both operations maintained the integrity of United Nations policy, but it was very clear that Japan called the shots. The Japanese constitution has been suitably amended to allow the dispatch of troops abroad. In the Asian Pacific, the Japanese, flushed with success, have gained face. Mr. Vasuehi Akashi, in charge of the Cambodian operation and now head of the UN in Zagreb, suggested the idea of a joint training center for peacekeeping in Asia in an interview to *Newsweek* (24 January 1994). The idea is intriguing, but there are no details of the form this center would adopt, its location, its leadership and whether or not it would have a military role. He also opined that Japan should have a permanent seat on the United Nations Security Council, and said, "The time has come for Japan to contribute personnel who will sweat for peace". Perhaps in Mr. Akashi's Thesaurus, sweating and bleeding are synonyms. Before a Pacific Treaty organisation sees the light of day, there are existing currents on the same lines to be considered.

On 25 July 1994, the foreign ministers of the six ASEAN countries met with their seven dialogue partners in Singapore. They announced the formation of an ASEAN Regional Forum The seven dialogue partners (Australia, Canada, the EC, Japan, New Zealand, South Korea and the U.S.) and five other regional states (China, Laos, Papua New Guinea, Russia and Vietnam) were invited to participate. The relationship between Mr. Akashi's proposed center and the forum is open to speculation.

According to the London-based *Institute of Strategic Studies, most East Asian* states have been "expanding and improving" their armed forces, with the emphasis on "naval and air forces which are the most suitable for projecting military force in a region where distances are great". The French military magazine *Raids* offers a breakdown of the abundant marine forces of the Asian Pacific: China, 3 divisions—Taiwan, 2 divisions—Thailand, 2 brigades—Indonesia, 6 battalions—South Korea, 2 divisions—North Korea, 13 battalions—Philippines, 4 brigades — Vietnam—6 brigades. India is the only Asian country with aircraft carriers, but has only one regiment of marines.

China has marine forces, but no aircraft carriers, and is reputed to have two under construction, while the Indians are reportedly expanding their marines and improving facilities at their naval bases on the Andaman and Laccadive islands. China projects power in the region by opening up historic land routes without drawing attention to their strategic value. Chinese support for the Maoist guerrilla movement in Oman's Dhofar province oddly coincided with the construction of the Karakoram Highway, leading from Sinkiang province through the northern Karakorams of Pakistan (the old Silk Route) down to the Arabian Sea overlooking the Hormuz Straits to the Gulf. China has now exhumed the old caravan trail from Yunnan through Myanmar (formerly Burma), to Thailand, eventually allowing China to threaten the Malacca Straits. When the road is metalled to allow heavy traffic, South Asia itself will have been neatly outflanked. Sun Tzu did stress the importance of "diversion" and "march by a indirect route" (retained in General Tao Hanzhang's modern interpretation).

The Chinese double envelopment from the Persian Gulf to the Malacca Straits will influence the structure of Mr. Akashi's proposed Center for Peacekeeping, and the degree of Chinese participation. In its Regional Overview of East Asia and Australasia, the London-based Institute of Strategic Studies observes "the countries of the region see an American presence as essential to their continued stability."

However, the Pacific is not the only region liable to come under threat. Other areas have their own forces of instability—they need careful watching. Dorinda Elliot, writing for *Newsweek* in January 1994, categorically stated: "The Russian empire is rising again".

American responsibilities in the Pacific cannot be shouldered by reducing the European payload. Partnership for Peace as a U.S. response to a possible renaissance of the Russian empire is concession, with potentially volatile consequences. Decreasing commitment in Europe to meet the needs in the Pacific is evasion of responsibility. Lacking an integral mechanism for self resolution, a shelved problem festers.

Western economies have successfully tackled the Japanese economic juggernaut by a series of hard decisions. The people who bite the bullet have shown their mettle, and high calibre leadership still flourishes in the Atlantic basin.

Continuing American involvement with Europe ensures stability both in Europe and the Pacific, reducing the chances of indigestion caused by Russian, Chinese and Japanese appetites.

China's Entry Into WTO—March 1996.

On the evening of February 28, European Union and East Asian leaders met in Bangkok for the first ever Euro-Asian summit. 15 European and 10 East Asian leaders clad in open-necked Asian silk shirts sat around laden banquet tables. They were warming up to the formal trade discussions over the next two days. By presenting the visiting EU Leaders with local semi-formal garb, the East Asians were able to have everybody dressed alike, thereby determining the pitch, and to some extent, the rules of the game.

The leaders met to discuss trade relations between the European Union (EU) and East Asia. During a visit to Paris in 1994, Singapore's neo-Confucianist Prime Minister, Goh Chok Tong had broached the idea of a summit between East Asian countries and European Union leaders.

In 1994, East Asia accounted for 23 percent of the EU's total volume of international trade, with North America at 17 percent. Yet direct investment from EU countries in East Asia is only 1 percent of its foreign investments elsewhere, and this 1 percent investment only constitutes one-tenth of all foreign investment in East Asia.

The next decade is estimated to offer investment possibilities of 130 to 150 billion dollars per year in East Asian infrastructure, namely telecommunications and financial services.

The Brussels whiz-kids, and their counterparts in the capitals and think-tanks of the EU member countries either failed to estimate this market, or were unable to offer cogent plans to exploit this information, or else were incapable of putting together a coherent approach. Which perhaps explains why their bosses had to wear open-necked silk shirts, guzzle sake and cross arms for mediagenic handshakes with neo-Confucians who hold western values in contempt, in order to serve their electorate a slice of hot Asian pie.

No doubt the estimated dimensions of the East Asian market for investment in telecommunications and financial services is close to the mark. The missing link in *this* theory is the guarantee that EU member countries will be able to obtain more than a token share of the market. Neo-Confucians of the Pacific Rim, well versed in Sun Tzu, are playing off the EU's need against the Clinton administration's greed. With even banks chary of lending money, EU member countries need a mediagenic success to stimulate investment and tackle unemployment. In view of the U.S. election, the Clinton administration is greedy for a mediagenic success to offset the half-hearted peace it brokered with enthusiasm in Bosnia, Palestine and Ireland.

If the investment share awarded to the European Union does not threaten American prognostics, the Clinton administration will be able to claim victory. If the investment share of the EU can be shown as respectable competition vis à vis the U.S., the EU leaders' Bangkok visit can be spun as a success. On the heels of this summit, sale of non-nuclear high-tech weapons to this "nuclear-free" zone should come as no surprise: as plans to "digitalize" EU armies mature, existing weapons systems need a market, and people who build them need to keep their jobs. As the summiteers concentrated on drafting an appropriate communiqué, certain East Asian countries held naval exercises in the South China Sea. With the next summit scheduled in London for 1998, the same exercises, if repeated, would be able to display East Asian proficiency with EU weapons.

The neo-Confucians' victory is manifold. Their electorate has seen leaders come all the way from Western Europe seeking contracts: they were made to dress and shake hands to local specifications. Eminent analysts in France and Germany are publishing articles showing the common values of Confucianism and Franco-German "tempered capitalism"! The biggest coup of all is that the EU leaders, by keeping human rights off the agenda, have accepted the de facto validity of the anti-western neo-

Confucian stance (*National Educator* issues of February and July 1994). They have also accepted that future rules of economic competition will be jointly made, and that social welfare, human rights and trade are not synonyms. This will disallow EU "unfair competition" rules to be operative in the imposition of trade barriers.

In December, after successfully eliminating one-third of the Christian population of Timor, Indonesia got Australia to accept Timor as *de jeure* Indonesian territory, subsequently excluding Australia from the summit. When Antonio Guterres, the Portuguese Prime Minister, tried to broach the subject of Timor during the silk-shirted dinner of the 28th, Suharto of Indonesia "promised to think about it". In bilateral talks with China and Vietnam, however, the French President "notably insisted" that the condition of Christian minorities occupy a prominent place on the agenda.

World Trade Organization talks are scheduled for December. If the Euro-Asian summit is a preview of what is to come, the United States might have its hands full trying to face down a stacked deck held by East Asians backed by Western Europeans.

Communists Take Over Hong Kong In Year Of Ox—. March 1997.

In 1899, foreseeing the end of the British Empire, Nobel laureate Rudyard Kipling urged Americans to "Take up the white man's burden" in his celebrated poem. A half-century later, John Masters, a third-generation colonel of the British Indian Army, chose to write his novels as an American citizen in Texas. Like Kipling in *The Man Who Would Be King*, Masters immortalized the fine relationship between South Asian warriors and their white leaders. With a writer's insight, Kipling presaged the end of a waning Empire, and Masters, as the commanding officer of a mercenary Gurkha regiment, oversaw it during the Independence celebrations of India, the "biggest jewel" in the British Monarch's crown.

Hong Kong, with border patrols ensured by Royal Gurkha mercenaries, is the second-biggest jewel in the British crown: growth rate nearly a steady 5 percent, exports touching 200 billion dollars, foreign trade at nearly 150 percent of 152 billion dollars GNP. It is also an example of the universality of western Judeo-Christian values like liberty, equality, fraternity, rule of law and plain common-sense decency: infant mortality is 7 percent, life expectancy 80 years, and literacy 100 percent. In comparison, China's foreign trade is only 25 percent of GNP, economic growth is uncontrolled, exports are approximately 150 billion dollars, infant mortality is 44 percent, life expectancy 68.5 years, and illiteracy 20 percent. Chinese standards will shortly grip Hong Kong in a chokehold. The Chinese government has announced that the electoral system and civil liberties initiated by the British government in Hong Kong will be scrapped after the British colony reverts to China on July 1, 1997. Chris Patten, the governor of Hong Kong, found the Chinese decision "disturbing", according to a *BBC*

World Service broadcast. Writing on Asia's Future in the British establishment weekly *The Economist*, Chris Patten had remarked: "If we accept the concept of Asian values, we have to deny the universality of human rights". From the Rule of Law and Court of Appeals, the 6.2 million people of Hong Kong will regress to totalitarianism.

As an outpost of western civilization in a boiling sea of Confucianism and communism, Hong Kong's strategic value to the stock markets of the west is comparable to the value of Rhodes and Malta to crusaders in the 11th and 12th centuries.

British withdrawal from Hong Kong will place this strategic value into communist hands. Unprecedented financial resources will rejuvenate the communist capacity for international mischief. The recent Sino-Russian-Indian tripartite under process is a case in point. Britain had seen its special relationship with the United States written on the wall. As early as 1982, talks on the future of Hong Kong began between the British and the Chinese. On December 19, 1984, the British and Chinese Prime Ministers signed an agreement outlining terms for the reversion of Hong Kong as a special administrative region of China in 1997.

In 1991 a Bill of Rights was passed in the Hong Kong Legislative Council (Legco), contested by the pro-Beijing Preliminary Working Committee. In 1994, Chris Patten, ex-governor of Northern Ireland and Head of the British Conservative Party, was appointed governor of Hong Kong (*National Educator*, February 1994). A skilled puppet-master, he discreetly orchestrated structural changes within the legislative system. The Democracy movement thus established is now well entrenched. In the September elections of 1996, the people of Hong Kong expressed their desire to maintain a western democratic structure. The pro-Beijing Alliance for Betterment of Hong Kong won a pathetic 16 out of 68 seats, while the Barrister Martin Lee's United Democrats, Allen Lee's Liberal Party and affiliated independents formed a coalition to express the will of the people of Hong Kong. The struggle between the forces of totalitarianism and democracy will begin after the British have packed up: British de-colonizers are well versed in nattily skipping a colony, leaving the natives to carry their own burden.

In another three months, the 99-year lease agreement under which the British held Hong Kong's 1067 square kilometers after the opium war, will come to term. In 1896, the British had the power to force the lease on the Chinese—the Chinese now have the power to make Washington withdraw its support, incapacitating the British ability to negotiate a second lease.

On July 1, 1997, the crown-appointed British governor of Hong Kong will supervise the last pageant of the British Empire. Her majesty's crack Gurkha mercenaries will kiss their long-bladed Kukris with the trident of Shiva, their war-god, notched into the battle-blade. They will present arms to the Chinese whom they have historically held in contempt, and watch the Union Jack come down. That evening, in the mess halls, there will be no tall tales. Loyal to their salt, these legendary mercenaries, romanticized by John Masters, Kipling and James Clavel, will savor their British *da'al* and *chappaties* in silence. Residents of Hong Kong's 6.2 million population whose bank accounts disqualify them from holding British passports will also contemplate their future in silence. The Gurkhas will understand: even after 20 years meritorious crown service to conserve English blood, they are denied the resident status accorded to opportunists from South Asia.

Yet, the expiry of the Hong Kong lease signals more than just the swan song of the British Empire. Assimilation of Hong Kong into the Chinese communist empire will further increase the disparity among Chinese regions, which has, historically, led to a break-up (*National Educator*, February 1994). India, despite its recent rapprochement with the Chinese, continues to maintain its 20,000-strong force of Para-qualified and commando-trained Tibetan refugees, waiting for the Chinese Achilles heel in Tibet to expose itself (*National Educator* February 1994). And the lads and lasses who brought down the "evil empire" have not yet written their memoirs—one may wonder whether they are still fighting communism, or have had their teeth drawn by Clinton's back-room boys in their desperate zeal to appease China and maintain youthful pledges. The Clinton administration's hopeless failure to wean India into the western alliance, and orchestrate a re-negotiation of the Hong Kong lease has germinated a new alliance between China, India and Russia which bodes ill for the west. The novelist Han Suyin, short-listed for the Nobel Prize, believes that the four poles of the 21st century are the United States, the European Union, China and India. Washington's inability to harmonize the four poles into the "music of the spheres" that synergizes world policy is a tragedy that will start unfolding in several acts after July 1, 1997. World leadership *is* a heavy "burden" to "take up."

South Asia's Nuclear Blasts Destabilize Region—July 1998.

Since the "Indian dream" pursued by Christopher Columbus, and the bloodletting in 1947 when British management lost its credibility, South Asia has not attracted more world attention than by the nuclear tests conducted by India and Pakistan. In between these three events, only India's poverty has maintained the interest of India-watchers. No flattering comment on India's great past and superb future can be complete without a reference to its inability to evolve into a welfare state. India's brainpower and ability to acquire and manage wealth are also expressed in the same breath, as is its "exceptionally efficient" army, and scientific and technological development. India's humanists seduced an entire generation of backpackers in the sixties, in keen pursuit of values and wisdom they felt were absent in the west. Mahatma Gandhi's non-violent culture indulging in frightening pyrotechnics while millions of its masses live below the poverty line is puzzling indeed. As far as conventional defense is concerned, India should be capable of defending itself with around 1.1 million battle-tested professional soldiers, descendants of the mythical warriors in the legendary British Indian Army. India is also practically self-sufficient in most of its military hardware: two aircraft carriers, a state-of-the-art fighter plane, a new main battle tank, and nuclear submarines are in the works. A spy satellite entirely designed and built by India can reportedly peep into hidden corners. In Sri Lanka, the Indians displayed wisdom in puling out their troops on the verge of a Vietnam-style quagmire. In the Maldives, Indian paratroopers were felicitated for their action in restoring democracy. In Somalia, Indian troops pacified their sector with aplomb, leaving, as they had arrived, on their own ships. These credentials should be enough to allow India to feel secure against its best-known adversary, Pakistan, which is at best a country desperately striving to pay its bills and stay together.

The answer is yes and no. Against India's might, Pakistan comes across as the little guy, especially when viewed against the dismemberment of East and West Pakistan which created Bangladesh on Indian bayonets and Pakistani rape. Yes, but India only succeeded where Pakistan had failed in 1965 by launching Operation Gibraltar in Kashmir, hoping to start an insurgency and thereby divest India of its northern state of Kashmir. Thus, Pakistan is only the little guy by virtue of a failed result, and not as whipping boy.

India's biggest concern is China, and in this respect Indian thinking is in line with that of the American Pentagon. China defeated India in a cowardly border war in 1962, shortly after seizing Tibet. China and Pakistan developed a cozy relationship, outflanking India. The Karakoram Highway now links the Chinese province of Sinkiang with the entrance to the Persian Gulf, passing as it does through the length of Pakistan. The Chinese are also busy building a road through Burma to link up with the Bay of Bengal. Once complete, India will be strategically outflanked. It is already under the scrutiny of China's spy satellites and threat of its nuclear missiles. And China is a member of the Security Council. Despite the precariousness of its economy, China continues to be courted by the west as an international VIP, whereas India still feels it is treated like a coolie.

If the Indian tests were designed to provoke Pakistan into conducting its own tests, then it was a success.

India and Pakistan's nuclear tests in May have now raised disturbing questions about the causes and consequences of the South Asian nuclear arms race.

Washington reacted with immediate economic sanctions against India. A senate investigation committee was initiated to probe into why, on the day India conducted its tests, there was no Electronic or Human intelligence to indicate what was coming. India analysts at the CIA were off-duty.

If all this is not a coincidence, then India's ability goes beyond nuclear explosions to outwit the American government.

That, however, only establishes that India is more than just a poor country loudly proclaiming its manhood! In pursuit of the *Rajiv Doctrine,* India is seeking to stand up to China and Pakistan, and maintain hegemony in the Indian Ocean. The U.S. Pentagon rates China as the single most important threat to U.S. interests in the next century, with ballistic missiles reportedly pointed at American women and children. By means of a road running through Pakistan, and another shortly to be completed through Burma, China has almost succeeded in outflanking India, and in the process gaining land-access to the Arabian Gulf and Bay of Bengal, while threatening the Malacca Straits. Its nuclear-tipped missiles in Tibet are pointed at India's teeming poor. And despite the Pentagon's analyses, Washington continues to pay court to Beijing, to the extent of allegedly letting satellite technology slip into Chinese hands through political myopia or greed.

Over the past half-century, China has assiduously cultivated India's fratricidal enemy, Pakistan, who has adroitly played Washington and Beijing against India. With the probable knowledge of the U.S. Military Mission in Islamabad, Pakistan would seek to raise a regiment, knowing that India would then have to raise three of its own to maintain a doctrinal military balance. In the case of fighter aircraft and undetectable submarines, it allowed Pakistan to time its military expansion with India's economic projects, several of which, especially in education, health and family planning, it succeeded in disrupting.

India's nuclear tests will reverse this same policy on Pakistan. With an economy mainly indigenous, limited material ambitions and friends other than the U.S., India can hope to weather U.S. displeasure. Pakistan, however, is incapable of confronting Washington's wrath. Its economy was reported to be in a "spin" by early June due to American sanctions (*The Times* of London, June 8, 1998). Isolated from the west, Pakistan will have to apply for more aid to the Gulf countries, Libya and Saudi Arabia its committed financiers for acquiring nuclear power since the Islamic Conference of 1973 held in Lahore, Pakistan, one year prior to India's first nuclear test. Pakistan will now extend the export of military expertise in personnel and equipment to the Gulf and Saudi Arabia, by offering its latest military accomplishment. The Associated Press reported jubilation in the Islamic world at Pakistan's nuclear test, and *Arabic News.com* lent its approval to the event in a well-argued editorial. Pakistan's bomb is the Islamic bomb, which its ally Turkey is capable of carrying on one of its F-16's manufactured under license. Israel has just lost the *strategic depth* afforded it by Pakistan (Pakistan's late Prime Minister Z.A.Bhutto in last speech to the National Assembly, 1977).

Shortly before the Gulf War, Israel had reportedly made an offer to the Indians: in return for refueling facilities, they would destroy Pakistan's nuclear plants. The plan, leaked to the U.S., inconvenienced Washington at that time. The day Pakistan tested its device in May this year, it claims to have detected unknown aircraft above its skies (British *Daily Telegraph*). If true, this only works to the Indian advantage, revealing either Pakistan's own ability to detect hostile aircraft, or Washington's willingness to continue propping up Pakistan. After all, the oil pumped out from the Caspian by U.S. oil companies is scheduled to be piped through Afghanistan and Pakistan: in May, the Taliban of Afghanistan were feted in Washington to secure the proposed pipeline. That, of course, after the petro-dollars, will be the second reason Pakistan might just escape India's full wrath.

In 1965, under the aegis of its failed Operation Gibraltar, Pakistan sent highly trained members of its Special Services Group into Kashmir, hoping to foment a rebellion and wrest Kashmir from India. In 1971, India retaliated by helping East Pakistan to become Bangladesh, and the Indian General who planned the operation was hailed by the Reader's Digest as a *Soldier for Peace*. Over the past few years, India has consistently accused Pakistan of stirring up trouble in Kashmir, causing thousands of deaths and tying down approximately 100,000 Indian troops.

Fears of a pre-emptive nuclear strike by Pakistan are mostly groundless: Pakistan has no strategic depth, whereas India can survive a first strike to annihilate Pakistan. The equation with China is different. Both India and China would like to be legitimate players on the world stage, and realize that they have not yet exhausted the possibilities of diplomacy. China's economy reached a watershed three years ago, and is now said to be over-heated. India has sensed the coming fissures, and when China begins to show large cracks, would like to be a partner in the decision-making process for China's future (*National Educator*, July 994).

India also has an interest in the Indian Ocean. In 1987 it intervened in Sri Lanka, and had the wisdom to pull out in 1990 before it got bogged down. In 1989 Indian paratroopers restored democracy in the Maldives, and were applauded by the world community. To give its ambitions credibility, in the late seventies and early eighties, it started production of its own aircraft carriers, submarines, main battle tank, helicopters and an advanced tactical fighter, called a "fighter pilot's dream" by Nicholas Nugent of the BBC. This last was due in 2002, but is now announced to be ready for 2000: unless India is planning an earlier surprise. India's timetable conforms to the perception of its own interest. However, India needs to navigate with care in the Indian Ocean in case it tempts Australia and others into the nuclear power game.

Asia's Smouldering Hot Spot—October 1998.

Iran remains ready to attack Afghanistan after inconclusive talks in New York between the United States, Russia and six of Afghanistan's neighbors. Whether Iran is saber-rattling with 200,000 troops on the border remains unclear, but the fundamentalist Islamic Taliban militia, which controls most of Afghanistan, is prepared to receive a massive ground assault. Sources told *The National Educator* an attack by Iran would be a risky tactic given the Afghan genius for guerrilla warfare.

Peace is not an option in Afghanistan despite the near conquest of the nation by the Taliban. Hatred of Iran is historic, explaining the Taliban's belligerent rhetoric against Iran and its arming of civilians close to the border.

The furious independence of clans and tribes in Afghanistan means that domination by the Pashtuns of the Taliban will, in due course, be violently resistant. It is probably already happening in some pockets and Iran is certain to sponsor terrorism against the Taliban.

The Taliban has no hope of building a nation given the enormous number of tribes and ethnic groups. Continued warfare is inevitable—if not with outsiders, then with other Afghans who resent Pashtun rule. The ultimate solution might be a division of the country along ethnic lines. The tradition of deceit in negotiations and reneging on deals insures that agreements are usually temporary.

The United Nations has little chance of brokering a deal among people for whom alliances are opportunistic. The "six plus two" meeting's decision to send a mediator to defuse tensions between Teheran and Kabul is an almost meaningless gesture. It is not even clear that the Taliban will accept the mediator since it was not allowed to participate in the New York session. Only three countries recognize the Taliban as the government of

Afghanistan—Pakistan, Saudi Arabia and the United Arab Emirates. In reality, there is no semblance of government of any hue in Afghanistan despite rival claims for legitimacy.

Pakistan has urged the international community to engage in direct talks with the Taliban, saying that would make it more responsible. Having helped to create the Taliban, Pakistan is worried that it is a source for regional instability, especially for instability in Pakistan. No intelligentsia is left in Afghanistan to moderate the largely illiterate soldiers of the Taliban. Negotiations with the Taliban are further complicated by divisions and hierarchies in its ranks, of which the rank and file is made up of young and overwhelmingly illiterate peasants and tribesmen from the *madrassas (Islamic schools). At the top of the double-tiered hierarchy are experienced Mujahidin fighters who opposed the former occupation by the Soviet Union, followed by fighters who actively opposed the communist regime of President Najibullah*, toppled in 1992.

The Taliban militia has warned Iran that it has deployed American-made Stinger anti-aircraft missiles on its border and will use them if attacked. The movement's acting foreign Minister, Mullah Mohammed Hassan, was quoted as saying, "Our forces will follow the enemy into his territory." Actually, in addition to U.S.-made stinger missiles, the Taliban has also deployed Russian-built, short-range, ground-to-ground Lunar rockets. The militia, while stating it does not want war with Iran, is prepared to fight any Iranian invasion.

Meanwhile, Iran's supreme leader Ayatollah Khameinei has told military and top civilian officials that the nation must be ready for "speedy, timely and decisive implementation of whatever decisions the senior political and security authorities deem necessary." He has ordered the armed forces to be prepared to take action against the Taliban Islamic militia. Khamenei, who is also the commander-in-chief of the armed forces, described the Taliban as a "brutal, dogmatic and ignorant group that relies on foreigners and seeks to serve their interests."

Sino-Russian Axis A Dangerous Global Reality—June 1999.

Napoleon Bonaparte said that when China awakes, it will shake the world. The tragic flaw of all predictions and prophecies being the absence of a date, the world is still waiting for the planet's most populous totalitarian country to awake. On the other hand, misunderstanding China's twilight state between sleep and wakefulness, the British daily *The Economist* predicted its almost imminent demise in 1998. Thus, a completely awake China is a threat to world stability, just as a China broken up into a number of regions implies another nightmare scenario.

With an insolvent banking system, over 11 percent unemployment, and increasing disparity between regions, China is a prime candidate for implosion. That would mean that the Islamic regions of China bordering Central Asia and Pakistan would form a solid bloc all the way to Turkey. The Eurasian space that Mr. Brzezinsky believes is central to western geopolitical interest would be replaced by a hostile bloc equipped with nuclear weapons and intercontinental ballistic missiles contributed by the Muslim-majority Chinese province of Zhinkiang with its missile bases. Although the initial breakup of China would offer more markets to world trade, the strategic negatives inspire little interest.

A fully awake China presents a threat to world stability by outright use of military means. According to Professor Walter A. McDougall, "the Chinese seem to understand, as never before over 3,000 years, the influence of sea power on history". The U.S. Naval War College is reported to have simulated a Sino-American conflict for the year 2010. Although the simulation is reportedly still secret, it is clear that Chinese ability to confront the United States is based on its economic capacity to fuel its military industry.

Once this level of industrial technology is attained, China will start making its presence felt in the Pacific, just as the West turned towards the same basin in the fourteenth and fifteenth centuries when the Ottoman Turks denied it complete access to the Mediterranean.

According to historian Paul Kennedy, the seafaring exploits of the west at that time were possible due to the separation of Church and State in Europe, leading to intense competition among warring states, thereby accelerating the level of technological competence to hitherto unknown levels in history. The consequent ascendancy of western Judeo-Christian civilization, with its accent on democracy, free trade and human rights needs no telling.

The Chinese now hope to turn this tide of history against the west, by buying surplus technology from the Russians, making it imperative for this new Sino-Russian rapprochement to be closely watched for any signs of "gentlemen's agreements" detrimental to world peace. A case in point is the purchase of the aircraft carrier "Varyag, almost as "hefty as America's largest carrier", which cannot get into the shallow waters of Macao's harbor, to which it was destined for conversion into a "hotel and casino"! According to the London-based Institute of Strategic Studies, China's own aircraft carriers are still under construction, and no date for their completion can as yet be given. Thus, in the absence of its own renaissance, China is trying to accelerate history by the purchase of foreign technology, and where it cannot buy, it does not hesitate to steal. The policy is similar to that of some Islamic countries observed by Gibbs namely, that Islam, linking the rise of the west to its own decline ignores the effect of Mongol invasions, and seeks to bypass the need for a renaissance by buying western military technology to turn it against the west. Such a policy can only be pursued at the expense of economic development, engendering domestic discontent.

Chinese ambitions in the Pacific deserve to be guided in a healthy direction. On land, its neighbor India needs to be dealt with in such a way that it feels an equal partner of the west, and not a "little brother".

Increased Indian self-confidence will encourage the Chinese to allocate resources to the Himalayas. However, decreased resources for mischief in the Pacific should not allow the Chinese to feel desperate. Increased trade between South Korea, Japan, China, Taiwan and India, with encouragement from the U.S., should allow the Chinese to appreciate alternatives to Pacific hegemony. Ariel and Will Durant, the American philosophers, predicted that the dimension of air power would eventually decrease the significance of sea-lanes. The galloping advance of technology gives credence to this analysis. It is thus essential for the west to maintain its lead in air and space technology. In the future, the strategic importance of sea-lanes might be no more significant than that of land-routes. Until that time, it is hoped that no new factors rear their head to menace the Pacific peoples struggling for democratic and trade institutions in a laudable effort to wrest dignity from their authoritarian history.

Riding Tigers—November 99, unpublished

In October, media images showed Pakistanis dancing with joy and distributing sweetmeats to welcome a change from civilian to military mismanagement. Since the Reagan era, such images have usually meant the opposite. Pakistan's new strongman, General Parvaiz Musharraf, has offered a "new deal"—an end to corruption. In the context of Pakistan, his promise is an oxymoron. From the sordid little bribe in the grubby fist of a traffic policeman, to the. BCCl bank scam and "procurement" of nuclear spare parts, corruption is a way of life in Pakistan.

Although General Musharraf knows all this, he was not motivated by a hunger for power or the desire to loot and plunder. A career General in a third-world professional army with service in its elite Special Services Group, he is expected to be -and probably is -a dedicated professional in the Kshatriya tradition. Therefore, the timing of the coup and the events that led up to it are significant.

Over the past fifty years, Pakistan and India have kept each other -and the world's leadership- busy over the unresolved issue of Kashmir. Last year, following their nuclear tests, both countries opened avenues towards a closer relationship. Officers who faced Indian might in 1965 and 1971, and are now of very senior rank, became alarmed. In a well-planned move, guerrillas consisting of Kashmiris, Pakistanis, a handful of Afghans and Arabs—and members of Pakistan's crack Northern Light Infantry, infiltrated and occupied the strategic heights of Kargil on the Line of Control (LOC) in Kashmir. In 1947, 1965and 1971, there had been bitter fighting over Kargil. Following Pakistan's defeat in 1971, it ceded Kargil to India. In a wargame shortly before this year's occupation of Kargil, the Indian High Command is reported to have concluded that Pakistan would never occupy Kargil. Perhaps because this information became available to the Pakistanis, that is precisely what they did. The operation was a credit to the Pakistan Army, known among professionals for its tactical soundness and strategic clumsiness.

Accordingly, anticipating, and seeking to obstruct the eventual Indian counter-attack (for which Pakistan Army military doctrine maintains a healthy respect), Pakistan bought up 50,000 pairs of snow boots all over Europe. The infiltrators dug in, built concrete bunkers, and were supplied by helicopters applying innovative, high-risk ground navigation techniques. Although caught napping, and unable to shift either their remarkably well-equipped, trained and experienced mountain troops from the Chinese border, or hastily buy mountain boots in Europe, the Indians reacted well. They showed up Pakistan's diplomatic and strategic ineptitude by mobilizing international support. Once the G-8 condemnation came through, the Indians made short work of the Pakistanis. Former Prime Minister Nawaz Sharif, while on a visit to Washington, declared that Pakistan would withdraw "support" of the infiltrators. The Army leadership apparently went ballistic. It would have wanted nothing better than to prolong the incident, with outnumbered Pakistanis fighting a last-man last-round battle to the point where the local conflict would have had to conflagrate, with or without nawaz Sharif's consent.

After a series of rows with the Prime Minister, General Musharraf was sent on a trip to Sri Lanka. In his absence, Nawaz Sharif decided to appoint another general as Chief of Army Staff. When Parvaiz Musharraf returned from Sri Lanka, he was presented with a fait accompli by his officers and practically told that he was Pakistan's new leader. Nawaz Sharif and his military advisors had totally miscalculated the influence of the shadowy Young Officers' Groups that pervaded the Pakistan Army in the aftermath of the 1971 defeat.

These officers, with thirty-odd years of service, are now field and general officers. In 1973, under Ali Bhutto's socialist government, fourteen of them were tried and convicted for sedition in what was known as the

Attock Conspiracy, but they were only the tip of the iceberg of discontent the government hoped to contain by dissuasion. The officers blamed politicians, led by Ali Bhutto for the Bangladesh debacle. While their preparation for and participation in the Afghan war gave their professionalism an outlet, the bitterness only increased. Once the Russians had been ousted from Afghanistan, the Pakistanis involved expected to be the western world's pets, hoping, in return, to square accounts with India. The resulting disappointment turned into bitter disillusion, expressed by strong anti-Americanism.

On the day following the coup in Pakistan, the impeccably groomed President of the London-based Pakistan Forum appeared on CNN to suggest men of probity who could complement General Musharraf's government. Among those mentioned were retired Air Marshall Asghar Khan and General Hamid Gul. Asghar Khan was rumoured to have been sympathetic to the sentiments of the Attock Conspiracy and General Hamid Gul led Pakistan's Inter-Services Intelligence (ISI), in its devastating operations during the Afghan war. ISI are probably current managers of the 50,000-strong Taliban beefed up by an estimated 8,000 Pakistani ex-servicemen. The training of non-Pakistani volunteers is reportedly conducted at at the Pakistan Army's 7 Division Headquarters at Rishkor, a facility "bigger and better organized" than Osama bin Laden's Khost camps in Afghanistan, target of American reprisals where a couple of Tomahawk Cruise Missiles failed to explode, allowing themselves to be examined by vested interests.

Immediately after the coup, the Indian Army went on alert, but K. Ragunath, the Indian Foreign Secretary, had no comment to offer. The Council of Commonwealth Ministers suspended Pakistan's membership. General Musharraf announced a reduction of troops on the Kashmir Line of Control, a naïve response to Pakistan's exclusion by the comity of nations. Akbar Ahmed, of Selwyn College, Cambridge, referred to a "new generation" of leadership, with greater "integrity"—perhaps Asghar Khan and Hamid Gul representing the aspirations of the Young Officers'

Groups of the '70's? At the same time, Mr. Ahmed described General Musharraf as "riding a tiger". However, this tiger's stomach is filled with terrorist training camps, ballistic missiles, nuclear power and little else. The tiger is hungry. Since tigers do not beg, this tiger will have to go hunting soon. What and where will it hunt, and with which of its resources? Governments come and go, but the continuity of Pakistan's policy is manifest in the steady acquisition of nuclear power and delivery systems. In the geopolitical strategic confrontation that is around the corner, Sunni Pakistan will jockey for position with Shiite Iran to spearhead the Islamic world. The west, too, is riding a tiger in its relations with Pakistan. Isolate it, and it is further radicalised. Stroke it with dollars, and the aid money that does not slip into private coffers slithers its way into nuclear and missile development. Pakistan's long-term strategic policy is on an irrevocable collision course with the west. It needs to be seriously taken into account.

Information Technology Bodes Well For India, Not Pakistan—January 2000

At the dawn of a new millennium, predictions on the direction of global Information Technology (IT) have become a hot topic. Comparing the length of mankind's history, with the infancy of IT, discourages definitive prognostics on the subject. However, most of the significant factors affecting IT can be identified.

The future of IT will be decided by the extent to which it is mastered by its managers and end-users, the available investment capital to keep fuelling research, the purchasing power of end-users to acquire hardware and software updates, the political freedom to communicate, the wisdom not to misuse this liberty, and language abilities.

The cumulative and accelerated passage of information facilitates the mastery of IT. Tools are getting more user friendly, cyberspace is a congenial environment for all ages to be in, and IT figures early and prominently in school syllabi. Economically, world trade is booming, and Federal Reserve Banks are slowly learning to do their job. Invested capital is hard to lose, and the interchange of government sponsored and private research complement each other. Since the Reagan era, during which IT played a key role in liberating Poland from the communist yoke, the third world Joe Bloggs appreciates the freedom to choose. Reagan's legacy is in the expectations of oppressed peoples. States all over the world have learnt that educational standards lead to an educated workforce, a prerequisite to a competitive modern economy, which, when healthy, is the best guarantee of a government's continuity. Mahathir Mohammed, President of Malaysia and Lee Kuan Yew, the patriarch of Singapore tried to challenge the universality of human rights by institutionalising neo-Confucianism across East Asia through a series of forums, think tanks and research institutions. There have been no significant results of this misplaced effort. The foundations of Poland's communism crumbled under the onslaught of tracts and pamphlets spewed out by portable computers. China knows this, and keeps a close eye on its inter-net, even though in Tibet, its own Poland, the ground is not yet ready for IT to serve the cause of human rights.

The cyber world has no sovereign states. Communication cuts across state boundaries to create centres of interest communicating with each other. In time, this will create an alternative version of freemasonry and guilds. Whether it will actually threaten the existing spatial bases of the modern nation-state is open to discussion. Marshall McLuhan identified Gutenberg as the cause of the modern nation-state, and the computer is often referred to as another Gutenberg. That comparison is hard to refute, but the exact duplication of the consequences of Gutenberg cannot come about, since however analgous the circumstances may appear to be, history does not lend itself to copy and paste operations.

There are, however, parts of the developing world where conditions are closer to the period between Gutenberg (15th century) and Westphalia (1648 which is generally reckoned to be the birth of the modern nation-state) than anywhere else on the planet. But a word of caution: during these two centuries of economic, social and intellectual change, there was little outside inspiration: after all, the Mongol, Mughal, Turkish or Chinese states were not a model for Europe! Europeans went beyond the statements of judeo-christianism to express them in electoral democracy, universal suffrage and education. The third-world mass now has a model to look upto beyond its own restrictive environment. That is a challenge governments of developing countries have to meet. Cyber-space, more than Hollywood glitz, forces them to face upto the realities of their environment. South Asia, with its ethnic and religious diversity and vast pool of talented elites at all levels and in all sectors of activity makes it an interesting area to study. The two main South Asian actors are India and Pakistan. Both have a half-century of modern history. Pakistan's raison d'être has been hatred for India over Kashmir, and Islam. India's main concerns have been to model a society based on western affluence and a place within the moral leadership of the world.

As a consequence of Pakistan's chosen concerns, 25 percent of its budget goes into defense, and in recovering from its periodical bouts of military and civilian mis-rule. The black-market economy is healthy, but the legal economy is a contradiction in terms. GDP growth is at 3.5 percent and inflation at 8.5 percent. The electorate is dormant, class division is as sharp as caste in India, and the rural-urban divide a stark reality. As IT hits Pakistan, this rural-urban divide will widen, leading to the creation of a small class of urban elite hated by traditional rich and poor alike. Whatever form of cyberspace that exists will also become a battle-ground for militant and tolerant voices of Islam. Pakistan being Pakistan, they will fight it out in the streets and in the countryside with hockey sticks and Kalashnikovs, forcing the hand of authoritarian forces. A lot of Pakistan's IT talent will go into its trans-border interests, from Central Asia to the South of India. It is estimated that Pakistan's Inter-Services Intelligence (ISI) master-minded the cyber attack on the Indian government's Kashmir website in October 1999, and is busy stirring up trouble for India in places as far away as Assam and Kerala. An IT-cyberspace boom in Pakistan will cause further destabilization

In India, business is so good that despite Pakistan's provocations, and Indian might, nobody wants war with Pakistan. Population growth in India has slowed, GDP growth is at 6.1 percent and inflation at 8 percent. In 10 years, adult literacy has gone up from 52 percent to 64 percent. The urban-rural and male-female literacy gaps are shrinking. However, in corruption, the political and judicial systems rival those of Pakistan. IT is doing what the government of India has not been able to do: really bettering the lot of people. As more people communicate with each other, a new virtual caste that cuts across traditional lines of ethnicity, geography and religion is beginning to emerge. This class in India might be the ultimate cement to hold it together and end the protracted series of civil wars flaring up over the past fifty years. It might eventually check corruption. This cyber-space IT class will grow on itself as it creates interlocking internal and external links. IT will shore up India's economic, political and social structures.

The wild card is the volatility of India-Pakistan relations.

Chinese Dragon Roars Across Taiwan Straits—
April 2000.

In February of this year, China published its White Paper on Taiwan, unambiguously reiterating its intention to bring a capitalist democracy under the communist yoke. Chinese intentions betray an ambition well beyond simply influencing the forthcoming elections in Taiwan. This time, Beijing's bellicosity is backed by the Sino-Russian strategic partnership, purchase of Russian strategic military equipment and technology plus large-scale espionage and outright theft of western technology. The Chinese are also reassessing their doctrine in terms of enlarged, strategic joint operations covering a spectrum of intelligence, finance, terrorism, crime cartels and cyberspace.

As the Chinese dragon roars across the Taiwan straits, the Russian bear is rearing its head in the Mediterranean. The aircraft carrier Admiral Kuznetsov and the rest of its Fleet Task group will hold exercises in the Mediterranean and other "unspecified parts of the world" (French establishment daily *Le Monde*). Without the move being very original, it can still tie-up enough NATO forces to give the Chinese more elbowroom in the Taiwan straits—were it to come to that. And, with the Chinese purchase of Russian submarines, warships, cruise missiles and sophisticated fighter aircraft, the Kremlin would appear to have been well-paid for this service.

Beijing's shopping bags contain the forthcoming Type 094 SSBNs & 093 SSNs, 039 Song-class diesel electric submarines, 40 Shkval nuclear torpedoes and 2 Sovremenny-class guided missile destroyers. The Australian aircraft carrier HMAS Melbourne has been acquired for "scrap" in order to study it. The Russian aircraft carrier Admiral Kuznetov has been inspected. Beijing has approved advanced funding for an entire class of carriers commencing in 2001. By 2005, Beijing hopes to have the Jianji-10 Fighter aircraft (F-10) in the air, and land-attack missile capability is growing.

According to the authoritative weekly *Jane's Intelligence Review*, China intends to "resubordinate Taiwan to mainland Chinese rule by force if necessary and to promote its long-range power projection strategy".

Accordingly, new missile bases are being rapidly built in the province of Fujian for the DF-AA/M-AA missile. Fujian's coastline faces Taiwan, making it vulnerable to the DF-AA/M-AA. China's "long-term power projection strategy" is also being well looked after. One of the goals is to develop a family of land, sea and air-launched cruise missiles. In the meantime, it is suspected that China might buy the Russian stealth missile NPO Machinostroyena 3K 55E Yakhant.

All this brawn is not without a brain. *Unrestricted War*, co-authored by Colonels Qiao Liang and Wang Xiangrui, is the current hot book circulating within Chinese military circles and among the keen foreign military attachés. The ethos of the book recognises that China cannot technologically outpace the west in any foreseeable future and, as such, should look for weaknesses within the American military machine and the non-military infrastructure on which it depends for its existence. The biggest American weakness perceived by the two Colonels is the high value placed on human life. That is seen to influence a decrease in the political will to get involved in conflicts, with increased reliance on high-quality, high-tech weapons. The infrastructure that supports all this involves financial and industrial institutions, technocrats, hackers, drug cartels and terrorists. The authors go on to justify a weaker country flouting universal human values by disregarding the conventions and traditions of warfare, a logical extension of the Chinese "human wave" attacks practised with devastating effect against Indians and Americans. The current doctrine promotes attacks on the entire non-military infrastructure by mobilizing all available means from hackers to terrorists. The colonels suggest that had Milosevic sent teams of terrorists to Italy, France, Germany and Belgium, and targeted U.S. bases in Europe in response to last year's bombing campaign in Bosnia, the political result would have been different.

The breadth and range of this total war vision making the rounds in Beijing is awe-inspiring. It betrays Chinese intentions. Obviously considering peacetime as a period of preparation for war, with spurious motives in their commercial relations with the west, they have not abandoned their belief in Mao Zedong's guiding principle of all political power coming from the barrel of a gun. The direct threat to China only came from Russia, which is now their strategic partner. Thus, all the expense and effort the Chinese are expending has only one target—western civilization, which they hope to replace with their Confucian brand of communism. We not only need to stay at the cutting edge of technology and deny access to potentially hostile countries, but also ensure that our military personnel can adequately cope with its breakdown.

New Alliances Preparing To Confront The West—June 2000.

The recent rapprochement between China, India, Russia and Iran, the success of Chen Shui-bian's Democratic Progressive Party in Taiwan and the South Asian Kashmir dispute have heightened tension in the Taiwan straits and increased the chances of an Indo-Pakistan war.

According to N.B Naqvi writing in the *Pakistan Defence Journal*, last year India, "playing on Iran's wounded pride" floated the idea of an anti-American "axis" of India, Iran and Russia with China as an eventual partner. Central Asia's strategic raw materials including oil and gas have drawn the attention of international interests. Radical Islam, patronised by Pakistan's Inter-Services Intelligence (ISI) has stepped up destabilisation operations from Chechnya to Kashmir to Zhinkiang to Shiite Iran. Pakistan is keen to reserve a place at the bargaining counter when the big contracts for oil derricks and pipelines go out. In the long term, these Kiplingesque "Great Game" antics are well beyond Pakistan's economic, military, social or cultural reach. In the short and medium term, Pakistan has been able to divert its IMF loans and foreign workers' remittances from pressing domestic problems to international intrigue in order to assert its nuisance value. This means that countries, which feel the tentacles of the Pakistani octopus, will react: in or out of proportion to the threat in the medium and long term.

Iran is the only Shiite state in the world, and Pakistan's radicals and Afghanistan's Talibans being Sunni dominated, makes them dedicated enemies of Iran. Taliban Afghanistan is a Pakistani client state, affording Pakistan, in the words of Pakistan's General Hamid Gul, former head of Inter Services Intelligence (ISI), "strategic depth". Partially seeking to appease Taliban and Pakistani radicals' expectations and also to contain the restlessness of what Colonel Cloughly, writing in *Jane's Intelligence Weekly* calls "young zealots" among the Pakistan army's officer corps, Pakistan is not averse to shaking down Iran for a few petrodollars by encouraging anti-Shia activity. The Shah, after all, always paid up over the Baluchistan bogey.

Whilst the Soviets were in Afghanistan, they felt the bite of the estimated 100,000 Pakistanis who actively participated in that war. The Chechens are now rewriting recent Soviet-Afghan history for the Russians. China, Pakistan's long-time ally, is having to sit up and take notice of the considerable inflow of radical Islamic literature from across the Karakorams and the Celestial mountains from Pakistan and Uzbekistan. This literature is aimed at Islamic secessionists in communism's last major redoubt. India, of course is facing Pakistan-backed unrest from Kashmir to Cochin. According to Indian Interior Minister Advani, Pakistan has established a "covert network" in India.

Russia, Iran, China and India have a common enemy in radical Islam. Pakistan, a long-time Chinese and Iranian associate, is inexorably losing this status, while its relationship with Russia and India has always been confrontational. India's success in reminding Russia, Iran and China of this state of affairs was a case of preaching to converts. Thereafter it conveniently withdrew from active participation to organise Mr Clinton's 80-curry welcome in Delhi.

In 1962, China summarily bloodied India's nose and shattered Nehru-inspired visions of a non-aligned socialist bloc leading the world from its moral high horse. China subsequently became an atomic power, and went on to show the U.S. its teeth in Korea and Vietnam. As it rose in stature, the Nehru jacket became the Mao jacket, and U.S. recognition of China gave it a seat in the Security Council. India hopes that by treading the same path it can arrive at the same destination as the Chinese.

China and India have started getting cosy. China recently thanked India for its support in response to the UN Human Rights Commission's attempt to condemn it for human rights violations, and in other ways China is treating India as an imminent Security Council member. According to the French daily *Le Monde*, Britain and France are lending their support to India for a permanent Security Council seat. While France has firmly declared India a "strategic partner", Britain has implied a cause-effect relationship between the resolution of the Kashmir problem and India's attainment of a permanent Security Council Seat. Baroness Asthal of Scotland, Foreign Office Minister in the House of Lords, replying to a question on Kashmir by Lord Nazir Ahmed, stated that compliance with UN resolutions—which means a plebiscite in Kashmir—would enforce the credentials of a candidacy for a permanent seat in the Security Council.

India's ambition has obviously reassured China that it's neighbours' mountain divisions and nuclear arsenal are meant for defence and not vengeance against China, allowing it to divert resources to the Taiwan straits, thereby improving U.S. Defense Secretary Cohen's chances of selling the Taiwanese a Missile Defense Shield instead of the Aegis cruiser they would prefer. Addressing *Vijnan Bharati* (the association of scientists who took part in India's 1974 and 1998 atomic tests) in Mumbai on May 1 this year, the Indian Atomic Energy Commission's former chairman, Dr. P.K.Iyengar called for India to test a neutron bomb before signing the Comprehensive Test Ban Treaty (CTBT). This has further reassured China that to play in the Big League, India will forego revenge for its 1962 border defeat. Regionally, India's immediate interest is to settle its dispute with Pakistan in an effort to stabilise domestic unrest. Were this to lead to an armed conflict with Pakistan, India would like to ensure its northern front. Thus, India and China have a mutual interest in maintaining calm across the Himalayan watershed and India will encourage Taiwanese belligerence to instigate the Chinese to divert military resources from the Himalayas. With the snows melted and before the monsoon rains, India might well be tempted to test a neutron bomb and then quickly follow it up with a strike against Pakistan to dismantle the latter's covert network.

Section Nine—Terrorism

Russia Still Exporting Nuclear Materials To Terrorists—October 1994.

The conventional threat to the European Community (EC) of a resurgent Russia in search of historical mischief is compounded by the illicit export of enriched nuclear material from Russia, its use by destined countries, and their plans to exploit their eventual nuclear power status. Importers of contraband nuclear material are also exporters and/or supporters of terrorism. Commenting on the fifth seizure of uranium/plutonium in Germany in the past two years, the French daily *Le Monde* observed: "Potential customers are states desirous of being nuclear powers, and some of them support terrorism."

Instability in the Mediterranean is too close to the EC for comfort. Tunisia and Morocco are dormant, but the lava from Algeria's fundamentalists laps European shores. In August, fundamentalists in Algeria brazenly shot dead five French citizens on consular soil, bringing the total of European deaths to 52 (including 15 French). Charles Pasqua, France's Corsican home minister, ordered a crack down on fundamentalists in France suspected of links with extremists in Algeria. To the dismay of nearly five million Muslims in France, and the approval of 70 percent French (supporting national anti-terrorist policy), around 20,000 identity checks were carried out and 25 suspects interned. Algeria's Islamic Armed Groups issued a "declaration of war" against France. The conservative British daily, *The Daily Telegraph*, believes the Islamic Armed Groups possess "the determination, personnel and weapons to open a terrorist campaign in France...the challenge must be taken seriously."

On July 24, French police arrested a group of six Algerians and Tunisians armed to the teeth, and bound for Barcelona, with the logistical support of the Palestinian Hamas. According to the French daily *Le Figaro*, they had planned an attack against the Jewish community in Spain. An unambiguous link has been established between the Islamic terrorist groups operating on an international scale. The arrest came only a week after the bombing of the Israeli embassy in Buenos Aires, and two days before the blast in London.

Just before the London bang, Mrs. Stella Rimington, head of the British Secret Intelligence Service, had boasted in the Dimbleby Lecture that London had been denied to Middle East terrorists as an operating base. Shortly after the London blast, an 8,000-strong rally of Muslims in Wembley stadium near London called for the resurrection of the Islamic Caliphate. In 1922, dissatisfied British Muslim jurists had demanded a separate, Islamic parliament.

A Saudi Arabian defector, Mohammed al-Khileur, a former official at the UNO, has accused Saudi Arabia, the west's closest Mideastern ally, of giving financial aid to terrorists spying in the U.S., and "a secret attempt to acquire nuclear weapons" by "trying to buy parts and technology to build nuclear weapons," in deadly mimesis of Pakistan, Iran and Iraq's methods.

According to the German dailies *Der Spiegel* and *Welt am Sontag*, the August seizure of 50 grams of plutonium 239 in Germany from the hold of a Russian airliner involved the arrest of a Columbian and two Spaniards. Victor Sidorenko, Russia's deputy minister for atomic energy, was reportedly on the same plane.

Clearly, unity of method and objective form the bridge between the theft of nuclear enriched material, organized crime, terrorist groups and their sponsors.

In view of security threats ranging from backyard conflagrations and "Russia Rising" to "Hostile Islam" bent on nuclear weapons and delivery systems, EC defense is steadily moving towards self-reliance. In the Bastille Day parade in France, 36 Fuchs and Marden vehicles of the Bundeswher rolled down the Champs Elysees as part of the Eurocorps. Television commentators referred to Eurocorps as the Foreign Legion of Europe.

In view of the EC's Mediterranean interests, exercise Farfadet was held in 1992. It involved 12,000 troops from France, Italy, Spain and Britain, including Special Forces. As an inter-army coordination exercise, culminating in hostage scenarios, it was a success. Today, a European Mediterranean Force—comprising France, Italy and Spain—is reportedly in the works.

Jacques Sauter of Luxembourg was selected as Jaques Delor's successor to the European Commission presidency in an atmosphere of political farce, which reflects on EC squabbles, and not Sauter's competence. EC defense policy is not based on a personality cult but in response to the ratio of defense needs versus available resources. The dimensions of the EC's security concerns demand a high standard of cooperation between military forces, all special forces, intelligence agencies and police forces assisted by relevant academic circles and think tanks linked by a coordinating body.

Islamic Terorism Stoppable? U.S. Foreign Policy May Be Key —February 1995.

As European families gathered to celebrate good cheer on Christmas Eve, the harsh realities of the Mediterranean basin were rudely brought home to them. At Algiers airport, Paris bound Air France Airbus A-300 with 227 people including crew members was taken over by four young Algerian gunmen. In a well planned operation, the four terrorists boarded the aircraft dressed as ground staff engaged in a last minute passport check. They revealed themselves when they shot an Algerian policeman and Bui Giang To, the commercial attaché of the Vietnamese embassy to Algeria. The bodies were unceremoniously flung onto the tarmac.

The young gunmen addressed each other by predetermined numbers and claimed affiliation with the Islamic Armed Groups of Algeria, engaged in a bitter civil war that has so far claimed an estimated 17,000 lives. They demanded that the Oxford educated Abassi Madani, leader of the Islamic Salvation Front, and his deputy Ali Benhadj, be freed from house arrest. The young radicals wanted the plane to fly to Paris where they hoped to convert it into a lethal Christmas cracker by blowing it up in the skies.

The French and Algerian governments immediately formed crisis cells. At the diplomatic level, the French government succeeded in convincing the Algerians to keep their anti-terrorist forces at bay. On Christmas Day itself, the hijackers chose to kill Yannick Beugnet, a French citizen and cook at the French embassy in Algiers.

On Boxing Day, with relations frazzled between Paris and Algiers, the Algerian government reluctantly allowed the plane to take off. It landed in Marseilles with the intention of refuelling before taking off for Paris.

The hijackers threatened to kill a fourth passenger if all their demands were not met.

Minutes after the ultimatum expired, elite GIGN hostage rescue commandos led by Major Favier stormed Airbus A-300 in what the BBC called a "carefully planned" operation. In one minute and fifteen seconds, passengers were sliding down the emergency chutes. At the end of the operation, all four terrorists lay dead. Élan, after all, is a French word.

The following day, the Islamic Armed Groups executed four priests (three French and one Belgian) in Algeria, in macabre reminiscence of the Belgian Congo between 1960 and 1964, when nuns and priests became innocent victims of the resentment of people to whom they had devoted their lives.

A week before the hijacking, the Islamic Foreign Ministers' Conference in Casablanca had unprecedentedly backed a code of conduct for combating terrorism and its sponsor countries. The hijacking of Airbus A-300 was the response of young radicals (and perhaps their sponsors) to a resolution passed by a pro-western and older generation. In Washington, Anouar Haddam, President of the Parliamentary delegation of the Islamic Salvation Front, categorically condemned hostage taking, but referred to the frustration of Algeria with France. Haddam's condemnation recognizes the importance of the West in whatever future the ISF hopes to build in Algeria. His reference to "frustration" defers to the muscle of young radicals. In Israel, too, the mainstream Palestinian leadership appears to walk a tightrope between the exigencies of its radical constituents and political realities. Hardliners and softliners are actually in lockstep on principle. The differences might very well be superficial and part of undeclared policy.

Islamic conflicts are inexorably nearing Europe. Bosnia, Armenia-Azerbaijan, Chechnya and North Africa are conflicts involving Muslims. Albania is waiting to explode. The EU and the Russians recognize the nature of the threat, and almost share the same approach. In view of the ISF parliamentary delegation visiting Washington, the United States is seeking to establish bilateral relations in the Mediterranean independent of EU interests. If the EU feels its long term strategic needs are excluded from the United States' foreign policy agenda, new alliances based on shared defense needs are liable to emerge.

Oklahoma Bombing And Tokyo Gas Attack—June and July 1995.

In the first part, this article presents a reaction of the European press to the Oklahoma city bombing, the possibility of an Islamic fundamentalist angle explored by the European press, and its implications. The second part weighs the implications of the Tokyo gas attack by the sect Aum Shinrikyo , and evokes an Indian angle. Both parts suggest that international terrorism is entering a new phase.

Part I

In *Special Warfare (1993), Dr Bruce Hoffman*, director of the Arroyo Center's Strategy and Doctrine Program in RAND's Army Research Division, stated "despite the end of both the Cold War and the ideological polarization that divided the world, the United States will nonetheless remain an attractive target for terrorists seeking to attract attention." On April 19, the bomb that exploded in Oklahoma City sadly proved the verity of his words. This time it was not a far away place, but the American heartland where terrorists chose to strike mercilessly at women and children. A single bomb, manufactured with products that reduced hunger in the third world through scrupulous use, barbarically wrenched away the lives of under a hundred innocent victims. The shock waves reverberated beyond the shores of the United States. The German daily *Frankfurter Allgemeine Zeitung* rightly referred to the "shock" felt by the entire European Union. The Italian daily *Republica* said, "Europe feels revolted"

The French, and British press also condemned the act in no uncertain terms. Europeans are inured to proxy wars popping up on their landscape with depressing regularity. The overriding question is whether the apparent act of vengeance by the Branch Davidians is indigenous from conception to execution, or whether it was aided by external impulsion. According to the *International Herald Tribune*, Geary County Sheriff Bill Deppish said the pair who rented the truck that is alleged to have been the delivery system for the bomb "used aliases and some kind of false identification other than a driver's license"—which Mr. Deppish declined to describe. One may be excused the liberty of wondering why.

Although the Branch Davidians have taken center-stage as prime villains, the European press reports that professional investigators in the United States are examining the possibility of a link with Islamic fundamentalists. The conservative French daily *Le Figaro*, sees the "hand of the mid-east" in the Oklahoma incident. The paper links last year's bomb in Buenos Aires which left a hundred dead, the 1983 bomb in Beirut that killed 241 Americans and the 1993 WTC bombing that killed eight. In these major attacks, and in others, the same explosive mix was used. The high-brow *Le Monde* goes a step further in examining the modus operandi, down to the elements of delivery system, van rental, detonators etc.

While the arrest of members of the Branch Davidians would suggest home-grown motives, the modus operandi points at foreign planning. After all, homegrown U.S. terrorism has a tragi-comic record of efficiency: In 1969-70 U.S. leftists exploded 250 bombs that caused only one death. Warriors of Islam have a more deadly record.

Weldon Kennedy of the FBI was quoted by *Le Monde* as saying to the effect that if the FBI had been looking for two white men they had not given up looking for people of mid-eastern appearance. The *Herald Tribune* quotes a former CIA official: "don't forget the IRA turned to the Libyans for help when they needed it". The U.S. President, in his address to the nation in the aftermath of the Oklahoma bombing, clearly referred to different Middle East groups with a vested interest in destroying the Middle East peace process.

The Times of London took into account the modus operandi of the WTC bombing and the links of its mastermind, Ramzi Ahmed, with

Denmark, the Philippines, and above all Pakistan. Ramzi and his friend Kahim Murad both admit membership of the 5th Battalion of the Liberation Army based in Pakistan, which seeks to subvert the Middle East peace process referred to in the U.S. President's speech. The daily *Times* goes on to refer to Ramzi's membership in the Warriors of the Prophet, a Pakistan-based organization. BBC 2 reports lead one to believe that this very organization is a pivotal force in enforcing the blasphemy laws which led to the passing of the death sentence on two Christians, who are even now under sentence by a "fatwa", hiding "somewhere in Europe". *Le Monde* claims: "The trail leading to Pakistan is the most serious line of investigation being pursued by U.S. investigators".

In view of the Islamic fundamentalist angle to the Oklahoma bomb, other aspects beg to be taken into consideration. State-sponsored terrorism may be official, or unofficial, retaining in either case, a low or high profile. Terrorism by proxy which used to be a Soviet prerogative, is now being rivaled by Islamic fundamentalists. The political maturity of Islamic fundamentalists, and their global scope marks a turning point in their worldview. They feel confident enough to sub-contract individual operations to their theological enemies.

This new turn in the policy of Islamic fundamentalists was only to be expected. Just as a left-wing international brigade fought in the Spanish Civil War, an Islamic brigade fought in Afghanistan. At the end of the Spanish civil war, the veterans of the international brigade continued fighting fascism during the Second World War. Following the end of the Second World War, these veterans turned their attention to fighting capitalist democracy, becoming, in the process, witting or unwitting agents of Soviet policy. Where are the veterans of the Islamic International Brigade that had its headquarters in Pakistan for over a decade? Flushed with victory against the Russian bear, they lethally thumb their noses at the west whose war they think they fought in Afghanistan. Some of them are fighting domestic pro-western governments in Algeria, Egypt and Pakistan. Others are tasting adventure in Chechnya, Tajikistan, Ajerbaijan, Bosnia,

Chechnya, Kashmir, the Philippines and Myanmar. Just as a lot of veterans of the Spanish civil war became witting or unwitting extensions of Soviet foreign policy, are veterans of the International Islamic Brigade extensions of a centralized global policy of Islamic fundamentalism? And if they carry on taking a cue from the old Soviet policy, they will seek to further enlarge their front.

As such, unacknowledged terrorist acts committed by client groups will define global terrorism in the next ten years. Shifting alliances in the Islamic world should be expected, anticipated and accounted for. The day after the Oklahoma bomb, Turkish intelligence foiled a plot to assassinate Mrs. Tansu Ciller, Turkey's mediagenic pro-western Prime Minister. The same day, Saudi Arabia, one of the western world's closest allies, refused to cooperate in the extradition of Imad Mughnya, alleged to have masterminded the 1983 suicide attack in Beirut. The excuse that the royal family are afraid of radicals is getting a little stale now. It is time to admit that the Saudis now feel no fear of showing where their true loyalties lie.

In February, Willy Claes, the Secretary-General of NATO, blurted out in an off-the-cuff remark "Islamic fundamentalism is just as dangerous as communism was". Within and outside the EU the remark was only criticized for its indiscretion. One is led to wonder what information the Secretary-General of NATO had in his possession.

Part II

Islamic fundamentalism is not the only form of terrorism moving into a more dangerous phase. The Japanese sect Aum Shinrikyo was allegedly responsible for the sarin gas attack in Tokyo that left 12 dead on March 20, 1995. On 5 April 1995, there was an attempt on the life of Mr. Kunimatsu, Japan's Chief of Police. The same day the bomb exploded in Oklahoma City, Aum were apparently responsible for the poison gas attack in Yokohama, and channel 1 of French TV reports that the day following the Oklahoma bombing, U.S. law enforcement agencies foiled an attempt to blow up Disneyland, reportedly planned by Aum.

The Economist draws attention to the sect's worship of the Hindu god Shiva, spouse of Kali, the goddess of death and destruction. The British establishment weekly speculates on the link between Shiva-Kali worship and the thugs, a brotherhood of assassins who killed by strangulation in the name of the goddess Kali.

The British declared that they had destroyed them just at the beginning of the second half of the nineteenth century, but bazaar rumors in India had always persisted that they only went underground. Are they raising their heads above ground now? In *Holy Terror (Rand, 1993), Dr Bruce Hoffman*, Director of the Arroyo Center's Strategy and Doctrine program in Rand's Army Division, recognizes the importance of studying the thugs in any history of terrorist groups. In view of Aum Shinrikyo's renaissance of Kali worship through the shedding of blood, Hindu-inspired sects that have been flourishing since the sixties, take on a threatening dimension. Even discounting Indian government sponsorship, the potential for mischief is large. The method, chronology and impetus of attacks do not imply freak accidents but deliberate policy. Therefore these people are moving from the acquisition of influence through wealth into a phase of acquisition of power through terror.

In India itself, Hinduism is regressing from Mahatma Gandhi's stance of moral persuasion. Shiv Sena is the militant armed wing of Hindu extremism. Its headquarters are in Pune, and it is said to be closely linked with the RSSK, which also has its headquarters in Pune. Mahatma Gandhi's assassin belonged to the RSSK. The Shiv Sena has now won political power in Maharashtra state. Pune and Bombay form part of Maharashtra state. Three weeks after seizing power, the Shiv Sena "launched a drive to deport Bombay's 43,000 illegal Muslim immigrants" (*Time* Magazine). In response to an anonymous phone threat from a purported Muslim, Bal Thackeray, leader of the Shiv Sena, threatened the entire Muslim community with total elimination if a hair of his head was harmed.

Shiv Sena means the army of Shiva. The ideological godhead of Aum Shirinkyo and the Hindu right in India is the same. Kali, the spouse of Shiva, looms in the background of this menacing cabal, and the possibility of the dreaded Thugs rearing their heads on a socio-political platform is frightening. For decades the thugs, under different names, have been the source of drug smuggling from the Indian sub-continent to Europe. Let us not forget that until the Appalachian raid, nobody was willing to believe in the existence of the Italian-American mafia. If the essence of Bal Thackeray's cold-blooded threat of mass extermination is to be carried out by high-tech, up-dated thugs such as Aum Shinrikyo and other sects, the scenario is worrying.

It would indicate that despite internecine rivalry, anti-western sentiment in Asia has a unity of objectives. In that case, East Asian attitudes of hostility towards the west need to be taken into consideration for their inspirational, and eventually nuisance value, certainly in influencing and molding fundamental attitudes. The disdainful position of Malaysia's Mahathir Mohammed and Singapore's Kishore Mahbubani towards western civilization and values is not encouraging. These are not future partners, and the grass roots they influence are liable to synthesize this arrogance with the terrorist methods chosen by others in the Asian neighborhood.

In twenty year's time, with the blessing of East Asia's neo-Confucianism, Hindu and Islamic fundamentalism could be in lockstep in an effort to rid Asia of any vestiges of western influence. Hong Kong and the Philippines are taken as modern manifestations of Gibraltar and Malta, outposts of the orders of warrior monks who battled Saracens for the preservation of Christendom. In that case, Ramzi Ahmed's (alleged mastermind of the WTC bombing extradited to the U.S. from Pakistan and currently on trial) choice of Hong Kong and the Philippines as targets of sustained terrorist attacks brings to mind Jeanne Kirpatrick's remark in an interview with *Newsweek* following the 1983 suicide bombing of American soldiers in Beirut. Reagan's ambassador to the UN said to the effect that the attack was part of an overall plan to rid the mid-east of an

American presence. In *Holy Terror* (Rand, 1993), Dr. Bruce Hoffman concludes "Finally, we may also be on the cusp of a new, and potentially more dangerous, era of terrorism as the year 2000—the literal millennium—approaches. One cannot predict the effect that this pivotal symbolic watershed might have on religion-inspired terrorist groups who feel impelled either to hasten the redemption associated with the millennium through acts of violence or, in the event that the year 2000 passes and redemption does not occur, to attempt to implement Armageddon by the apocalyptic use of weapons of mass destruction"

It is in this context that Yitzhak Rabin (Prime Minister of Israel)'s advice to President Clinton following the Oklahoma City bomb to "hit terrorists before they hit U.S." assumes importance.

Relentless Islamic Terrorism Aimed At French—December 1995.

In a communiqué issued in London in 1994, the Islamic Armed Group (IAG) of Algeria declared war on France. In the first phase French expatriates were killed in Algeria. In the second phase, which started last Christmas, an airbus was hijacked with the intention of blowing it up over Paris.

On July 11th Sheikh Sahraouvi, Imam of the Paris mosque, one of the founders of the Islamic Salvation Front and politically opposed to the IAG, became, along with an innocent bystander, the first victims of the summer attacks on French soil. Although a shocking cold-blooded murder, it did not appear to be a precursor of a spate of terrorist attacks. *La Tribune*, an Algerian Daily, had warned on July 1st that a battle-hardened five-man IAG commando was on its way from Bosnia to France.

Nine terrorist attacks took place over an approximately 15-week period between July 11th and October 17th, —an average of about one attack every twelfth day with staggered intervals. On Aug 19, the IAG demanded that President Chirac convert to Islam. On October 7, the Reuters office in Cairo received a communiqué from the IAG promising "no respite" until Islam had conquered France.

Symbols have been omnipresent during the attacks. Christmas and summer vacations represent western Christendom's affluence. The explosive material used was camping gas bottles that proliferate summer campsites. Apart from simplicity and availability, camping gas bottles symbolize liberty, affluence and technological proficiency.

The first summer bomb exploded at St. Michel (St Michael) underground station in Paris. It is the station for the Latin Quarter, symbolic home of the '60s revolution. The leadership of terrorist groups today is in the hands of middle-aged men bitterly cynical about the '60s. The choice of the Latin Quarter's underground station indicates disheartened idealism.

A terrorist, Khaled Kelkaal, 24, an Algerian-born resident of Lyons, was shot dead at a place called Maison Blanche in Lyon. Consequently, a bomb exploded at a Paris underground station of the same name. Maison Blanche in English means White House, from where the "Great Satan" rules. And then a second bomb exploded at Saint Michel underground station. Saint Michel is the patron saint of paratroopers, and Khaled Kelkaal had been shot at Maison Blanche by paratroopers. October 17th, the date of the second explosion at Saint Michel, marks the day, thirty-four years ago, when French police are alleged to have killed a sizeable number of Algerians demonstrating in Paris for Algerian independence.

The second explosion at Saint Michel also implies a commander well versed in Irregular Operations. Hitting the same target when least expected denotes a commander with flair and a solid grounding in military doctrine. These guerillas are getting sound military-academy and infantry school type training from somewhere. They are also selected by the same standards. This sort of training cannot be imparted in the course of a civil war where the guerrilla does not have enough control of territory to ensure the application of a military curriculum over a period of six months to two years. In Algeria, the IAG can only run short, intensive courses to impart combat skills. Algeria is therefore not their Secure Area, and the clusters of immigrant communities in France, which provide them with support, are only their forward bases.

On November 3, in a television interview, a spokesman for French Intelligence affirmed that the head of the terrorists' organizational pyramid was outside France. The evening Khaled Kelkaal was shot, Channel 1 of French TV reported that Kelkaal and his buddy had both been "trained, broken in and battle-hardened" in Pakistan. The TV report added that recruits from Algeria and the North African communities in Europe regularly went to Germany, from where, on fake passports, they entered Pakistan and Afghanistan. On October 28, in Paris, Investigating Judge

Bruguiere opened a judicial inquiry into a terrorist conspiracy involving training centers in Pakistan and Afghanistan. A naturalized French citizen of German origin was also arrested in France for aiding terrorists. The sort of people who abetted Baader-Meinhof, and ran the terrorist camps in former East Germany, are now involved with other terrorist organizations. Extradition warrants are out for suspects in Sweden, Switzerland Belgium and Britain. Britain is alleged to harbor 200 to 400 terrorists wanted for questioning by French security services. Following President Chirac's meeting with John Major in London on October 30, the British Prime Minister declared that refugees in Britain committing terrorist acts in France would not be tolerated. Accordingly, on November 4, MI5 (counter-intelligence) and Scotland Yard arrested Abou Fares, the "IAG officer" alleged to have coordinated the summer bombings. This clearly identifies Britain as a secure area for the terrorists, which will now be denied to them, making Britain itself vulnerable to hostile acts.

The reaction to the summer bombings by French security forces was competent. In October, they actually nipped one attack in the bud, arresting a terrorist ready to explode a bomb in Lille. Vigipirate, a defensive plan against terrorists, was activated, and is still in effect. Among other measures, it involves the entire population, and the deployment of over 10,000 troops.

However, the essential question remains of identifying and rendering unusable the guerrillas' Secure Area for high-quality training that builds military thinking. The fundamental rule of anti-guerrilla warfare demands the destruction of secure areas, isolating guerrillas with a view to rendering them vulnerable to search and destroy missions. The British in Malaya and the French in Algeria managed to apply this rule with success.

It seems highly unlikely that military measures will be initiated against secure areas outside France. Diplomatic measures are being tried. Hoping to appease the IAG, President Chirac cancelled his meeting with the Algerian President at the United Nations' celebrations in New York. The ploy failed, with the Algerian government able to express indignation and the IAG triumph. Within France, it has become politically incorrect to talk of terrorism without convoluted semantics to avoid charges of racism. Since the gun battle between paratroopers and Khaled Kelkaal there have been riots by North African youth. A series of chat shows and films are being studiously broadcast by French TV to reassure North Africans in France that there is compassion and understanding for their culture and heritage. There is also a "Marshall Plan" in the works to improve conditions in North African neighborhoods. The plan is a sound "hearts and minds" approach. Fundamentalist talent scouts have been succeeding in recruiting disgruntled and alienated youth in predominantly North African neighborhoods. However, no "hearts and minds" campaign can be successful unless backed by measures to deny the guerrilla his secure areas.

The declared objective of the IAG is the Islamic conquest of France, a resurrection of the Great Moorish Dream destroyed by Charles Martel at Poitiers in 732 AD. This Dream strikes a chord in the hearts of North Africans immigrants in France putting them in a classic conflict-of-interest situation between their God and their Caesar. In the absence of a ceasefire, Christmas celebrations are liable to be interrupted by attacks on communication centers.

G-7 Communique Puts World Leaders To Test—July 1996.

The G-7 Summit of seven of the world's most industrialized nations (The United States, Japan, Canada, France, Germany, Britain and Italy) representing two-thirds of the world economy and half of its trade took place in Lyons, France on June 27 and 28. It grandly reminded the world of barbarians at its gates, emitted rallying cries, evoked principles, disagreed over the means of implementing the principles, and failed to reassure the world with kingly solutions.

On June 26, one day before the G-7 summit, the murder of 19 Americans in pursuit of their legitimate duties perpetrated by extremists in Saudi Arabia projected terrorism to the forefront of world news. Terrorists are now here to stay, helped unwittingly by an American President with a track record of vacillation, determined to set the record straight during an election year. In the G-7 communiqué issued on June 28, the world economy had to take a backseat while last year's G-7 communiqué in Halifax was resurrected as this year's resolve.

Last year's G-7 communiqué targeted terrorism and organized crime. While action on the former is still awaited, some progress has been made to contain international organized crime, notably against money-laundering operations. Hoping to achieve success against terrorism, the U.S. passed the Helms-Burton law, which aims to penalize an American ally trading with a country that sponsors terrorism. While recognizing the necessity of fighting terrorism, the EU leadership see this law as creative semantics designed to contain multilateral trade links. There is a strong feeling within European academic circles that the U.S. is in a weak moral position to offer this kind of advice. From the World Trade Center bomb in 1993 to the Dhahran bomb last year which killed 5 Americans, Islamic fundamentalist veterans of the Afghan war have been the main suspects, which implies American training and patronage. Thus, evoking the terms of the Helms-Burton law puts the U.S. in an ineffective position vis à vis its allies, while terrorists realize that economic sanctions and dissension within allied ranks rather than the Delta Force is their biggest worry.

That concerted, allied action is required to contain terrorism in view of its global dimensions is the subject of consensus, but achieving this goal within the framework of the Helms-Burton law is the object of contention. The G-7 communiqué, in reaffirming the "primacy of multilateral trade…rebuked" the Helms-Burton law (*The Daily Telegraph*). The reported "tension" between Bill Clinton and the French President, Jacques Chirac was a clash over the method of applying a principle equally dear to both.

However, the U.S. was relatively well positioned to lecture its allies on economics. In the past four years, the U.S. has created approximately 10 million jobs, and its unemployment rate is under 6 percent, compared with the EU's 10 percent. According to the OECD (Organization for Economic Cooperation and Development)'s last report quoted by the French daily *Le Monde*, the EU will only see about 1.6 percent economic growth by the end of this year, and tight fiscal policies designed to ease the pressure of budget deficits are liable to stagnate growth for 1997. By reminding the EU leaders of the merits of low deficit and increased interest rates, a Democratic President was able to bask in the sunshine of his Republican predecessors.

The G-7 leaders unanimously applauded the new markets of Asia and Latin America for opening up to the world economy, and expressed concern about the third world by agreeing to provide debt relief to the poorest countries. Although the humanitarian and public relational aspect of this resolution is undebateable, the economic consequences are open to question. To give body to this resolution, the International Monetary Fund will have to sell about 5 million ounces of its stock of 103 million ounces of gold reserves.

Opinion was divided over the wisdom of reducing IMF gold reserves. Germany fears that insofar as increased globalization threatens the fragility of interlocked monetary systems, decreasing IMF gold reserves might be imprudent.

Regrettably, when the semantics are peeled off the core of the communiqué, the kings stand naked in a tremulous world. The G-7 Summit raised issues and consequent fears, without offering solutions. As the Catholic daily *La Croix* expressed it: "leaders are not expected to enrich the catalogue of fears but to share (with the led) the means chosen to decrease the fears"

Economic growth in ratio to demographic explosion can alleviate the misery of billions. The dimensions of terrorism today threaten the economic—and by consequence the social fiber of the world. A concerted, serious and pragmatic effort to wipe out terrorism is imperative. The G-7 leaders have the power. The coming years will be a test of their resolve.

Terrorism Main Threat To Civilized Societies— September 1998.

True to habit, terrorists once again projected themselves into world headlines during the vacation period. In two well-coordinated, determined and professional attacks on August 7, United States embassies were simultaneously bombed in two different countries. The death toll of the Nairobi and Dar-es-Salaam tragedies exceeded 250, with over 5000 wounded. If the objective of the terrorists was to shock western vacationers out of their relaxed complacency, it succeeded. These people also applied Mao Tse Dong's guerrilla rules to perfection: they struck where they were least expected.

According to the London-based Al-Mouhajiroun movement (movement of exiles), the two attacks were probably carried out by the Islamic International Front, in application of the decisions taken at the Peshawar (Pakistan) conference held in June. In Dubai and Cairo, an organization hitherto apparently unknown, calling itself "The Islamic Army for the Liberation of Sacred Places" claimed credit for the two bombings. Nearly twenty years ago, there was an attempt to seize the Mecca in Saudi Arabia. The attack was foiled, but the ideas are still alive, carried by a new generation.

The French press agency, AFP, quoting an "Islamic official", reported that it was decided at the Peshawar conference to hit American targets worldwide. AFP further declares that the Peshawar conference was held under the sponsorship of one Osama Bin Laden, a renegade Saudi billionaire who actively supported anti-Soviet insurgency in Afghanistan, hastening the demise of the Soviet empire. On May 28, this same Osama Bin Laden had been interviewed by John Miller for ABC News. Bin Laden unequivocally declared his contempt for the U.S.' inability to sustain human casualties, adding that "Nato…did not fire a single shot" to bring down the Soviet empire. He called on Muslims to hit Americans wherever they could. Bin Laden is now suspected of being behind the bombings in Africa. This may or may not be true—he is not the only person in the world to have mouthed violent anti-Americanisms, and who has the resources to convert nasty semantics into lethal action.

Ms Albright, the American Secretary of State, warned of her country's long memory and reach. In a pointed reference to Iran and others of its ilk, U.S. Defense Secretary Mr. Cohen declared, "it was important to establish whether a nation was involved in either sponsoring or harboring bombers" (BBC *News Service*). After the Beirut bombing in 1983 Jean Kirpatrick's statement was less hysterical and more cogent. She said that it was an attempt to get the United States out of the Middle East, and confirmed that it would not happen.

The volume of press speculation and politicians' statements confirms that either very little is known about terrorism, or what is known is not taken into account. If a proven link emerges between Osama Bin Laden, the Peshawar conference of June, and the Nairobi and Dar-es-Salaam bombings, perhaps it is time for the United States and its allies to reassess their counter-terrorism policy, especially rules of evidence.

The next attack might not necessarily be an embassy, but another soft target with a minority of Americans and a majority of other nationalities working for the Americans. At the Peshawar conference, the International Islamic Front for the Jihad against Jews and Crusaders was formed. According to Bin Laden, "it has a higher council to coordinate...". The African attacks certainly showed coordination and strategic purpose. The next targets will have strategic significance for the perpetrators, even if it is not perceived as such by their adversaries. The challenge is to sharpen perception, accept that there are patterns of reasoning outside the known framework used by analysts, to pursue a logic of prevention, avoid a staggered Maginot Line mentality, and wrest initiative from the adversary in the field, without ignoring the imperative of political sagacity.

Dominique Moïsi, Deputy Director of the French Institute of International Relations, in a broadcast interview with RTL radio-TV, bluntly dubbed the two bombings in Africa the harvest of the United States' sanctions policy. On August 10, Ms. Albright addressed a packed auditorium of diplomats. "One diplomat questioned whether the United States sets such a heavy standard of evidence…that punishment is unlikely".

In its issue of July 31, 1996, *The European* reported that "The Group of Seven are planning to hit back at terrorists…and create centers of excellence in anti-terrorist expertise". If these centers are alive and kicking, it is time for the politicians to let professionals do their job.

Europe Bureau Report : *Allah's Networks—* September 1998.

Two recent books compared worldwide are *In The Shadow of the Prophet* by Milton Viorst, and *Beyond Belief* by V.S.Naipaul. In a joint review of both books for the *Los Angeles Times* (August 2), Nikki R. Keddie of UCLA draws out the difference between the approaches of both writers. While Viorst searches for moderate forces and forces of change in Islamic countries, Naipaul seeks to pinpoint forces that explain the unmitigated militancy that inspires terrorists. Neither writer touches on the subject of organization and objectives.

In 1997, the French investigative journalist Antoine Sfeir wrote *Les Reseaux d'Allah* (Allah's Networks), detailing the Islamic networks in France and Western Europe. The author's grasp and synthesis of history, sociology, religion, politics and modern guerrilla warfare is backed up by statistical information. The clear graphs and tables make it a work of scholarly investigative journalism. It was one of the few such books to be reviewed on the front page of the prestigious French daily *Le Monde*. Sfeir's work makes it clear that Islamic missionary organizations operating within the liberal socio-political environment of western democracies provide a resource of sympathizers. He also provides a list of twenty international Islamic socio-religious organizations suspected of terrorist activities. Sfeir provides their addresses and telephone numbers. They are all headquartered in Peshawar, Pakistan.

Scourge Of Neo-Terrorists Must Be Obliterated—November-December 1999.

Just as the British Army had to learn 20th century warfare during the Boer War, counter-terrorist organizations are going to have to learn to fight 21st century terrorism that encompasses the Special Forces of sponsor countries and their ballistic missile programs. At times it is easy to be misled by the sloppy appearances of some terrorists and equate them with Castro's 1956 rebels. The wild-eyed teenagers of Hamas using sling shots against the Israel security forces have matured into computer-smart managers using Internet chat rooms across the U.S.A., coordinating their operations across Gaza by e-mail. Flight simulation programs offer terrorists the skills to use drones and update their knowledge of an aircraft's vulnerable points. Like NATO officers honing their operational skills in warfare using sophisticated, cost-effective computer programs, terrorists are free to adapt any management or war game to their training objectives.

The commercialisation of satellite imagery allows terrorists to assess their targets and plan operations with the same facility as armed forces. Encryption programs available on the market ensure the security of terrorist communications. And since efficient money laundering lies at the heart of successful terrorism, cyberspace offers secure, faceless banking for the conduct of spurious financial transactions.

According to a 1999 Rand Corporation report, old-style terrorists with ideological commitment, a political agenda, and direct state sponsorship are on the way out. New terrorists rely less on vertical chains of command and personality cults that offered astute intelligence officers backtracking and infiltration opportunities. The use of hire-and-fire amateur talent is also on the wane. This means current methods of intelligence-gathering, analyses and counter-terrorism will need to be reassessed. We may expect flatter, decentralized transnational terrorist structures. The U.S. recently set up National Security Study Group, also known as the Boren-Rudman Commission, a think tank which will study three items on its agenda over a two and one-half year period. It will determine the global security environment of the 21st century, develop an appropriate national security strategy in the light of its analyses of the national character and recommend alternatives to the current strategy.

The need for alternatives admits the declining relevance of current approaches. Although the weapons likely to be pointed at anti-terrorist forces might not be liable to radical change, restructuring and other factors mentioned above represent a de facto force multiplier. The Tamil Tigers (Sri Lanka) and their spectacular success in diverting a ship full of arms from its destination to their purposes (without a conventional hijacking operation) and the supposed coordination of Islamic insurgency in Kashmir are two cases in point. In both cases, the guerrillas have shown an equal expertise in playing with people's minds as with their bodies. Psychological warfare and related applications of psychology are now being recognized as weapons by terrorists. With the carnage spread by the bombs in Russia, leading to Yeltsin's latest lumbering invasion of Chechnya, there has been a spate of charges, countercharges and speculation on the possibility of transnational links between Islamic militants from Pakistan to Dagestan. Taking into account the factors generated by the use of cyberspace by terrorist groups lends credence to the existence of a well-knit international order of Islamic militancy.

The Rumsfeld Commission in the United States describes another role for terrorists and Special Forces of hostile nations: namely, as an alternative delivery system for nuclear, chemical and biological (NBC) warheads. The nightmare scenario of fiction is seriously considered by a government commission. Thus, NBC, terrorism and ballistic missiles are linked, and ergo, forces to counter them must also be linked. Since a large part of the intra and intercommunications has harnessed cyberspace to its nefarious ends, only intensive and extensive cooperation among the agencies will keep malignant forces at bay.

It would also be well to remember that according to *Jane's Intelligence Review*, of a total of 600 RGM/AJGM-109 Tomahawk Cruise Missiles launched between 1991 and 1999, "There are at least six recorded instances when Tomahawk missiles have gone off course and landed without their warheads exploding. In some cases these missiles have been auctioned to the highest bidder, but reports have indicated that Chinese Iranian and Pakistani experts have all examined these missiles in detail." Of these three countries, China has been identified by the Pentagon as a possible adversary, and Pakistan missed being on the U.S. list of terrorist countries by a hair's breadth during the Bush administration's last days. Lately, reports have mentioned the presence of Pakistani and Iranian volunteers in conflicts from Kashmir to Dagestan.

The latter half of this year, to date, has been relatively quiet. Despite attention centered on Kosovo, East Timor and Russia, there was a relative absence of the usual terrorist bombs of resentment against western affluence during the holiday season. Therefore, at a tactical level, terrorism might be planning a spectacular *danse macabre* for the millennium celebrations, and at the strategic level, its antics from Kashmir to Dagestan and Chechnya possibly indicate a concerted effort to retain control of (or at the lease maintain a nuisance value in) Brzezinsky's "Eurasian Space." This should allow their sponsor countries to further improve the efficiency of their missiles and crease out transnational command and control problems before they announce all-out strategic confrontation. This is a period of preparation in which these forces are playing on the logic of planners bound by time-space…and judicial standards of evidence. Yet, pre-emptive action for defensive purposes has been recognized since 1967. This preparation period should be denied them by all appropriate means.

CONCLUSION

The pertinence of the welfare state created by Britain's 1911 Insurance Act has been replaced by the principles of public welfare and the preservation of a way of life on the basis of national economic well being. The fall of the Berlin Wall blurred the sharpness of the left and right-wing divide, leading to a zigzag pattern in which both strive to manage the national interest in step with public expectations. Thus it is, that conservatives scrabble to establish their credentials as the managers of public welfare, while progressives seek to advance their claims as executives of market economics. In Italy, Silvio Berlusconi, a conservative with a controversial history, has been entrusted to lead the nation. Britain has once again chosen Mr. Blair's "new left" with its socialist past to maintain a healthy economic climate. The American people retained the services of the Democrats under Mr Clinton in the interest of their wallets, which has now been conferred on the Republicans under Mr Bush. The link between politics, finance, high technology, public welfare and the defense industry dictates its own logic, leading to the belief of little practical difference between the mainstream left and right, decreasing electorate commitment and in turn explaining low voter turnout in western democracies. Party politics has reached a watershed, and personality cults are on the rise.

The charm of Mr. Clinton's personality obscured his administation's mishandling of relations with China. *The New York Times* identified China as former President Clinton's "greatest challenge", which he failed to measure up to, inexcusable in the light of the Pentagon's analyses clearly identifying

China as more foe than friend. The Chinese made the most of this inconsistency within the American government, spreading their wings with glee until rudely brought to earth by India's nuclear tests in 1998. The European Union felt it was being put on the back seat, and plowed ahead to maintain its own relations with China, which, de facto, found itself perhaps the world's most favored nation for economic and cultural ties.

Tempting though it might have been to consider otherwise, the Cold War never really ended. It was based on a confrontation between the forces of liberty and those of oppression. The implosion of the Soviet Union still left communism flourishing in China, North Korea and Cuba. In their eagerness to harvest the Chinese market, American vested interests led their electorate to believe that China was just a cuddly panda. This panda is now a roaring dragon in the Republican lap—and we know of lion-tamers, but history only reveals dragon-killers. The reality of the cold war just moved house to Beijing, obscured by the hype of booming business and the arts.

Multiculturalism in the United States started as an expression of good will intended to counter the undesirable effects of cultural introversion. Overtaken by the terror of political correctness taken to absurd limits, it could create a scenario as frightening as that offered in the movie *Civil War*. The beauty of the American cultural melting pot is the end of diversity towards a single goal, whereas a tossed salad celebrates the virtues of diversity. Excessive zeal in totally eliminating the gap between what is said and what is done is only noble in the intention, as it will lead to newer, more vicious hypocrisies.

Despite Russia's apparently fragile domestic institutions, its foreign policy is doing well under Vladimir Putin. As the Bush administration seeks to position assets to deal with China, the Russians will take full advantage of their new-found position. They learned their lessons over two decades ago in their successful orchestration of the Campaign for Nuclear Disarmament, and are ready to apply them to the current situation.

President Vladimir Putin of Russia speaks beautiful words, but in the act, rather than consolidating institutional reforms undertaken by Mikhael Gorbachev, he is regressing to authoritarianism. By omission, the *Mafyia* continues to flourish. Yet, Russian nationalism is viewed by certain Europeans as a counter-force to American hegemony. By default, Russia's current domestic and foreign policies meet with mitigated opposition. The Putin administration has lost none of the lessons it learned during the cold war on managing disinformation. Its response to the American National Missile Defense proposal has been two-pronged: an offer to cooperate with the Americans in the development of this system, and an offer to the European countries to produce a cut-price version for them. Realizing that it cannot change American policy, Russia seeks to influence it by offering alternatives with a view to modifying U.S. programmes to its own advantage. At the same time, Russia has resuscitated its relationship with China, and re-established its friendship with India: the recent Indo-U.S. rapprochment did not interfere with the Indo-Russian joint testing of a cruise missile in the Bay of Bengal in June 2001. Russia has also agreed to supply military hardware and technology to Iran. Russia has centuries of an assertive culture and a fine capacity for organisation. To underestimate it would be a blunder.

The European Union cannot develop an integrated missile defense before it has its own army or at least a command, control and intelligence system to direct its various forces. Mr. Putin's offer of a Missile Defense Shield and the American determination to go ahead with their own, skilfully exploit this vacuum. It goes without saying that the American offer has a better chance of success. Most of the EU countries are NATO members. They have small, but well-equipped military forces. The U.S. Armed Forces, however, constitute NATO's center of gravity, a prerequisite to a credible defense of Europe. On the other hand, the United States also needs the Atlantic partnership for strategic reasons of trade and diplomacy. Military reforms in Europe are moving in the direction of professionalization and force projection. This should lead to enhanced competence in fighting terrorism. At the highest levels of strategic military thinking, a second lieutenant multiplied to the rank of General, finds it difficult to think laterally. He reasons symmetrically in time-space translated to territorial boundaries and declarations of war, whereas the terrorist thinks transnationally and therefore acts asymmetrically. Analytical systems of threat analyses must not be subordinate to the method itself. Identification of the threat must be clear, unequivocal and unhampered by constraints of politically correct mediaspeak.

The idea of the French Foreign Legion providing an infrastructure for a European Army was first proposed by me in the editorial columns of *The European* in 1991. France has the expertise in moulding cohesion out of disparate elements. The problem is, the other EU countries, would never entrust this task to a single member-state. France itself might not be that keen on an idea that starts well but ends up with the Legion under European command!

Turkey has this enticing offer of a large, well-trained army and trade opportunities in return for membership of the European Union. It is not a question of the Turks' ethnic or geographical credentials, but ambiguity over their singularity of interest. If the west were embroiled in a conflict with a coalition of Islamic countries, which bloc would Turkey choose? Until the resolution of that doubt in the hearts and minds of the concerned parties, and the emergence of clear indicators, Turkey will remain a privileged trading partner of the European Union.

But what really threatens the European Union and the United States at par with the consequences of terrorism is unbridled immigration across frontiers. If it exceeds the tolerance level of the electorate, western democracies will lose the level of fine enlightenment Judeo-Christian civilization took centuries to achieve. It is not at the level of porous frontiers that this issue will be decided—it will be legislated in the sacrosanct corridors of power.

Power also assumes responsibility for social engineering, whether it be in pursuance of Antonio Gramsci's theory to take over national education as a strategy for engineering a socialist society, or its prevention. Myth and legend that sustain a society's past and its self-image are under threat, from the media and the educational system. To recreate the past is regression, to deny it criminal. Communism has not disappeared, but continues in different forms in Italy, Russia, Romania, Bulgaria, Poland, North Korea and China. The fall of the Berlin wall was the end of a battle, not the war.

In many ways, such a war is now easier to fight. Technology, research into the human sciences and finance allow both sides a fair advantage to convince an increasingly better educated public of the values in content and form being offered them. Losers and winners will be declared, history will be rewritten, and the victors' values will be considered to have prevailed. Actually, it might just be a question of degrees of competence, efficiency and mediocrity.

Economy is the telling factor. An economic slowdown will lead to protectionism, endangering free trade and the framework of trading zones and alliances. This will also endanger the delicate structure of enlightened thought in public life. Man is born in sin, and raised from it by the Grace of God. The history of mankind reveals punctual nobility in moments of time, preserved in myth and legend—the rest is savagery. It is this natural instinct that western civilisation has fought for centuries to overcome, and the degree of success achieved is greater than any other known civilisation—retractors may call this hypocrisy, but the very force that enslaved other peoples decided to outlaw the practice and make rule of law available to all. I thought of this when I stood in front of the piece of the Berlin wall in the entrance hall of the Reagan Memorial Library, and read the names of all the countries where President Reagan's policies had brought about change with the intention of giving every man not just a fistful of dollars, but an equal chance to make a few with dignity.

In 1998, only eleven years after the Berlin wall was smashed down by German youth, thirteen of the fifteen EU countries were led by left-wing governments or coalitions. President Reagan, Dame Thatcher and Pope John Paul II's legacy fell under the management policies of people who were either not upto scratch, or careerists eager to claim the victory of another's battle. In the United States as in Europe, the feeling among a new, educated populace was that they had only been courted for the fight against communism, and that their usefulness was over. Starting with the Democrats in the United States, conservatives were swept from power. In 1997 in France, when a conservative President, Jacques Chirac, called an early parliamentary election only to find himself cohabiting with a socialist parliament and Prime Minister, it was a verdict passed by the French for being taken for granted. Attitudes to conservatives in power also hardened in other European countries. People felt the conservatives message was "now we've gotten rid of that bunch, let's put you guys back in place"! Yet, the tide has now turned, with the same electorates realising, starting with the United States, that conservatives might just do it better.

Thus it was that during these stormy years, the National Front party of France, led by the charismatic and reviled Monsieur Jean-Marie Le Pen, inserted itself into the left-right breach and managed to attain 15 percent of the national vote in 1995. The party and its leaders stayed in headlines of the international press, and I felt that through studying that one single phenomena, light could be shed on much of what was happening in Europe at that time. Traumatic stress from the perceived loss of sovereignty within the EU, the debate over the Euro and frontier barriers, the end of the cold war, the emergence of the Commonwealth of Independent States, the threat of terrorism, rogue nations rearing their heads, highhanded attitudes of leaders, unemployment, unchecked immigration and insecurity in the streets were weakening the psyche of the average European.

France has been at the vanguard of nations determined to be an integral part of the western alliance without being taken for granted. This requires adroit diplomacy and leadership with sang-froid, a French word. On the eve of the Gulf War, Dame Thatcher reportedly is said to have soothed a worried George Bush about France's perceived vacillations.

"France", she is reported to have said, "will hum and haw, but when the ship sails, she will be on it".

The rise of Germany as a power within and without the EU is another matter, and not to be taken lightly. While France is accused of its Gaullist self-image of grandeur, it is Germany with its MittelEuropa and control of the Central Bank that pursues grandeur in the act. The square-headed, brutal but bumbling Germans outwitted by the daring courage of a handful of gifted amateurs is Hollywood hype about the Second World War. A big economic powerhouse at the disposal of other Europeans because of their Second World War genocide is another fallacy. Crafty diplomacy, skilful leadership and a determination to put the past behind them is the reality. They plan to face their future responsibilities with a professional army trained for power projection. That, of course, does not stop anxiety within Germany's political leadership about civilian control over a professional army that can guarantee the stature of its economy. The Generals fret that disappearance of military service will lead to a recession of national values. There is also the fear that the presence of civilians will put them at the mercy of trade unions, which, if opposed to power projection in a particular part of the world, can call a strike by its members and paralyse the German Army. All in all, a balanced, self-confident Germany is in the interest of all its neighbours who have little desire to see a frustrated Germany redefine itself.

Britain does not talk about grandeur either, but goes much further than Germany in its efforts to realize it, betraying symptoms of Post-Empire-Traumatic-Stress-Disorder. Its approach to reliving empire is based on the financial power of the City of London and its usefulness to the United States. The power of the post-empire City is analogous with that of Venice after the Roman Empire. The circumnavigation of the Cape of Good Hope rendered that influence obsolete, and the Euro might have the same effect on Britain. The Special Relationship with the United States is the centerpiece of British foreign policy. The United States needs an ally within the EU, and a clear link with its European cultural roots.

Britain needs to rub itself against American power. Both countries promote the English language as an international industry. However, culture being a tributary of power, American phonology and lexicon exert a strong influence on British English . Yet the British maintain their efforts in the promotion of British English as an international language, little realising that increased internationalisation leads to a proportionate decrease in jurisdiction over the language. The losing battle is fought with renowned British obstinacy in a quest for grandeur.

The conservative rhetoric of the Tories has been taken over by Mr. Tony Blair's repackaged Labor, much like the corporate takeover of an ailing company. This year's election victory by the Labor party once again confirms the singularity of conservative values in market economics and sings the swan song of socialist dialectics. Britain never had a French or American style revolution. The British working classes obediently waited for perks trickling down from the aristocracy. Today, their illiterate past is well behind them, although gratitude has yet to come. The vicarious thrill enjoyed by the public by delving into the private lives of their erstwhile "betters" is more than what Salman Rushdie defines as public voyeurism—following Lady Diana's tragic death, they were vultures led in their flight by a vulpine tabloid press.

As the European Parliament debates the ramifications of the Echelon electronic system, Britain finds itself at a crossroads, with the BBC predicting that it might have to finally make a clear choice between the EU and the United States. Echelon is the system of electronic eavesdropping managed by UKUSA, a single-purpose affiliation of the United States, Canada, Britain, Australia and New Zealand. The composition is based neither on common national interests, nor on language. If the former, why not France, and if the latter, why not India and Nigeria? The glue is a common Anglo-Saxon heredity, and the inclusion of New Zealand clinches it—just a small island of wealthy immigrant sheep farmers thousands of miles away from the United States with no international reach on its own. At the end of the day, then, the age of enlightenment has yet to overcome ethnic considerations. This is the final argument that will decide Britain's fate vis a vis the EU and the United States. If push comes to shove, who will Britain stand up and be counted with?

The disposition of the Asian chessboard will not be entirely determined in Washington, but by its ability to handle the two big players—China and India. The fundamentals of the Nehru and Rajiv Doctrines, which sought to maintain Indian hegemony in the Indian Ocean and a presence in space as an expression of the historical bee in the Indian bonnet for having ignored its coastal frontier and succumbed to foreign rule have been maintained by successive governments. That said, India's immediate interest beyond its frontiers lies in settling its dispute with Pakistan in an effort to stabilize domestic unrest. Otherwise, its overriding concern is in international trade and a permanent seat in the United Nations' Security Council.

China cannot offer the world any comfort by a similar analyses. Its "lost territory" policy was applied in Tibet because resources allowed it, and has not been applied to Peru and Zanzibar because China's reach cannot yet extend that far. However, China is taking steps to lengthen its reach. Its military forces are rapidly converting to digitilazed systems and high-tech warfare to replace their traditional reliance on human waves, without abandoning Mao's dictum of all political power coming from the barrel of a gun. Their missiles are targeted at American cities and their host of cyber warriors continues to flourish.

The greatest challenge in the coming years will be terrorism. In 1996, the Group of Seven were planning to create "centres of excellence in anti-terrorist expertise". Certain think tanks such as the one at the British Universities of Keele and St. Andrews are doing good work, but the effect on terrorism itself can only be gauged by arrest records or a decrease in activity. Neither has been forthcoming. In February 1995, Willy Claes, NATO Secretary General had to apologize and explain for saying that Islamic Fundamentalism was just as dangerous as communism had been in the past. If that is the case, then the threat should be clearly defined and announced, otherwise it will contain the efficiency of law and order forces. The idea of Western security at the expense of maintaining the pre-conceived and untested notional theories of a group of expensively mis-educated social engineers needs to be revised. The threat of biological and nuclear terrorism is too real to be shelved for political expediency. The "new threats" to NATO referred to by President Bush during his spring 2001 European tour also need to be unambiguously stated, studied and tackled.

The United States has the economic, technological and military where-withal to put its National Missile Defense System (NMD) into place. Its fundamentals will remain constant, but the modification of its structure, and the degree of participation by allies will determine its form. Russia realizes it cannot overturn American policy: it will seek to alter it to its advantage. The Western allies will maintain their critical rhetoric until substantial sub-contracts for the development of NMD and U.S. acquies-cence on the modalities of the European Defense Force are forthcoming.

These are the issues which will challenge the managers of the World Order and continue to preoccupy their analysts in the years to come. They make the world an exciting and dangerous place to live in, with the unfolding of daily news bringing the strengths and foibles of mortals into the living room to remind us to remain in the world without becoming of it, to studiously ask for God's guidance in determining our dues to Him and Caesar, to not sit in a glass house and hurl stones at others and pray that world leaders reflect on the price to pay for gaining the world, that their minds may constantly seek to be renewed.

ABOUT THE AUTHOR

French by adoption, Gill was born in Pakistan. Member of the minority Christian community, he is the son of the renowned jurist and leader of the Christian community, Arthur Paul Gill, and a school headmistress and playwright, Susan Gill. A former Paratrooper, commissioned officer of the Punjab Regiment, and Brigadier of the French Foreign Legion, Azam Gill holds a PhD in American Studies from Grenoble University, France. He wrote his doctoral dissertation on William Faulkner and Master's thesis on Mario Puzo's *The Godfather*. He published two books—*Jail Reforms* and *Army Reforms*—in Pakistan. He has also published a novel on international terrorism, *The Bugle Sounds No More*, praised as *a first-class thriller* by Len Deighton, author of the trilogy *Faith*, *Hope* and *Charity*. After serving as an associate lecturer in English at Grenoble University, he is now under secondment to the French Ministry of Defence. His hobbies are reading, writing, cooking, swimming and French Boxing (also known as Savate).

BIBLIOGRAPHY

Bibliography Of Sources And Documents Consulted

AHLQUIST Roberts, King, Marvin, Weitzman & Dwiggins, eds. **Addison-Wesley United States History**. California, USA: Addison-Wesley, 1984.

ARON Raymond. **Sur Clauswitz**. Pref. Pierre Hassner. Brussels, Belgium: Editions Complexe, 1987, pbk.

Asahi Shimbun, issues of. Japan. http://www.asahi.com/english/english.html .

BAUD Jacques. **Encyclopédie du Renseignement et des Services Secrets**. Paris, France : Editions Lavauzelle, 1998, pbk.

BIGEARD Marcel. **De la Brousse à la Jungle**. France : Hachette / Carrère, 1994, pbk.

BLOOM Allan. **The Closing of the American Mind**. New York, USA: Simon & Schuster Trade, 1988, pbk.

BLOOM Allan. **The Republic of Plato**. 2nd ed. New york, USA: Simon & Schuster, 1991.

BOCK Alan W. **Ambush at Ruby Ridge: How Government Agents Set Randy Weaver Up and Took His Family Down**. New York, USA: Berkley Books, 1995, pbk.

BONIFACE, Pascal. **La France Est-elle Une Grande Puissance?** Paris, France : Preses de la Fondation Nationale des Sciences Politiques, 1998, pbk.

BRADLEE Benjamin C. **Conversations With Kennedy**. New York, USA: Pocket Books, 1976, pbk.

BRZEZINSKY Zbigniew. **The Grand Chessboard : American Primacy and Its Geostrategic Imperatives**. London, UK: Harper Collins (Basic Books), 1997.

BULL George, trans. **Niccolo Machiavelli: The Prince**. Harmondsworth, U.K.: Penguin, 1982, pbk.

Cato Institute, The, publications of. 1000 Massachusetts Ave., N.W., Washington D.C. 20001.

Center for the Study of American Business, publications of. Washington University, Campus Box 1027, One Brookings Drive, St. Louis, Missouri 63130-4899, USA.

CLANCY Tom. **Fighter Wing**. London, UK: Harper Collins, 1995, pbk.

CLANCY Tom. **Submarine**. New York, USA: Berkley Books, 1993.

CONBOY Ken. **Elite Forces of India and Pakistan.** London, UK: Osprey Publishing, 1992, pbk.

CONDON Richard—**Mile High.** New York, USA: Dial, 1969.

CONDON Richard—**The Manchurian Candidate.** New York, USA: Jove Pubns, 1991 (orig. 1959).

Corriera Della Serra, issues of. Via Solferino 28-20121 Milano, Italy. http://www.corriere.it/

Courrier Internationa, issues of *l.* B.O. 80, 70732, Sainte Geneviève Cedex, France. www.courrierinternational.com.

Daily Telegraph, The, issues of.

DARMAN Peter. **Warfare at Sea.** Osceola, WI, USA: Motorbooks International, 1997.

Dawn, issues of. http://www.dawn.com

DE LA BILLIERE General Sir Peter. **Storm Command: a Personal Account of the Gulf War.** London, U.K.: Harper & Collins, 1992.

De TOCQUEVILLE Alexis. **Democracy in America (vols I & II).** New York, USA: Random House, 1954, pbk.

DEACON Richard. **The French Secret Service.** London, UK: Collins (Grafton Books), 1990, pbk.

DICKIE, John **Inside the Foreign Office.** London, Uk: Chapmans Publishers, 1992, pbk.

DURANT Ariel and Will: **The Story of Civilization (vols I—X).** New York, USA: Simon & Schuster, 1935—1967).

DURANT Ariel and Will: **The Story of Philosophy.** New York, USA: Simon & Schuster, 1961, pbk.

Economist, The, issues of. P.O. Box 14, Harold Hill, Romford RM3 8EQ, U.K. http://www.economist.com/

El Mundo, issues of. Pradillo 42, 28002 Madrid, Spain. http://www.el-mundo.es/

El Pais , issues of. Miguel Yuste 40, 28037 Madrid, Spain. http://www.elpais.es/

ETAT du Monde. Paris, France : Editions Découverte, 1993—2001.

European, The. Out of Print.

EVANS G. Russell. **Death Knell of the Panama Canal ? Fairfax, Virginia, USA: National Security Center, 1997, pbk.**

FACTS ON FILE, issues of. 11 Pen Plaza, 15th Floor, New York, NY 10001, USA.

Far Eastern Economic Review, issues of. Citicorp Centre, 25th Floor, 18 Whitfield Rd-Causeway Bay, Hong Kong. http://www.feer.com

Foreign Affairs. 58 East 78th St., New York, NY 10021. www.foreignaffairs.org/

Foreign Policy Research Institute, publications of. 1528 Walnut Street, Suite 610, Philadelphia, PA 19102, USA.

Frankfurter Allgemeine Zeitung, issues of. Hellerhofstrasse 2-4, 60327 Frankfurt, Germany. http://www.faz.de

FUKUYAMA Francis. **The End of History and the Last Man**. New York, USA: Avon, 1993.

FUKUYAMA Francis. **Trust: The Social Virtues and the Creation of Prosperity**. London, U.K.: The Free Press, 1996.

GANDY Alain. **Royal Etranger: Légionnaires Cavaliers au Combat** (1914—1984). France: Presses de la Cité, 1985, pbk.

GILL Shaista. « The Quenchless Light: Universalism in Selected Short Fiction and Drama of Rabindranath Tagore». Diss. University of the Philippines, 1984.

GRIFFITH Kenneth. **The Discovery of Nehru : an Experience of India**. London, UK: Michael Joseph, 1989.

Guardian Weekly, The, issues of. 119 Farringdon Rd., London EC1 3ER, U.K. http://www.guardian.co.uk/

HANZHANG, Tao. **Sun Tzu's Art of War**. Trans. Yuan Shibing. New York, USA: Sterling, 1987, pbk.

HAWKING Stephen. **Black Holes and Baby Universes and other essays**. London, UK: Bantam, 1993, pbk.

HAWKING Stephen W. **A Brief History of Time: From the Big Bang to Black Holes**. London, U.K.: Guild Publishing, 1990.

Heritage Foundation, The, publications of. 214 Massachusetts Ave., N.E. Washington D.C., 20002-4999, USA. http://www.heritage.org

HOWARD Michael. **Studies in War and Peace**. New York, Viking Press, 1970. 262 p. The Classical Strategists, pp 154-183.

Independent, The, issues of. 1 Canada Square, Canary Wharf, London E14 5DL, U.K. http://www.independent.co.uk/

Institute of the Americas, publications of. 10111 North Torrey Pines Rd., La Jolla, CA 92037, USA.

International Herald Tribune, The , issues of. 6 bis rue des Graviers, 92521 Neuilly-sur-Seine, France. http://www.iht.com

IISS (International Institute for Strategic Studies), publications of. Arundel House, 13-15 Arundel Street, Temple Place, London WC2R 3DX, U.K.

JAMES Lawrence. **The Rise and Fall of the British Empire**. London, U.K.: Little, Brown & Company, 1994, pbk.

Jane's Intelligence Review , issues of. 1st Floor, The Quadrangle, 180 Wardour St., London W1F8FY, U.K. http://www.janes.com

JEREMIAH Books. **The Clinton Chronicles Book**. Hemet, CA, USA: Jeremiah, 1994, pbk.

Journal of Political Science, The, issues of.

KAPUR Rajiv A. **Sikh Separatism**. London, UK: Allen & Unwin, 1986.

KARNIK V.B., ed. **Chinese Invasion: Background and Sequel**. Bombay, India: Bharatiya Vidya Bhavan, 1966, pbk.

KAUTILYA. **Arthasastra**. Trans Gérard Challiard, François Richard. Paris, France : Editions du Félin, 1998, pbk.

Keesing's Archives, issues of. Keesing Capital Internatioal, Keesing Laan-2, B-2100 Deurne, Antwerp, Belgium.

KELLAND Gilbert. **Crime in London**. London, U.K.: Harper Collins, 1986, pbk.

KENNEDY Paul. **The Rise and Fall of the Great Powers: economic Change & Military Conflict from 1500 to 2000**. Brookfield, UT, USA: Random, 1987.

KIPLING Rudyard. **War Stories and Poems**. intro. A. Rutherford. Oxford, U.K: OUP, 1990.

KISSINGER Henry. **American Foreign Policy—A Global View**. Brookfield, UT, USA: Ashgate, 1983, pbk.

KISSINGER Henry. **Diplomacy**. New York, USA: Simon & Schuster, 1994.

L'Express, issues of. 17, rue de l'Arrivée, 75733 Paris Cedex 15, France.

La Republica, issues of. Piazza Indipendenza 11/b, 00185, Roma, Italy. http://www.republica.it/

La Stampa, issues of. Via Marenco 32, 10126 Torino, Italy. http://www.lastampa.it/

Le Figaro, issues of. 37, rue du Louvre 75002, Paris, France. www.le-figaro.com

LEGION Etranger. **Memorial de la Légion Etrangère**. Paris, France : Editions du Panthéon, 1966.

Le Monde, issues of. 21 bis, rue Claude-Bernard—B.P. 218, 75226 Paris Cedex 05, France. http://www.lemonde.fr

Le Nouvel Observateur, issues of. 8, rue Aboukir, 75002 Paris, France. www.nouvelobs.com

Le Point, issues of. www.lepoint.fr

LETIGRE Henri. **La Réaction du R.P.R. à la Percée du F.N.** Paris, France : La Pensée Universelle, 1988.

LEVEQUE Jean-Christophe. *Research Files and Personal Library*. Pommiers la Plaçette, France.

Libération, issues of. Pais, France. 11, rue Béranger, 75154, Paris, France. www.liberation.com

LIDDELL HART Sir Basil Henry. **Why Don't We Learn From History?** London, UK: George Allen and Unwin, 1946. 64 p.

LIDDELL HART Sir Basil Henry. **Great Captains Unveiled**. N. Stanford, NH, USA: Ayer, 1928.

Los Angeles Times, issues of. 145 Spring St., Los Angeles, CA 90012, USA. http://www.latimes.com/HOME/NEWS/

MAGRUDER'S AMERICAN GOVERNMENT. rev. William A Mclenaghan. Needham, Mass, USA: Prentice Hall, 1990.

MASON Philip. **A Matter of Honor:** An Account of the Indian Army, Its Officers and Men. London, U.K.: Jonathan Cape, 1974.

MASON, Philip. **The Men Who Ruled India**. London, U.K.: Jonathan Cape (Pan Books), 1985, pbk.

MASON, Philip. **A Matter of Honour.**

MAYER, Jean-Paul. **Rand, Brookings, Harvard et les Autres : Les Prophètes de la Stratégie des Etats-Unis**. Paris, France : ADDIM, 1997, pbk.

McCEARNEY James. **La Révolte des Cipayes**. Paris, France : Jean Picollec, 1999, pbk.

MCLUHAN Marshall. **Understanding Media: The Extension of Man**. New York, USA: NAL-Dutton, 1966, pbk.

MOREY Robert. **The Islamic Invasion**. Eurgene, Oregon, USA: Harvest House, 1992.

MORTON James. **Bent Coppers**. New York, USA: Warner Books, 1993, pbk.

NAIPAUL V.S. **Among The Unbelievers: an Islamic Journey**. Harmondsworth, UK: Penguin, 1982, pbk.

National Educator, The, issues of. 1216 North Tustin Avenue, Orange, CA92867 USA.

New York Times, The, issues of.

Newsweek, issues of. Newsweek Inc., 251 West 57th St., New York, NY 10019, USA.

NIXON Richard. **Leaders**. New York, USA: Warner Books, 1982, pbk.

Paris Match , issues of. 151, rue Anatole France, 92399 Le Vallois, France.

NUGENT Nicholas. **Rajiv Gandhi: son of a dynasty**. London, UK: BBC Books, 1990.

PARKER John. **Inside The Foreign Legion**. London, UK: Judy Piatkus, 1998.

PATTEN Chris. **East and West**. London, U.K.: Macmillan (Pan Books), 1998, pbk.

PEARSON John. **The Ultimate Family: The Making of the Royal House of Windsor**. Guldford, CT, USA: Ulverscroft, 1987.

PROVINCE Charles M. **The Unknown Patton**. New York, USA: Bonanza Books, 1983.

PUZO Mario. **The Godfather**. London, U.K: Pan, 1970.

Radio—All India Radio

Radio—Australian Broadcasting Corporation

Radio—Canadian Broadcasting Corporation

Radio—France-Info

Radio—France-Inter

Radio—Radio Netherlands

Rand Corporation, The, publications of. 1700, Main St., P.O. Box 2138, Santa Monica, CA 90407-2138, USA.

RAVENSCROFT Trevor. **The Spear of Destiny**. York Beach, Maine, USA: Samuel Weiser, Inc., pbk.

SAGAN Carl. **Broca's Brain**. New York, USA : Ballantine Books, 1980, pbk.

SERGENT Pierre. **La Légion Saute sur Kolweizi**. France : Presses de la Cité, 1978, pbk.

SCHWARZKOPF General H. Norman & Peter Petre. It Doesn't Take A Hero: The Autobiography of General Norman H. Schwarzkopf. New York, USA: Bantam Books, 1992.

SFEIR Antoine. **Les Réseaux d'Allah: Les Filières Islamistes en France et en Europe.** France : Plon, 1997, pbk.

SONTAG Sherry & DREW Christopher. **Blind Man's Bluff.** New York, USA: Harper Collins, 1999, pbk.

STARR Chester G. **The Influence of Sea Power on Ancient History.** New York, USA: Barnes & Noble, 1989.

STILLINGER Jack, ed. **The Poems of John Keats.** Cambridge, MA, USA: Belknap, 1978.

The Times of India. http://www.timesofindia.com

Time Magazine, issues of. 1271-Ave., of the Americas, New York, NY 10020 USA. http://www.pathfinder.com/time/

Times of India, The, issues of.

Times, The, issues of. 1- Pennington St., London E19XN, U.K. http://www.the-times.co.uk

TOYNBEE Arnold Joseph. **A Study of History.** Vols 1-10 abr. Oxford, U.K.: Oxford University Press, 1987, pbk.

TULLY Mark. **No Full Stops in India.** London, UK: Penguin, 1992, pbk.

TV—BBC Channel-1

TV—BBC Channel-2

TV—BBC Channel-4

TV—BBC World Service

TV—CNN News

TV—French TF-1

TV—French TF-2

TV—French TF-3

TV—French TF-5

TV—French TF-6

TV—Sky News

USA Today, issues of. 1000 Wilson Blvd. # 600 Arlington, VA 22229, USA. http:/www.usatoday.com

VOLKOFF Vladimir. **Désinformation Flagrant Délit**. Monaco: Editions du Rocher, 1999, pbk.

Wall Street Journal, The, issues of. 200 Liberty St., New York, NY 10281. http://www.interactive.wsj.com/

Washington Post, The, issues of. 1150 15th St. NW Washington D.C., USA. http://www.washingtonpost.com

WELLS Stanley & Gary Taylor, eds. **William Shakespeare: The Complete Works**. Oxford, U.K.: Oxford University Press, 1988.

WRIGHT Peter. **Spycatcher**. Richmond, Victoria, Australia: Peter Heinemann, 1987, pbk.

YOUNG John Robert (pref. Len Deighton). **The French Foreign Legion**. London, UK: Thames & Hudson, 1984.

ZIEGLER Philip. **Mountbatten: the official biography**. London, UK: Book Club Associates, 1985.

INDEX